# PUBLIC–PRIVATE PARTNERSHIP MONITOR

## PHILIPPINES

DECEMBER 2020

ASIAN DEVELOPMENT BANK

6 ADB Avenue, Mandaluyong City, 1550 Metro Manila, Philippines
Tel +63 2 8632 4444; Fax +63 2 8636 2444
www.adb.org


Printed in the Philippines

ISBN 978-92-9262-648-8 (print); 978-92-9262-649-5 (electronic); 978-92-9262-650-1 (ebook)
Publication Stock No. SGP200424-2
DOI: http://dx.doi.org/10.22617/SGP200424-2



Corrigenda to ADB publications may be found at http://www.adb.org/publications/corrigenda.

Notes:
In this publication, "$" refers to United States dollars and "₱" refers to pesos.
ADB recognizes "China" as the People's Republic of China.

On the cover: *Left side*: **Construction workers**, in Tublay, Benguet, Philippines, meticulously crafting metal lattices for the construction of beams and columns (photo by Al Benavente/ADB). *Center photo*: **The North Luzon Expressway Rehabilitation and Expansion Project** of the Asian Development Bank (ADB) helped renovate an 83.7-kilometer section of the road and build or rehabilitate 14 interchanges, 24 bridges, and 31 overpasses from Manila to the Clark Special Economic Zone in Pampanga province. (photo by Kevin Hamdorf/ADB). *Right side from top to bottom*: The newly opened **Terminal 2 of The Mactan Cebu International Airport (MCIA)** can accommodate an additional 4.5 million passengers which will boost the capacity of the airport to 12.5 million passengers per year. The MCIA is the Philippines second largest airport and serves as the southern air transportation hub for country (photo by Ariel Javellana/ADB); **Solar panels gathering sun power and turbines harvesting wind power** at the Burgos Wind and Solar Farm in Burgos, Ilocos Norte in the Philippines (photo by Al Benavente/ADB).

Cover design by Claudette Rodrigo.

# Contents

# Tables and Figures

## Tables

**Figures**

# Foreword

We are pleased to present the *Public–Private Partnership Monitor*, a detailed review of the current state of public–private partnership (PPP) enabling environment in selected countries in Asia and the Pacific.

Availability of adequate infrastructure is a measure of a country's ability to sustain its economic growth. For economies across Asia and the Pacific, provision of basic infrastructure services, including water, health, energy, transportation, and communications, is an important public sector activity. As demand for infrastructure has increased faster than government budgets, the public sector has increasingly considered partnership with the private sector as an alternate modality for financing infrastructure.

The Asian Development Bank (ADB) estimates that Asia and the Pacific must spend $1.7 trillion a year on infrastructure until 2030 to maintain growth, meet social needs, and respond to the effects of climate change. That amount is expected to go up. The traditional sources of finance for infrastructure—the government's budgetary allocations—have not been enough to meet the demand. Prior to COVID-19 pandemic, ADB estimated an annual infrastructure gap of $204 billion to be filled through private sector investment. That amount is also now expected to increase.

For the private sector, investment in infrastructure, whether through PPPs or otherwise, represents an investment avenue competing with various other investment options available. In order to compete, and to crowd in private capital into infrastructure, governments need to provide a conducive environment to adequately establish and protect the rights of the private sector, and the necessary support to ensure every asset brought to market provides returns that are commensurate with the risks.

*The PPP Monitor* provides the investor community with business intelligence on the enabling environment, policies, priority sectors, and deals to facilitate informed investment decisions. For ADB developing member countries (DMCs), *the PPP Monitor* serves as a diagnostic tool to identify gaps in their legal, regulatory, and institutional framework. ADB and other international development agencies can also benefit from *the PPP Monitor* as it could be useful in initiating dialogues to assess a country's readiness to tap PPPs as a means to develop and sustain its infrastructure.

Building on the success of the previous editions of *the PPP Monitor*, the new PPP Monitor is now being brought online to widen its reach. More countries will be continually added in *the PPP Monitor* and it is expected to become a primary knowledge base for assessing a country's PPP environment for the government and the business community. *The PPP Monitor* features an interactive online version which allows users to compare and contrast the key PPP parameters and features across the DMCs. The online version of *the PPP Monitor* may be accessed at www.pppmonitor.adb.org.

*The PPP Monitor* has been upgraded to provide a "one-stop" information source, derived from a consolidation of (i) the previous PPP Monitor; (ii) leading PPP databases of multilateral development banks like the World Bank and the International Finance Corporation (IFC) and organizations like EIU (Infrascope), and GI Hub (InfraCompass); (iii) reports of a country's PPP unit; (iv) a country's legal framework; and (v) consultations with leading technical experts and legal firms as well as financial institutions.

*The PPP Monitor* includes more than 500 qualitative and quantitative indicators to profile the national PPP environment, the sector-specific PPP landscape (for eight identified infrastructure sectors), and the PPP landscape for local government projects. The COVID-19 pandemic has pushed social infrastructure into the forefront of policy and planning; hence, where possible, this PPP Monitor takes a bigger focus on social and municipal aspects like health, education, and affordable housing.

The PPP market in most of ADB developing member countries is still at an emerging/developing stage, and continuous regulatory reforms and institutional strengthening are required to facilitate further private sector investment in infrastructure and to create a sustainable pipeline of bankable projects. Through *the PPP Monitor*, ADB continues to provide support for DMCs in addressing various infrastructure and PPP-related challenges, in developing sustainable infrastructure projects, and in delivering efficient and effective public services through PPPs. ADB also helps DMCs improve their investment climates, formulate sound market regulations, and build robust legal and institutional frameworks to encourage private sector participation in infrastructure through PPPs.

We hope that this PPP Monitor will pave the way for continued dialogue between the public and private sectors and stimulate the adoption of PPPs in the Asia and Pacific region.

**Yoji Morishita**
Head, Office of Public–Private Partnerships
Asian Development Bank

# Acknowledgments

The *Public–Private Partnership Monitor: Country Profile—Philippines* was prepared by the Asian Development Bank (ADB) Office of Public–Private Partnership (OPPP), in close coordination with the Philippines Country Office.

Sanjay Grover, PPP specialist, PPP Thematic Group Secretariat, led the preparation of *the PPP Monitor*. He also developed and streamlined the analytical framework for capturing the national, sectoral, and municipal PPP landscape presented in this report.

Yoji Morishita, head of the OPPP, and Srinivas Sampath, chief of the PPP Thematic Group, provided guidance and support in developing *the PPP Monitor*.

*The PPP Monitor* uses data published by the governments of ADB developing member countries—on their official websites and in reports, publications, laws, and regulations—as well as data published by other multilateral development agencies and included in industry publications and databases such as those of the World Bank, Organisation for Economic Co-operation and Development (OECD), World Economic Forum, International Monetary Fund (IMF), Inframation Group, IJGlobal, Economist Intelligence Unit (Infrascope Index), Global Infrastructure Hub, TheGlobalEconomy.com, Bloomberg, S&P Global, Trading Economics and PPP Knowledge Lab.

ADB partnered with CRISIL Infrastructure Advisory and Panapps Inc. in developing *the PPP Monitor*. CRISIL Infrastructure Advisory shared its expertise and provided inputs in developing *the PPP Monitor* for the Philippines while Panapps Inc. published this report online.

Ricardo McKlmon, Jezreel Pabia Uy, and Carmelia Godoy managed the contributors internal and external to ADB. With guidance from the Philippine Country Office, Cristina Lozano, Dionisio II D. Camango and Catherine Lopez Fong of OPPP reviewed the publication and provided quality control. *The PPP Monitor* has also benefited from the review inputs of Philippines PPP Center Executive Director Ferdinand Pecson and his team.

Several others provided help and support—Cyrel San Gabriel edited the report, Asiatype Inc. and Levi Rodolfo Lusterio performed typesetting and proofreading respectively, and Claudette Rodrigo designed the cover. April-Marie Gallega and Ayun Sundari of the Knowledge Support Division of ADB Department of Communications provided guidance and assistance in the publication process.

# Definition of Terms

| Term | Definition |
|---|---|
| Public–private partnership (PPP) | Contractual arrangement between public (national, state, provincial, or local) and private entities through which the skills, assets, and/or financial resources of each of the public and private sectors are allocated in a complementary manner, thereby sharing the risks and rewards, to seek to provide optimal service delivery and good value to citizens. In a PPP, the public sector retains the ultimate responsibility for service delivery, although the private sector provides the service for an extended time.<br><br>Within Asian Development Bank operations, all contracts such as performance-based contracts (management and service contracts), lease–operate–transfer, build–own–operate–transfer, design–build–finance–operate, variants, and concessions are considered as various forms of PPP.<br><br>Excluded are:<br>• contracts involving turnkey design and construction as part of public procurement (engineering, procurement, and construction contracts);<br>• simple service contracts that are not linked to performance standards (those that are more aligned with outsourcing to private contractor staff to operate public assets);<br>• construction contracts with extended warranties and/or maintenance provisions of, for example, up to five years post completion (wherein performance risk-sharing is minimal as the assets are new and need only basic maintenance); and<br>• all privatization and divestures. |
| Affermage or lease contracts | Under a lease contract, the private sector developer is responsible for the service in its entirety and undertakes obligations relating to quality and service standards. Except for new and replacement investments, which remain the responsibility of the government contracting agency, the operator provides the service at his expense and risk. The duration of the leasing contract is typically 10 years and may be renewed up to 20 years. Responsibility for service provision is transferred from the public sector to the private sector and the financial risk for operation and maintenance is borne entirely by the private sector operator. In particular, the operator is responsible for losses and for unpaid consumers' debts. Leases do not involve any sale of assets to the private sector. |
| Availability-/ performance-based payments | Method of investment recovery in PPP projects, when payments to the private party are made by the government contracting agency over the lifetime of a PPP contract in return for making infrastructure or services available for use at acceptable and contractually agreed performance standards. |

*continued on next page*

*continued from previous page*

| Term | Definition |
|---|---|
| Best and final offer (BAFO) | An incentive mechanism provided by the government contracting agency to the private sector developer initiating a PPP project through the unsolicited proposal route (USP proponent) to be automatically shortlisted for the final bidding round and provide its best and final offer to match the other bidders' best offer. |
| Build–lease–transfer | A PPP type whereby a private sector developer is authorized to finance and construct an infrastructure or development facility, and upon its completion hands it over to the government contracting agency on a lease arrangement for a fixed period after which ownership of the facility is automatically transferred to the government contracting agency. |
| Build–own–operate | A PPP type whereby a private sector developer is authorized to finance, construct, own, operate, and maintain an infrastructure or development facility from which the private sector developer is allowed to recover its total investment, operating and maintenance costs plus a reasonable return thereon by collecting tolls, fees, rentals or other charges from facility users. Under this PPP type, the private sector developer which owns the assets of the facility may assign its operation and maintenance to a facility operator. |
| Build–operate–transfer | Build–operate–transfer (BOT) and similar arrangements are a specialized concession in which a private firm or consortium finances and develops a new infrastructure project or a major component according to performance standards set by the government.<br><br>Under BOTs, the private sector developer provides the capital required to build a new facility. Importantly, the private operator now owns the assets for a period set by contract—sufficient to give the developer time to recover investment costs through user charges. |
| Build–transfer | A PPP type under which the private sector developer undertakes the financing and construction of a given infrastructure or development facility, and after its completion hands it over to the government contracting agency, which pays the private sector developer on an agreed schedule its total investments expended on the project, plus a reasonable rate of return thereon. This arrangement may be employed in the construction of any infrastructure or development project, including critical facilities which, for security or strategic reasons, must be operated directly by the government contracting agency. |
| Commercial close | Indicates the signing of the PPP contract between the government contract agency and the identified private sector developer. Usually occurs after the terms and conditions of the draft PPP contract are negotiated and agreed between the government contracting agency and the identified private sector developer. |
| Competitive bidding | A process under which the bidders submit information detailing their qualifications and detailed technical and financial proposals, which are evaluated according to defined criteria—often in a multi-stage process—to select a preferred bidder. Competitive bidding may also include competitive negotiations and license schemes. |
| Concession | A PPP type which makes the concessionaire (established by the selected private sector developer) responsible for the full delivery of services in a specified area, including operation, maintenance, collection, management, and construction and rehabilitation of the system. Importantly, the private sector developer is responsible for all capital investment. Although the concessionaire is responsible for providing the assets, such assets are publicly owned even during the concession period. The public sector is responsible for establishing performance standards and ensuring that the concessionaire meets them. In essence, the public sector's role shifts from being the service provider to regulating the price and quality of service. |
| Currency conversion swap fee | A premium which is paid by the borrower to settle on a swap in which the parties sell currencies to each other subject to an agreement to repurchase the same currency in the same amount, at the same exchange rate, and on a fixed date in the future. |
| Direct agreement | An agreement normally made between the concessionaire (established by the private sector developer), the government contracting agency, and the lenders. The agreement usually gives the lenders step-in rights to take over the operation of the key PPP contracts. |

*continued on next page*

*continued from previous page*

| Term | Definition |
|---|---|
| Direct negotiations | A type of PPP procurement under which the PPP contract is awarded on the basis of a direct agreement with a private sector developer without going through the competitive bidding process. |
| Dispute resolution | A process to resolve any dispute between the government contracting agency and the private sector developer as agreed in the PPP contract. The possible dispute resolution mechanisms in a PPP contract could include resolution through:<br>• discussion between both parties,<br>• dispute resolution board,<br>• expert determination,<br>• mediation or conciliation, or<br>• arbitration. |
| Environmental impact assessment | A process of evaluating the likely environmental impacts of a proposed project or development, taking into account interrelated socioeconomic, cultural, and human health impacts, both beneficial and adverse. |
| Feed-in tariff (FIT) | A policy mechanism designed to accelerate investment in renewable energy technologies by offering long-term purchase agreements for the sale of renewable energy electricity. |
| Financial close | An event whereby (i) a legally binding commitment of equity holders and/or debt financiers exists to provide or mobilize funding for the full cost of the project, and (ii) the conditions for funding have been met and the first tranche of funding is mobilized. If this information is not available, construction start date is used as an estimated financial closure date. |
| Financial equilibrium | A mechanism in a PPP agreement for dealing with changes, when changes in specified conditions and circumstances trigger compensating changes to the terms of the agreement. Some civil law jurisdictions emphasize economic or financial equilibrium provisions that entitle a partner to changes in the key financial terms of the contract to compensate for certain types of exogenous events that may otherwise impact returns. The partner is protected as the economic balance of the contract must be maintained and adequate compensation paid for damages suffered. Unexpected changes that merit financial equilibrium may arise from force majeure (major natural disasters or civil disturbances), government action, and unforeseen changes in economic conditions. |
| Force majeure | An event that is reasonably beyond the reasonable control of the affected party as a result of which such party's performance of its obligations under the PPP contract is prevented or rendered impossible. Force majeure events may include:<br>• war, civil war, armed conflict or terrorism;<br>• nuclear, chemical, or biological contamination unless the source or the cause of the contamination is the result of the actions of or breach by the concessionaire or its subcontractors;<br>• pressure waves caused by devices travelling at supersonic speeds, which directly causes either party (the "Affected Party") to be unable to comply with all or a material part of its obligations under the contract; or<br>• any other similar events that are beyond reasonable control of the affected party, and prevent or render impossible the performance by such party of its obligations under the PPP contract. |
| Government contracting agency | The ministry, department, or agency that enters into a PPP contract with the private sector and is responsible for ensuring that the relevant public assets or services are provided. |
| Government guarantee | Agreements under which the government agrees to bear some or all risks of a PPP project. It is a secondary obligation which legally binds the government to take on an obligation if a specified event occurs. A government guarantee constitutes a contingent liability, for which there is uncertainty as to whether the government may be required to make payments, and if so, how much and when it will be required to pay.<br>In practice, government guarantees are used when debt providers are unwilling to lend to a private party in a PPP because of concerns over credit risk and potential loan losses. Government guarantees can also be used to benefit equity investors in a PPP company when they require protection against the investment risks they bear. |

*continued on next page*

*continued from previous page*

| Term | Definition |
|---|---|
| Government pay (Off-take) | Represents the payment made by the government contracting agency to the concessionaire (established by the private sector developer) for the infrastructure assets provided and services delivered through a PPP project. These payments could be:<br>• usage-based—for example, shadow tolls or output-based subsidies;<br>• based on availability—that is, conditional on the availability of an asset or service to the specified quality; and<br>• upfront subsidies based on achieving certain agreed milestones. |
| Gross-cost contract | A type of PPP contract arrangement in the railway sector under which all revenues (from fares and other sources) are transferred to the government contracting agency, and the risks absorbed by the developer are confined to those associated with the cost of operations. |
| Hybrid arrangement | A method of investment recovery in PPP projects when payments to the private party are made as a combination of user charges and availability payments over the lifetime of a PPP contract, in return for making infrastructure or services available for use at acceptable and contractually agreed performance standards. |
| Independent power producer (IPP) scheme | A scheme whereby a producer of electrical energy, which is not a public utility, makes electric energy available for sale to utilities or the general public.<br>A scheme whereby a producer of electrical energy, which is a private entity, owns and/or operates facilities to generate electricity and then sells it to a utility, central government buyer, or end users. The IPP invests in generation technologies and recovers their cost from the sale of the electricity. |
| Interest rate swap fee | A premium paid by the borrower for a hedging contract to convert a floating interest rate into a fixed rate. The two parties agree to exchange interest rate payments based on a notional principal amount, with typically one paying a fixed rate and the other generally paying a floating rate. |
| Institutional arbitration | An arbitration process in which a specialized institution intervenes and takes on the role of administering the arbitration process between the government contracting agency and the private sector developer for a PPP project-related dispute. This institution would have its own set of rules which would provide a framework for the arbitration, and its own form of administration to assist in the process. |
| Joint venture | An alternative to full privatization in which the infrastructure is co-owned and operated by the public sector and private operators. Under a joint venture, the public and private sector partners can either form a new company or assume joint ownership of an existing company through a sale of shares to one or several private investors. The company may also be listed on the stock exchange. |
| Lender's step-in rights | Lender's rights in project-financed arrangements to "step in" to the project company's position in the contract to take control of the infrastructure project where the project company is not performing. |
| Management contract | A PPP type which expands the services to be contracted out to include some or all of the management and operation of the public service (i.e., utility, hospital, port authority). Although ultimate obligation for service provision remains in the public sector, daily management control and authority is assigned to the private partner or contractor. In most cases, the private partner provides working capital but no financing for investment. |
| Material adverse government action | An action by the government which directly and materially affects the private party of a PPP project in performing its obligations under the relevant PPP contract, and which would reasonably be expected to result in a material adverse effect. |
| Net-cost contract | A type of PPP contract arrangement in the railway sector under which all revenues (from fares and other sources) are retained by the developer, and traffic and revenue risks are absorbed either fully or as per a contractually agreed portion. |
| Nominal interest rate | The nominal interest rate is the interest rate applicable to a borrowing before taking inflation adjustment into account. In certain cases, nominal interest rate also refers to the advertised or stated interest rate on a borrowing, without taking into account any fees or compounding of interest.<br><br>Nominal interest rate = Real interest rate + Inflation rate |

*continued on next page*

*continued from previous page*

| Term | Definition |
|---|---|
| Nonrecourse/limited recourse project financing | The financing of the development or exploitation of a right, natural resource, or other assets where the bulk of the financing is to be provided by way of debt, and is to be repaid principally out of the assets being financed and their revenues. |
| Output-based aid (OBA) | Refers to development aid strategies that link the delivery of public services in developing countries to targeted performance-related subsidies. OBA provides a way in which international financial institutions can directly structure their financing to benefit poor people, even when the service provider is a private company. OBA is the use of explicit, performance-based subsidies funded by the donor agencies to complement or replace user fees. It involves the contracting out of basic service provision to a third party—such as private companies, nongovernment organizations, community-based organizations, and even public service providers—with subsidy payment tied to the delivery of specified outputs. This means that targeted and valuable subsidies to disadvantaged populations are funded through donor funds. The private partner, meanwhile, can only recover this funding by achieving specific performance outcomes. |
| Project bond financing | An alternative source of financing infrastructure project by placing bonds. |
| Project development | Indicates the stage of the PPP project lifecycle including PPP project identification, preparation, structuring, and procurement up to commercial close between the government contracting agency and the private sector developer. |
| Project development fund (PDF) | A fund dedicated to reimbursing the cost of feasibility studies, transaction advisers, and other costs of project development, to encourage contracting agencies to use high- quality transaction advisers and best practice. PDFs provide the specialized resources needed to conduct studies, to design and structure a PPP, and then to procure the PPP. |
| Real interest rate | The real interest rate is the interest rate applicable to a borrowing that takes inflation rate into account.<br><br>Real interest rate = Nominal interest rate – Inflation rate |
| Rehabilitate-operate-transfer | A PPP type whereby an existing facility is handed over to the private sector developer to refurbish, operate and maintain for a franchise period, at the expiry of which the legal title to the facility is turned over to the government contracting agency. |
| Regulatory framework | A framework encompassing all laws, regulations, policies, binding guidelines or instructions, other legal texts of general application, judicial decisions, and administrative rulings governing or setting precedent in connection with PPPs. In this context, the term "policies" refers to other government-issued documents, which are binding on all stakeholders, are enforced in a manner similar to laws and regulations, and provide detailed instructions for the implementation of PPPs. |
| Risk allocation matrix | Matrix indicating the allocation of the consequences of each risk to one of the parties in the PPP contract, or agreeing to deal with the risk through a specified mechanism which may involve sharing the risk. |
| Service contract | A PPP type under which the government contracting agency hires a private company or entity to carry out one or more specified tasks or services for a period, typically 1–3 years. The government contracting agency remains the primary provider of the infrastructure service and contracts out only portions of its operation to the private partner. The private partner must perform the service at the agreed cost and must typically meet performance standards set by the government contracting agency. Government contracting agencies generally use competitive bidding procedures to award service contracts, which tend to work well given the limited period and narrowly defined nature of these contracts. |
| Social impact assessment | Includes the processes of analyzing, monitoring, and managing the intended and unintended social consequences—both positive and negative—of planned interventions (policies, programs, plans, projects) and any social change processes invoked by those interventions. Its primary purpose is to bring about a more sustainable and equitable biophysical and human environment. |

*continued on next page*

*continued from previous page*

| Term | Definition |
|---|---|
| Social infrastructure | Covers social services, including hospitals, schools and universities, prisons, housing, and courts. |
| State-owned enterprise (SOE) | A company or enterprise owned by the government or in which the government has a controlling stake. |
| Swiss challenge | A process in public procurement when a government contracting agency that has received an unsolicited bid for a project publishes details of the bid and invites third parties to match or exceed it. |
| Tax holiday | A government incentive program that offers tax reduction or elimination to projects and/ or businesses. In the context of a PPP project, tax holidays are provided to exempt the concessionaire from making any tax payments during the initial demand ramp up period to make the project financially viable. |
| Unsolicited bid | A proposal made by a private party to undertake a PPP project. It is submitted at the initiative of the private party, rather than in response to a request from the government contracting agency. |
| User charges | A method of investment recovery in PPP projects when payments to the private party are fully derived from tariffs paid by users or off-takers over the lifetime of a PPP contract, in return for making infrastructure or services available for use at acceptable and contractually agreed performance standards. |
| Viability gap funding | A scheme wherein the projects with low financial viability are given grants (or other financial support from the government) up to a stipulated percentage of the project cost, making them financially viable as PPPs. |

# Abbreviations

| | | |
|---|---|---|
| ADB | – | Asian Development Bank |
| ARMM | – | Autonomous Region in Muslim Mindanao |
| ASEAN | – | Association of Southeast Asian Nations |
| BLGF | – | Bureau of Local Government Finance |
| BLT | – | build–lease–transfer |
| BOI | – | Board of Investments |
| BOO | – | build–own–operate |
| BOT | – | build–operate–transfer |
| BTO | – | build–transfer–operate |
| CAO | – | contract–add–operate |
| CBO | – | community-based organization |
| CCPAP | – | Coordinating Council of the Philippine Assistance Center |
| CCPSP | – | Coordinating Council for Private Sector Participation |
| CPI | – | consumer price index |
| CPIA | – | country policy and institutional assessment |
| CRISP | – | Credit Rating and Investors Services Philippines |
| CSU | – | Cagayan State University |
| DBM | – | Department of Budget and Management |
| DBP | – | Development Bank of the Philippines |
| DED | – | detailed engineering design |
| DENR | – | Department of Environment and Natural Resources |
| DILG | – | Department of the Interior and Local Government |
| DMC | – | developing member country |
| DOE | – | Department of Energy |
| DOF | – | Department of Finance |

| | | |
|---|---|---|
| DOH | – | Department of Health |
| DOT | – | develop–operate–transfer |
| DOTr | – | Department of Transportation |
| DPWH | – | Department of Public Works and Highways |
| DRT | – | Dispute Resolution Tribunal |
| DSCR | – | debt service cover ratio |
| DTI | – | Department of Trade and Industry |
| EGCO | – | Electricity Generating Company |
| EIA | – | environmental impact assessment |
| EIRR | – | economic internal rate of return |
| EIU | – | Economist Intelligence Unit |
| EPIRA | – | Electric Power Industry Reform Act |
| ERC | – | Energy Regulatory Commission |
| ESC | – | Education Service Contracting |
| EVAT | – | Expanded Value-Added Tax Act |
| EVOSS | – | Energy Virtual One-Stop Shop |
| EXCOM | – | Executive Committee |
| FDA | – | Food and Drug Administration |
| FDI | – | Foreign Direct Investment |
| FIRR | – | Financial Internal Rate of Return |
| FIT | – | feed-in-tariff |
| FIT-ALL | – | feed-in-tariff allowance |
| FNPV | – | financial net present value |
| FOB | – | freight on board |
| FOREX | – | foreign exchange |
| FPHC | – | First Philippine Holdings Corporation |
| GDP | – | gross domestic product |
| GNI | – | gross national income |
| GOCC | – | government-owned and controlled corporation |
| GPRAM | – | generic preferred risks allocation matrix |
| GRDP | – | gross regional domestic product |
| HFSRB | – | Health Facilities and Service Regulatory Bureau |

HGC – Home Guaranty Corporation
HMO – health maintenance organization
HUDCC – Housing and Urban Development Coordinating Council
Pag-IBIG – Pagtutulungan sa Kinabukasan: Ikaw, Bangko, Industriya at Gobyerno
ICC – Investment Coordination Committee
ICT – information and communications technology
IRA – internal revenue allotment
IRR – implementing rules and regulations
LBP – Land Bank of the Philippines
LGC – local government code
LGU – local government unit
LGUGC – Local Government Unit Guarantee Corporation
LIBOR – London Interbank Offered Rate
LOI – letter of instruction
LPI – logistics performance index
LRT – light rail transit
LWUA – Local Water Utilities Administration
MCA – multi-criteria analysis
MCIA – Mactan Cebu International Airport
MDC – Municipal Development Council
MDF – Municipal Development Fund
MDFO – Municipal Development Fund Office
MDG – millennium development goal
MFD – Macro Funders and Development Corporation
MOF – Ministry of Finance
MPIC – Metro Pacific Investments Corporation
MRT – metro rail transit
MSW – municipal solid waste
MTEF – medium term expenditure framework
MTPA – million metric tons per annum
MVA – multivariate analysis
MWSS – Metropolitan Waterworks and Sewerage System

MWSS-RO – MWSS Regulatory Office
NAIA – Ninoy Aquino International Airport
NAWASA – National Waterworks and Sewerage Authority
NBFC – non- banking financial corporation
NEDA – National Economic Development Authority
NGA – National Government Agency
NHIP – National Health Insurance Program
NLEX – North Luzon Expressway
NPC – National Power Corporation
NRW – non-revenue water
NSP – National Shelter Program
NSSMP – National Sewerage and Septage Management Program
NWRB – National Water Resources Board
ODA – official development assistance
OECD – Organisation for Economic Co-operation and Development
OPDS – Office of Project Development Services
PBIP – performance-based incentive policy
PCCI – Philippine Chamber of Commerce and Industry
PDC – Provincial Development Council
PDEX – Philippine Dealing and Exchange Corporation
PDF – Project Development Facility
PDMF – Project Development and Monitoring Facility
PDRCI – Philippine Dispute Resolution Center, Inc.
PDST – Philippine Dealing System Treasury
PEFA – Public Expenditure and Financial Accountability
PEMC – Philippine Electricity Market Corporation
PFMS – Public Financial Management System
PGH – Philippine General Hospital
PIPDF – Private Infrastructure Project Development Facility
PMC – Project Monitoring Committee
PNP – Philippine National Police
PNSDW – Philippine National Standards for Drinking Water

| | | |
|---|---|---|
| PPA | – | Power Purchase Agreement |
| PPI | – | private participation in infrastructure |
| PPP | – | public–private partnerships |
| PPPC | – | Public–Private Partnership Center |
| PPPGB | – | Public–Private Partnership Governing Board |
| PPPSF | – | Public–Private Partnership Support Fund (PPPSF) |
| PSALM | – | Power Sector Assets and Liabilities Management Corporation |
| PSE | – | Philippine Stock Exchange |
| PSIP | – | Public–Private Partnership for School Infrastructure Project |
| PSP | – | private sector participation |
| PSSP | – | Philippine Sustainable Sanitation Roadmap |
| PSSR | – | Philippine Sustainable Sanitation Plan |
| PTACF | – | Project Technical Assistance and Contingency Fund |
| PWSSR | – | Philippine Water Supply Sector Roadmap |
| RDC | – | Regional Development Council |
| REPA | – | Renewable Energy Payment Agreement |
| RFQ | – | request for qualification |
| ROO | – | rehabilitate–own–operate |
| ROT | – | rehabilitate–operate–transfer |
| RWA | – | Rural Water Supply Associations |
| SCBA | – | social cost–benefit analysis |
| SEC | – | Securities and Exchange Commission |
| SHFC | – | Social Housing Finance Corporation |
| SLEX | – | South Luzon Expressway |
| SMC | – | San Miguel Corporation |
| SPV | – | special purpose vehicle |
| SSS | – | Social Security System |
| TESDA | – | Technical Education and Skills Development Authority |
| TIEZA | – | Tourism Infrastructure and Enterprise Zone Authority |
| TPLEX | – | Tarlac–Pangasinan–La Union Expressway |
| TRB | – | Toll Regulatory Board |
| TVET | – | technical and vocational education and training |

| | | |
|---|---|---|
| UHC | – | Universal Health Care |
| USD | – | United States dollar |
| VGF | – | viability gap funding |
| WESM | – | wholesale electricity spot market |
| WSS | – | water supply and sanitation |
| WSSPMO | – | Water and Sanitation Program Management Office |

# Guide to Understanding the Public–Private Partnership Monitor

The *Public–Private Partnership Monitor*, a flagship publication of the Asian Development Bank (ADB), profiles the current state of the public–private partnerships (PPP) enabling environment in ADB's developing member countries (DMCs) in Asia and the Pacific. *The PPP Monitor* features, for the first time, a data driven, interactive online version which allows users to compare and contrast the key PPP parameters and features across the featured DMCs. While the featured countries are a small sample, more countries will be continually added in *the PPP Monitor*, which is expected to become a knowledge base for assessing a country's PPP environment for the government and the business community. The new PPP Monitor builds on the success of the first and second editions of *the PPP Monitor*.

*The PPP Monitor* provides a snapshot of the overall PPP landscape in the country. This downloadable guide also assesses more than 500 qualitative and quantitative indicators that have been structured per topic—the national PPP landscape, the sector-specific PPP landscape (for eight identified infrastructure sectors and a separate section for other sectors), and the PPP landscape for local government projects. *The PPP Monitor* also captures the critical macroeconomic and infrastructure sector indicators (including the *Ease of Doing Business* scores) from globally accepted sources.

Each of the topics and associated subtopics presented below are characterized by qualitative and quantitative indicators. Qualitative indicators take the form of a question to which "Yes," "No," "Not Applicable," or "Unavailable" answers can be given. Quantitative indicators are represented in the form of numbers, ratios, investment value, and duration.

For each of the developing member countries covered, the information and data are organized along the following topic clusters:

## Overview

| Topic | Subtopics |
|---|---|
| Overview | • Overview of the PPP legal and regulatory framework<br>• Number of PPP projects reaching financial close from 1990 till end of 2019 across sectors<br>• Total investment made in PPPs from 1990 to 2019 across sectors<br>• Features of past PPP projects including the number of PPPs procured through various modes<br>• Number of PPP projects under preparation and procurement<br>• Number of PPP projects supported by government<br>• Payment mechanism for PPPs<br>• Foreign sponsor participation in PPPs from 1990 to 2019<br>• Major sponsors active in the infrastructure sector in the country<br>• Challenges associated with the PPP landscape in the country |

# National Public–Private Partnership Landscape Indicators

To profile the national PPP landscape, the indicators are grouped into three major categories: national PPP enabling framework, government support for PPP projects, and maturity of the PPP market.

| Topic | Subtopics |
|---|---|
| National PPP legal and regulatory framework | Details on the legal and regulatory framework applicable to PPPs and its evolution since the introduction of PPPs in the country<br><br>Details on the other supporting laws and regulations governing PPPs in the country |
| PPP types | Details on the PPP types allowed to be used as per PPP legal and regulatory framework. In case the PPP legal and regulatory framework doesn't specify the PPP types, this section provides the details on the specific PPP types which have been adopted for various PPP projects at various stages of the PPP lifecycle. |
| Eligible sectors | Details on various infrastructure sectors for which projects could be procured through the PPP route as per the PPP legal and regulatory framework |
| Public–private partnership institutional framework | Details on the PPP institutional framework including the availability of a PPP Unit, the functions of the PPP Unit, the principal public entities associated with PPPs and their respective functions, and the details of the public entities responsible for PPP project identification, appraisal, approval, oversight, and monitoring |
| Entities responsible for PPP project identification, approval, and oversight | |
| Entities responsible for PPP project monitoring | |
| The public–private partnership process | Details on the various stages of the PPP process including PPP project identification, preparation, structuring, procurement, and management as per the PPP legal and regulatory framework in the country |
| PPP standard operating procedures, toolkits, templates, and model bid documents | Details on the standard operating procedures, and standard templates or model bidding documents available for PPPs (if any)<br><br>Details on the key clauses in a PPP Agreement based on the review of select PPP Agreements already executed, and/ or the review of the PPP legal and regulatory framework |
| Lender's security rights | Rights of lenders including the charge of project assets |
| Termination and compensation | Definition on whether the private player is eligible for compensation in case of PPP project termination due to various reasons |
| Unsolicited PPP proposals | Details on possibility of submission of unsolicited PPP proposals, and their treatment, including potential advantages provided to the unsolicited PPP proposal proponent at the PPP procurement stage |
| Foreign investor participation restrictions | Definition on whether there are any statutory restrictions on foreign equity investments and ownership in PPP projects |
| Dispute resolution | Definition of the dispute resolution process and the mechanisms available in the country |

*continued on next page*

*continued from previous page*

| Topic | Subtopics |
|---|---|
| Environmental and social issues | Details on whether the legal and regulatory framework governing PPPs stipulates a mechanism for managing the environmental and social impact of a PPP project, including the potential environmental and social issues which could be caused by a PPP project |
| Land rights | Definition of the various mechanisms through which land ownership and/or land use rights could be provided to the private partner in respect of the project site for a PPP project<br><br>Details on land records and registration which could be provided to the private partner |
| Government financial support for PPP projects | Details on the various mechanisms of government financial support available to make PPP projects financially viable<br><br>Salient features of government financial support mechanisms available |
| Project development funding support | Details on the various sources through which funding could be availed for the development activities (preparation, structuring, and procurement) of a PPP project<br><br>Details on stages of the PPP project development during which such funding could be availed and utilized, including payments to transaction advisors |
| PPP project statistics | Details on the key PPP statistics in the country such as the availability of (i) a PPP database showing distribution of PPP projects across sectors and across various stages of the PPP lifecycle, and (ii) a national PPP project pipeline and its alignment with the National Infrastructure Plan for the country |
| Sources of PPP financing | Details on the sources of financing for PPP projects in the country<br><br>Details on typical key financing terms for various sources of financing, banks active in project finance for the last 24 months, active PPP project sponsors in the country for the last 24 months, availability of derivatives market, and availability of credit rating agencies in the country |

# Sector-Specific Public–Private Partnership Landscape Indicators

To profile the sector-specific PPP landscape, the indicators are grouped into five major categories: (i) sector-specific PPP contracting agencies, (ii) sector laws and regulations, (iii) sector master plan (including sector-specific PPP pipeline), (iv) features of the past PPP projects in the sector, and (v) sector-specific challenges for PPPs. The sectors which do not appear consistently across the featured countries are covered under the 'Other Sectors' category in the sector-specific PPP landscape.

| Topic | Subtopics |
|---|---|
| Contracting agencies in the sector | Details on which government agencies could act as the contracting agencies for a PPP project |
| Sector laws and regulations | Details on the applicable sector laws and regulations for PPP projects, including the sector regulators and their respective functions. |
| Foreign investment restrictions in the sector | Details on the maximum allowed foreign equity investment in greenfield PPP projects in the sector |
| Standard contracts in the sector | Specification on whether standard contracts are available for PPP projects in the sector |
| Sector master plan | Details on the master plan and/or roadmap adopted for infrastructure development in the sector by the national government and the corresponding line ministry<br><br>Details on the pipeline of PPP projects for the sector aligned with this sector master plan and/or roadmap<br><br>Details on the PPP projects under preparation and procurement in the sector |
| Features of past PPP projects | Features of the past PPP projects based on supporting indicators in terms of the number and value (where applicable) of PPP projects for each supporting indicator |
| Tariffs applicable to the sector | Details on the indicative tariffs applicable in the sector based on the examples of select PPP or other projects operational in the sector |
| Typical risk allocation for PPP projects in the sector | Details on the typical risk allocation between the government contracting agency and the private partner based on examples of select PPP projects which have achieved commercial close |
| Financing details for PPP projects in the sector | Typical financing details based on past PPP projects on the lines of the supporting indicators |
| Challenges associated with PPPs in the sector | Details on the PPP-related and sector-specific challenges faced by PPP projects in the sector |
| Typical sector-specific infrastructure indicators for the country | Details on select sector-specific infrastructure indicators for the country |

## Local Government Public–Private Partnership Landscape

To profile the PPP landscape for local government projects, the indicators are grouped into seven major categories: (i) local governance system, (ii) infrastructure development plans for local governments, (iii) sectors in which local governments can implement PPPs, (iv) revenue sources for local governments, (v) borrowings by local governments, (vi) budgetary allocation to local governments, and (vii) credit rating of local governments.

| Topic | Subtopics |
|---|---|
| Key indicators related to local governments in the country | Details on the local governments using select key indicators on (i) the number and levels of local governments, (ii) the typical expenditure profile and heads, (iii) the typical revenue profile and heads, (iv) the typical debt profile and heads, and (v) grants and transfers from the higher levels of government |
| Local governance system | Details on the local governance system in the country, including the various levels of local governments; their roles, responsibilities, and functions; and the devolution of powers from the higher levels of government to the various levels of local governments |
| Infrastructure development plan for local governments | Details on the infrastructure development plans prepared by the local governments based on their capital investment projects in the pipeline, and the coverage of such infrastructure development plans |
| PPP enabling framework for local governments | Details on the PPP enabling framework applicable to local government PPP projects, including PPP legal and regulatory framework, PPP policy framework, and PPP institutional framework |
| Eligible sectors for PPPs for local governments | Details on the eligible sectors in which PPPs could be undertaken by the local government as government contracting agency |
| Revenues for local governments | Details on the typical sources of revenue for local governments |
| Borrowings by local governments | Details on the typical sources of debt financing available for local governments, the purpose for which borrowed funds could be used, the terms of such borrowings, and the borrowing exposure of select local governments |
| Budgetary allocation to local governments | Details on the budgetary allocations and transfers to the local governments from the higher levels of government |
| Credit rating of local governments | Details on the precedence of local governments being rated by credit rating agencies in the country, and the details of credit ratings obtained by select local governments in the past |
| Case study on a local government PPP | A case of a PPP project undertaken by a local government in the past covering details on project background, project assets, PPP structure for the project, risk allocation among the parties for the project, project finance and project revenue details, and key learnings from the PPP project |

# Critical Macroeconomic and Infrastructure Sector Indicators

This section captures the critical macroeconomic and infrastructure sector indicators (including the *Ease of Doing Business* scores) from globally accepted sources.

| Topic | Subtopics |
|---|---|
| Critical macroeconomic and infrastructure sector indicators | Details of the select key macroeconomic and infrastructure indicators for the country |
| *Ease of Doing Business* | Details on the various *Ease of Doing Business* parameters for the country based on the World Bank's *Ease of Doing Business* publication |

# Time Periods

The research was carried out in 2020 with the aim of reflecting the status as of the end of 2019. Therefore, some indicator data may have changed between the said period and the publication date of this report.

In country-level and sector-level sections, quantitative data in relation to the number of projects reflect the cumulative number of projects over the periods 1990–2017, 1990–2018, and 1990–2019. Otherwise, the data represent the status at each individual year.

# Currency Equivalents

(As of 7 April 2020)

₱1 = $ 0.01974
$1 = ₱ 50.37

# I. Overview

The Philippines is the first country in Asia to institutionalize private sector participation in infrastructure and development projects. In 1990, it enacted the build–operate–transfer (BOT) law (Republic Act 6957), which was amended and replaced by the Revised BOT Law and its Implementing Rules and Regulations (IRR) in 1994 (Republic Act 7718). The IRR was further revised in 2012, and the Revised BOT Law and its Revised IRR of 2012 form the legal and regulatory framework governing public–private partnerships (PPPs) in the Philippines. The Government of the Philippines also passed the Local Government Code in 1991 (Republic Act 7160) which encourages local government units (LGUs) to procure and implement infrastructure and development projects through PPP.

Over the last 3 decades, PPPs have been a key component of the overall strategy and development agenda of the Government of the Philippines for inclusive growth. The government has introduced many governance reforms to the BOT framework governing PPPs. These reforms include establishing the PPP Governing Board (PPPGB), a PPP Center, and a project development and monitoring facility (PDMF) to provide financial support for preparing PPP projects.[1] Executive orders and PPP-specific policy circulars have been issued clearly defining and detailing the PPP processes and mechanisms including the roles, responsibilities, and functions of various parties involved in a PPP. One such critical policy was Executive Order 136 of 2013, which reorganized the PPP Center and attached it to the National Economic and Development Authority (NEDA).

In 2016, the new government included the PPP program in its 10-point economic program highlighting the Philippines' commitment to facilitate private sector participation in infrastructure investment. The government adopted the 2017–2022 Development Plan with infrastructure as a top priority, and targeted spending on infrastructure projects to reach $180 billion between 2017 and 2022. PPPs at the LGU level is a priority investment area in the 2017–2022 Development Plan, consistent with the current administration's directive to accelerate infrastructure development in the countryside. LGUs are increasingly encouraged to pursue more PPPs based on the Local Government Code of 1991.

The PPP Center has proved to be working efficiently in facilitating PPP project preparation and development, building capacity of government contracting agencies, advocating policy reforms, monitoring implementation of PPP projects, and building up a PPP knowledge system. It also builds partnerships with organizations that aim to accelerate infrastructure development in the countryside, such as the Mindanao Development Authority, the Development Academy of the Philippines, and the League of Cities of the Philippines. The project preparation and bidding are generally carried out using experienced, international transaction advisers from the Project Development and Monitoring Facility (footnote 1).

From 1990 to 2019, about 116 PPP projects from different sectors (i.e., airports, electricity, information and communications technology, ports, railways, roads, and water and sewerage) have successfully achieved financial

1 ADB. 2019. *Public–Private Partnership Monitor. Second Edition.* Manila. https://www.adb.org/sites/default/files/publication/509426/ppp-monitor-second-edition.pdf.

closure. The total investment made in these PPP projects is approximately $43.95 billion. During this period, four PPP projects worth $5.06 billion were canceled (11.5% of total investment and 3.4% of total number of projects).[2] Figure 1 and Figure 2 show the number of PPP projects which have achieved financial closure, and which have been canceled.

**Figure 1: Public–Private Partnership Projects Financially Closed and Canceled, 1990–2019**

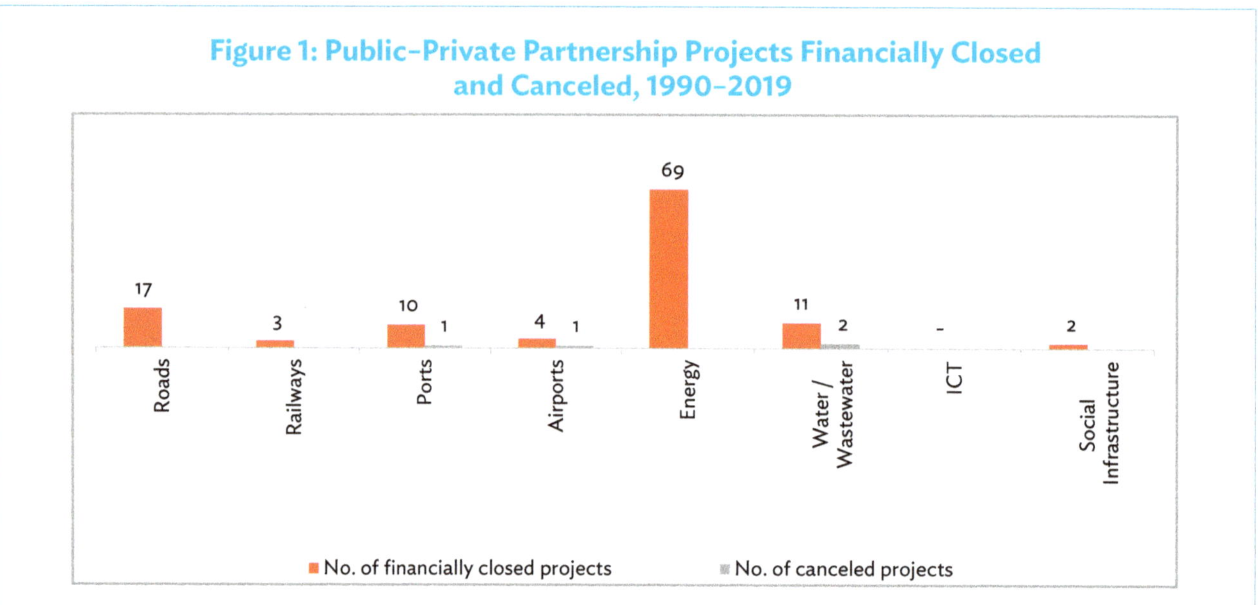


Note: Total projects include projects that are active, canceled, distressed, and concluded.

Source: World Bank. Infrastructure Finance, PPPs and Guarantees. Country Snapshots. Philippines. https://ppi.worldbank.org/en/snapshots/country/philippines (accessed 28 August 2020).

**Figure 2: Status of Public–Private Partnership Projects across Sectors**

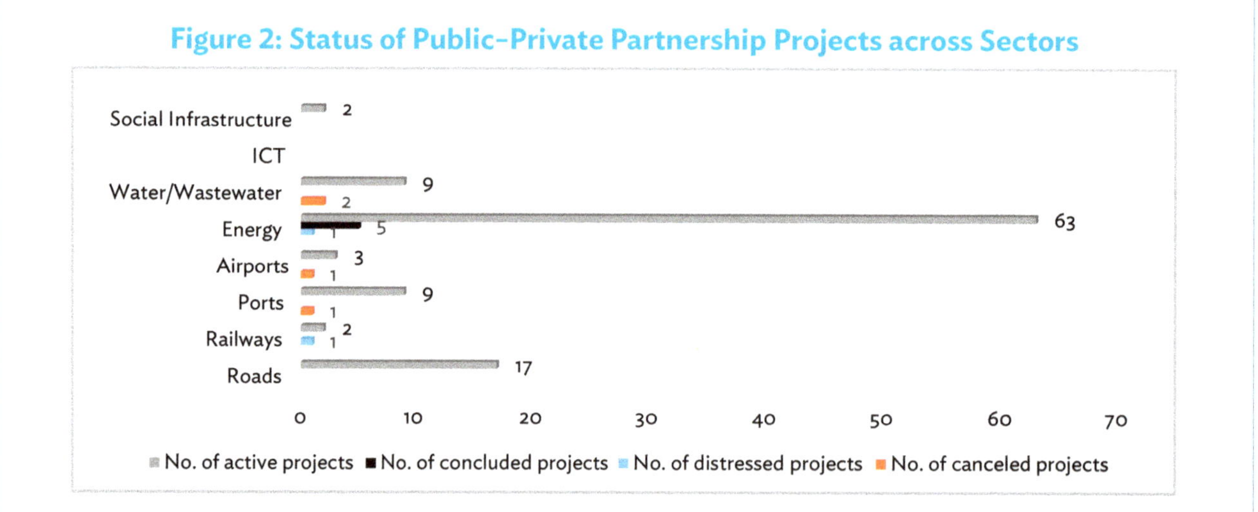


Note: Total projects include projects that are active, canceled, distressed, and concluded.

Source: World Bank. Infrastructure Finance, PPPs and Guarantees. Country Snapshots. Philippines. https://ppi.worldbank.org/en/snapshots/country/philippines (accessed 28 August 2020).

2 World Bank. Infrastructure Finance, PPPs and Guarantees. Country Snapshots. Philippines. https://ppi.worldbank.org/en/snapshots/country/philippines (accessed 28 August 2020).

PPPs are most dominant in the energy sector, and in roads and water and wastewater sectors. In the railways sector, the average size of a project reaching financial closure was highest at $1,058 million (₱53.29 billion as of April 2020), followed by that of the water and wastewater sector at $801 million (₱15.81 billion as of April 2020). Figure 3 depicts the total investment in each sector from 1990 to 2019, and the average size of a PPP project in each of these sectors. Table 1 lists the major sponsors that are active in the infrastructure sector.

## Figure 3: Investments in Public–Private Partnerships by Sector, 1990–2019

($ million)

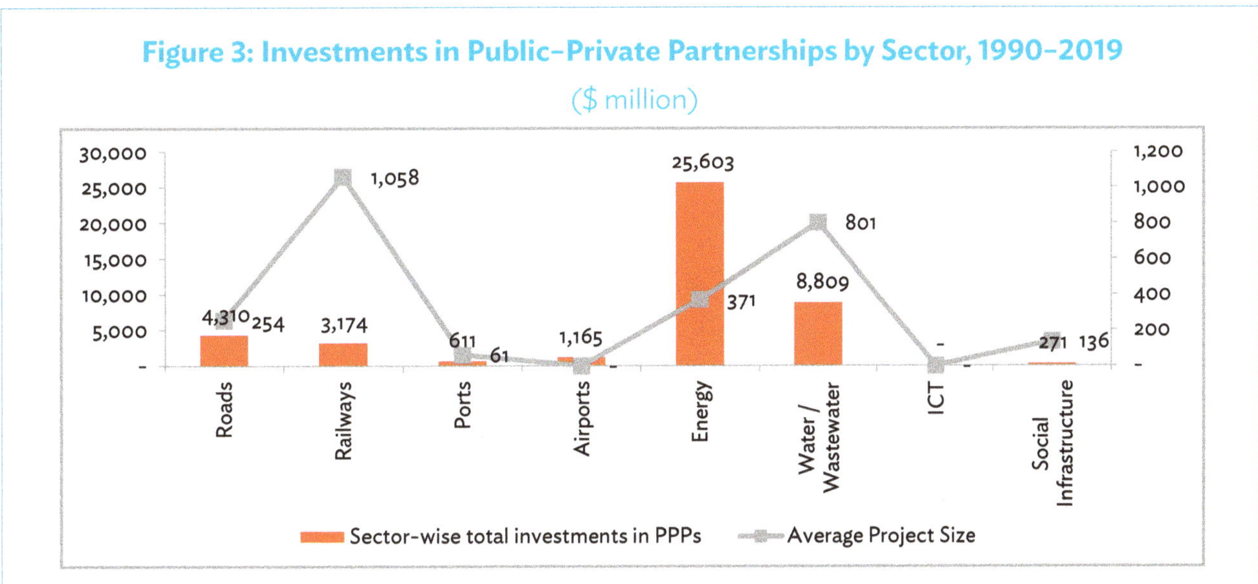


Note: Total projects include projects that are active, canceled, distressed, and concluded.

Source: World Bank. Infrastructure Finance, PPPs and Guarantees. Country Snapshots. Philippines. https://ppi.worldbank.org/en/snapshots/country/philippines (accessed 28 August 2020).

## Table 1: Major Sponsors Active in the Infrastructure Sector

| Private Sponsor | Country of Origin | Total Investment ($ million) | Total Investment (₱ billion) | Number of PPP Projects |
|---|---|---|---|---|
| Aboitiz Equity Ventures | Philippines | 8,186 | 412 | 21 |
| AES Corporation | United States of America | 1,757 | 89 | 2 |
| Ayala Corporation | Philippines | 8,234 | 415 | 8 |
| Lopez Holdings Corporation (formerly Benpres Holdings Corporation) | Philippines | 4,538 | 229 | 2 |
| Electricity Generating Company (EGCO) | Thailand | 2,923 | 147 | 5 |
| First Philippine Holdings Corporation (FPHC) | Philippines | 6,298 | 317 | 9 |
| Marubeni Corp. | Japan | 3,545 | 179 | 5 |
| Metro Pacific Investments Corporation (MPIC) | Philippines | 3,230 | 163 | 8 |
| San Miguel Corporation (SMC) | Philippines | 5,304 | 267 | 6 |
| SUEZ | United States of America | 5,218 | 263 | 2 |

Source: World Bank. Infrastructure Finance, PPPs and Guarantees. Country Snapshots. Philippines. https://ppi.worldbank.org/en/snapshots/country/philippines (accessed 28 August 2020).

From 1990 to 2019, nine PPP projects were procured through direct appointment, and 29 PPP projects through a competitive bidding process across various infrastructure sectors. Information on 56 projects is unavailable as per the World Bank database. Further, as per the database, a total of 57 projects have been procured through unsolicited route.

**Figure 4: Various Modes of Procuring Public–Private Partnership Projects, 1990–2019**

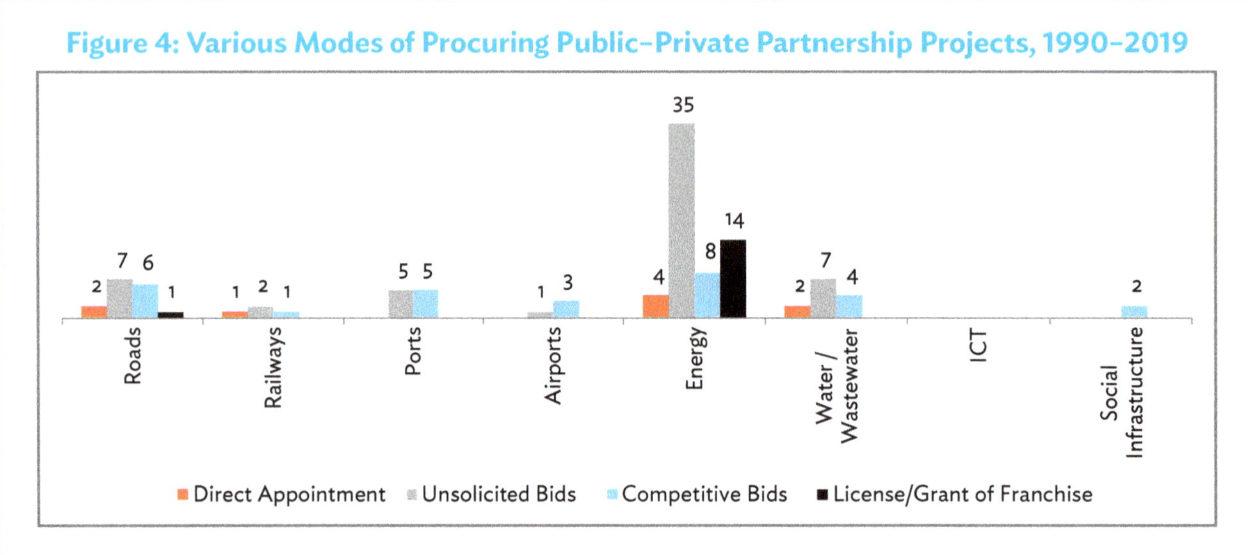


Note: Total projects include projects that are active, canceled, distressed, and concluded.

Source: World Bank. Infrastructure Finance, PPPs and Guarantees. Country Snapshots. Philippines. https://ppi.worldbank.org/en/snapshots/country/philippines (accessed 28 August 2020).

As of 2019, as per the PPP Center publications, there are 37 PPP projects at various stages of preparation, and three PPP projects under procurement across various infrastructure sectors including roads, railways, ports, airports, energy, water and wastewater, and social infrastructure (Figure 5).

**Figure 5: Public–Private Partnership Projects under Preparation and Procurement, 2019**

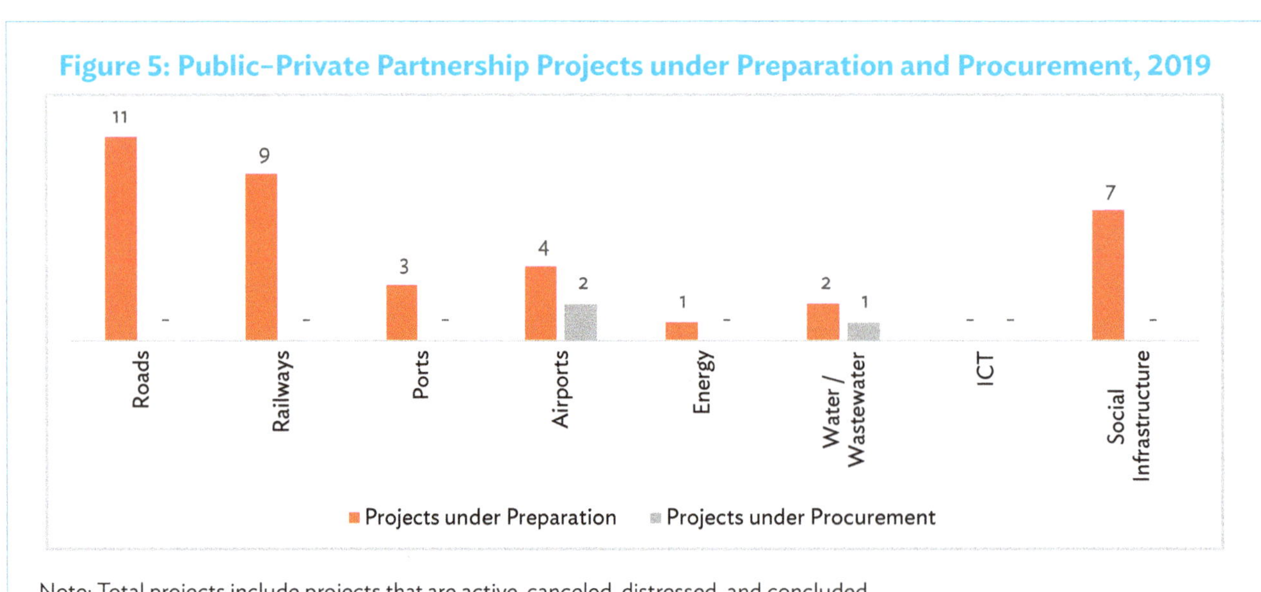


Note: Total projects include projects that are active, canceled, distressed, and concluded.

Source: Public–Private Partnership Center. https://ppp.gov.ph/

From 1990 to 2019, two projects have been supported through viability gap funding, 17 projects through government guarantees, and 43 projects through availability payments (Figure 6).

**Figure 6: Public–Private Partnership Projects with Government Support, 1990–2019**

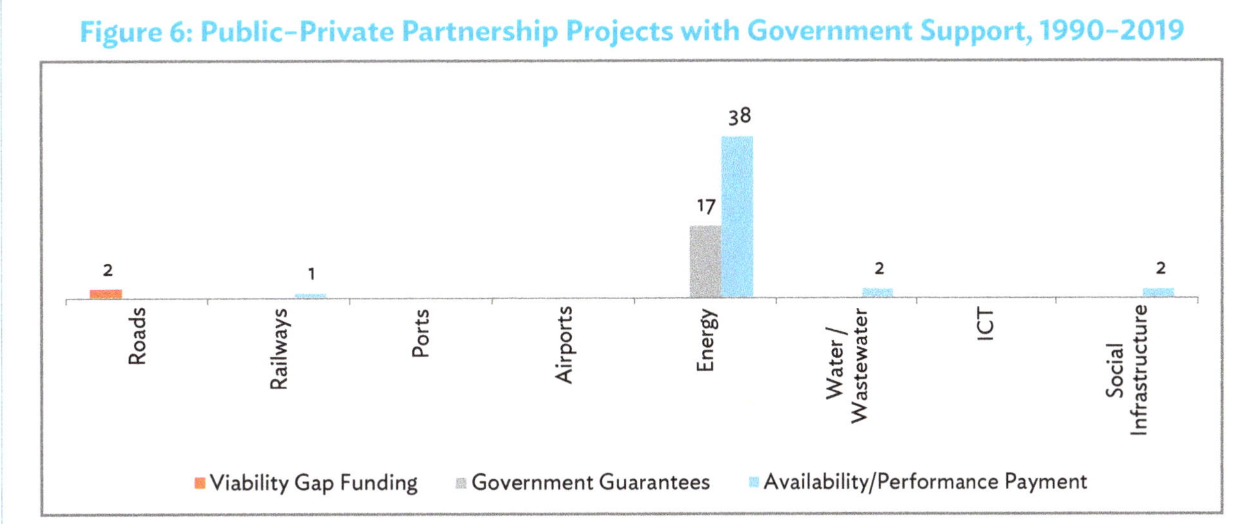


Note: Chart includes projects that are active, canceled, distressed, and concluded.

Source: World Bank. Infrastructure Finance, PPPs and Guarantees. Country Snapshots. Philippines. https://ppi.worldbank.org/en/snapshots/country/philippines (accessed 28 August 2020).

During the same period, 33 PPP projects were awarded based on user charges, and 43 PPP projects based on government pay (off-take). Information on 40 projects is unavailable or quoted "not applicable" on the database (Figure 7).

**Figure 7: Payment Mechanism for Public–Private Partnership Projects, 1990–2019**

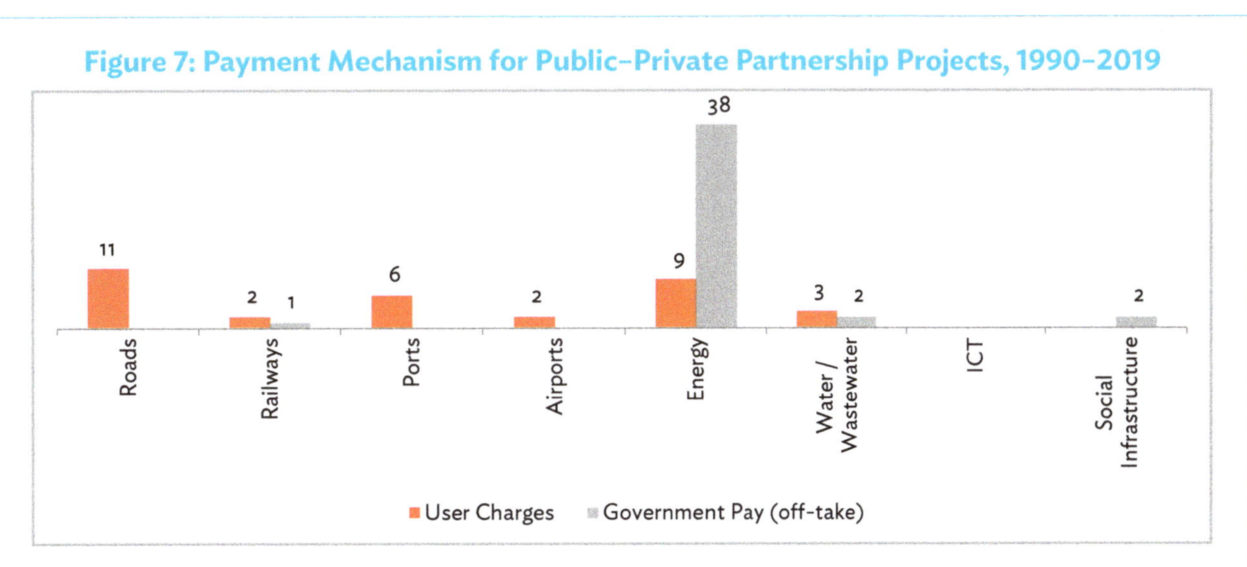


Note: Chart includes projects that are active, canceled, distressed, and concluded.

Source: World Bank. Infrastructure Finance, PPPs and Guarantees. Country Snapshots. Philippines. https://ppi.worldbank.org/en/snapshots/country/philippines (accessed 28 August 2020).

Over the last decade, the Philippines has witnessed the active participation of foreign sponsors. A total of 39 projects attracted participation from foreign sponsors predominantly in the energy sector. Figure 8 shows the distribution of PPP projects across various infrastructure sectors.

**Figure 8: Foreign Sponsor Participation, 1990–2019**

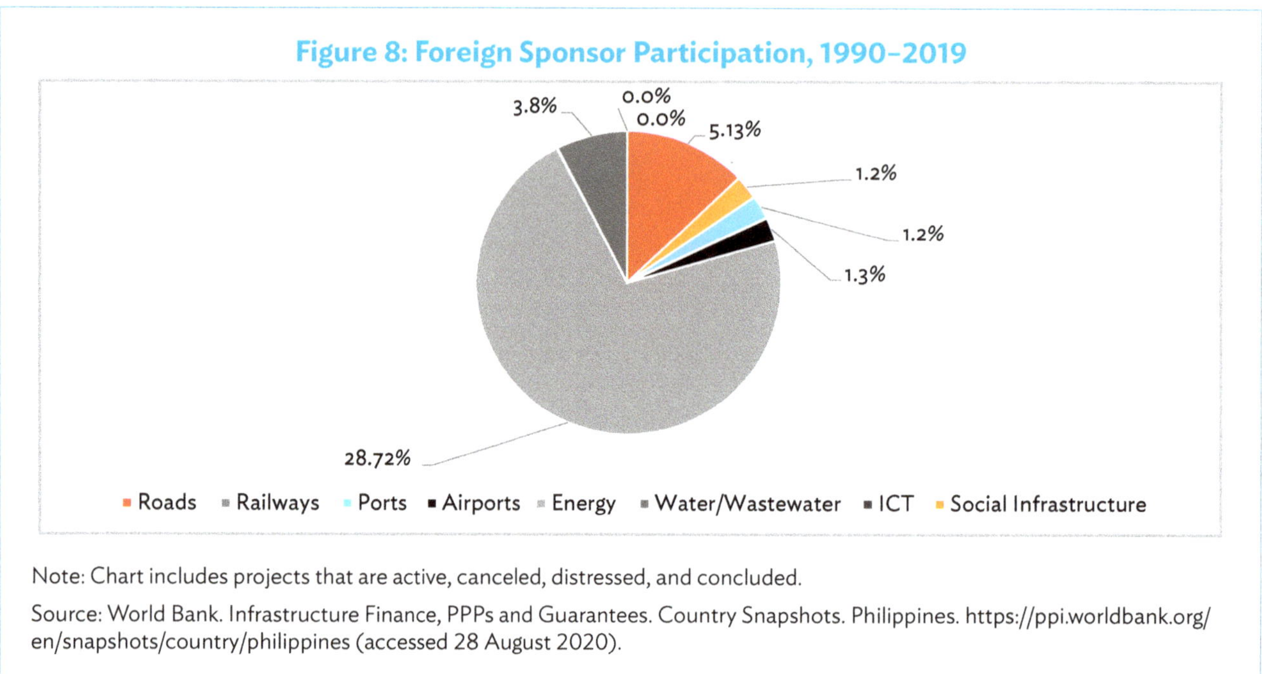


Note: Chart includes projects that are active, canceled, distressed, and concluded.

Source: World Bank. Infrastructure Finance, PPPs and Guarantees. Country Snapshots. Philippines. https://ppi.worldbank.org/en/snapshots/country/philippines (accessed 28 August 2020).

While much has been achieved in developing the PPP market in the Philippines, challenges still prevail. One of the critical impediments is the existing cap of 40% for foreign ownership in the PPP Project Special Purpose Vehicle for infrastructure PPPs, wherein the operation requires a public utility franchise. This may restrict competition and, as a result, may inhibit Philippine infrastructure development. According to the incumbent government, this issue is expected to be addressed through amendments to the 1987 Constitution.[3] There is a pending bill with the Congress of the Philippines to redefine what industries are considered public utilities.

Despite the restriction, a number of projects have witnessed foreign investors' participation over 1990–2019. The project financing scenario in the Philippines is dominated by local banks due to their aggressive lending backed by the very liquid debt market. The banks are uniquely positioned to lend to infrastructure PPPs on relatively attractive terms as compared to foreign loans, given their strong relationships with local conglomerates, and the requirement for loans to be in local currency. Furthermore, domestic banks do not require any political risk guarantee, unlike the international lenders, and they offer terms which are light on covenants (footnote 1).

The Philippines' bond market is another source of long-term financing for PPPs being explored by the government. In 2016, the Asian Development Bank (ADB) provided support for the issuance of the Philippines' first peso-denominated green project bond for the refinancing of the Tiwi and Makiling–Banahaw (Tiwi–MakBan) geothermal facilities (footnote 1).

[3] C. Jiao. 2017. *Businesses Look Forward to Government Relaxing Foreign Ownership Rules*. CNN. 7 January.

In late 2016, the Securities and Exchange Commission (SEC) approved the listing of PPP Project Special Purpose Vehicles on the stock exchange, which is expected to widen the source of equity funding for PPPs (footnote 1). Today, however, no PPP company has ever been listed on the stock exchange.

The slowing down of PPP project completion is also due to multiple government authorities that need coordination for decision making, delays in project procurement, changes in project structure and source of funding during the tender process, and engaging local governments in PPPs which have limited capacity to prepare, procure, and manage PPPs. These challenges are being addressed by the government and the PPP Center through various measures. The government is drafting amendments to the BOT Law through a PPP act, which would further improve the enabling environment for PPPs (footnote 1).

The other critical challenges in implementing PPPs in the Philippines are that PPP contracts are not required to be published, and the absence of an independent dispute resolution body. Alternative dispute resolution mechanisms are available in the Philippines, and while not specific to PPPs, they may be incorporated by reference to PPP contracts. Contractual arrangements that include the operation and maintenance of infrastructure and require regulatory authorization are also a challenge.[4]

The current administration has repeatedly expressed support for PPP projects. Among the various types of PPPs, the government has specific preference for "hybrid" PPPs, wherein the government develops the infrastructure project assets, and then involves the private sector in their operation and maintenance. The regulatory framework does not specifically require the prioritization of PPP projects. To accelerate its ambitious infrastructure plan, the current administration has been increasingly open to unsolicited proposals for PPPs. It seems to favor the traditional public procurement and financing mechanism, arguing that this reduces project preparation and implementation time and cost in a highly regulated PPP environment (footnote 4).

4 The Economist Intelligence Unit. Philippines. https://infrascope.eiu.com/.

# II. National Public–Private Partnership Landscape

Since the 1980s, the Government of the Philippines has been using PPPs as a mode of procurement, and has a comprehensive legal framework focusing on strengthening transparency and legal security. The PPP enabling framework in the Philippines includes the PPP law, along with related regulations, manuals, and policy guidelines. The Republic Act 7718 of 1994 (an amendment to Republic Act 6957 of 1990) provides the basic legal framework for PPPs. The new implementing rules and regulations for Republic Act 7718 were introduced in 2012. Several executive orders, including Executive Order 136 (2013) which reorganized the PPP Center and attached it to the National Economic and Development Authority (NEDA), have also been issued (footnote 4).

The PPP Center is the main facilitating and monitoring agency for PPPs in the Philippines, assisting both national and local agencies in their project selection and evaluation methods, value-for-money analyses, financial viability, and financial structuring. The PPP Center also manages a revolving Project Development and Monitoring Facility (PDMF) for the preparation of a business case, feasibility studies, and tender documentation for PPP projects. Executive Order 136 also created the PPP Governing Board (PPPGB) and institutionalized the PDMF. Since 2015, the PPPGB has issued multiple PPP-specific policy circulars, further detailing processes and mechanisms (footnote 4).

In February 2020, NEDA published the Revised List of Infrastructure Flagship Projects, indicating the projects to be implemented using PPP. The priority projects identified for the PPP mode of implementation mainly shapes the PPP environment in the Philippines.

The PPP ecosystem is guided by the priority projects identified for the PPP mode of implementation as per the *Revised List of Infrastructure Flagship Projects* published on 17 February 2020 by NEDA.

## National Public–Private Partnership Enabling Framework

### 1. Public–Private Partnership Legal and Regulatory Framework

| Parameter | |
|---|---|
| Does the country have— | |
| • National PPP laws and regulations? | ✓ |
| • Public financial management laws and regulations? | ✓ |
| • Sector-specific laws and regulations? | ✓ |
| • Procurement laws and regulations? | ✓ |
| • Environmental laws and regulations? | ✓ |

*continued on next page*

*continued from previous page*

| Parameter | |
|---|---|
| • Laws and regulations for social compliance? | ✓ |
| • Laws and regulations governing land acquisition and ownership? | ✓ |
| • Taxation laws and regulations? | ✓ |
| • Employment laws and regulations? | ✓ |
| • Licensing requirements? | × |
| What are the other components of the PPP legal and regulatory framework? | Other key supporting components (elaborated below) include:<br>• PPP Governing Board (PPPGB) Guidelines and Issuances;<br>• Presidential Executive Order 136, Series of 2013; and<br>• Presidential Executive Order 8, Series of 2010. |

✓ = Yes, × = No, NA = Not Applicable, UA = Unavailable

Sources: Public–Private Partnership Center. Legal and Regulatory Frameworks. https://ppp.gov.ph/ppp-program/legal-and-regulatory-frameworks/; Public–Private Partnership Center. Historical Background. https://ppp.gov.ph/ppp-program/historical-background.

## Evolution of the Public–Private Partnership Legal and Regulatory Framework in the Philippines

Over the last 3 decades, each government administration has introduced changes on the legal framework of PPPs in the Philippines (Figure 9). How the PPP framework has evolved and the key principles behind such evolution are discussed below.[5]

**In 1986**, the Government of the Philippines divested itself from non-essential business-related assets acquired during the martial law regime and enacted Presidential Proclamation 50 in December 1986, which created the Asset Privatization Trust and the Committee on Privatization to handle this disinvestment (footnote 5).

**In 1987**, the Philippine Constitution was passed which defined the role of the private sector as a valuable partner in achieving the country's development goals. The government recognizes "the indispensable role of the private sector as the main engine of national growth" (Section 20, Article II, of the Philippine Constitution) (footnote 5).

**In 1990**, the Build–Operate–Transfer (BOT) Law was passed, which brought the participation of the private sector into the frontline of development efforts.[6] The Philippines became the first country in Asia to enact a law specifically for the BOT process. The 1990 BOT Law provided the legal basis and mechanisms for the private sector to undertake capital investment projects that were traditionally implemented by government agencies, corporations, or local government units (LGUs). The 1990 BOT Law provided only two modalities for contracting between the public and the private sector: the build–operate–transfer (BOT) scheme and the build–transfer scheme.

5 Public–Private Partnership Center. Historical Background. https://ppp.gov.ph/ppp-program/historical-background/.

6 Republic Act 6957. An Act Authorizing the Financing, Construction, Operation and Maintenance of Infrastructure Projects by the Private Sector, and for other Purposes. https://ppp.gov.ph/ppp-program/historical-background/#:~:text=In%201986%2C%20right%20after%20the,also%20enacted%20Presidential%20Proclamation%20No.

**Figure 9: Timeline for the Public–Private Partnership Legal and Regulatory Framework in the Philippines**

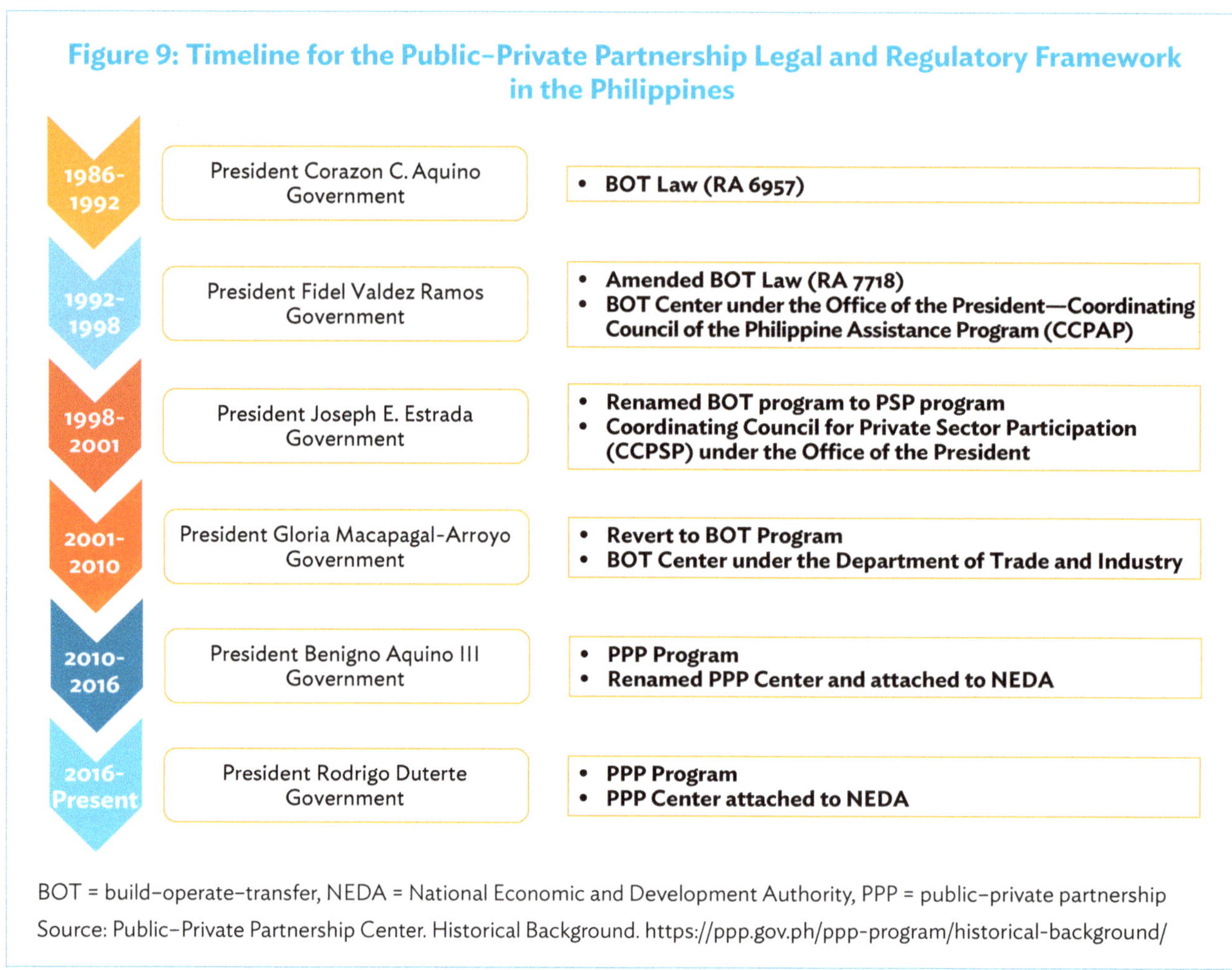


BOT = build–operate–transfer, NEDA = National Economic and Development Authority, PPP = public–private partnership

Source: Public–Private Partnership Center. Historical Background. https://ppp.gov.ph/ppp-program/historical-background/

The BOT scheme is a contractual arrangement wherein a contractor undertakes the construction, including financing, as well as operation and maintenance of a given infrastructure facility. The contractor operates the facility over a fixed term. During this term, it is allowed to charge the users with appropriate tolls, fees, and charges sufficient to recover its initial investment, operating and maintenance expenses, and a reasonable rate of return. The contractor transfers the facility back to the national government agency (NGA) or the LGU concerned at the end of the fixed term, which should not exceed 50 years (footnote 1).

In the build–transfer scheme, the facility is turned over to the NGA or the LGU concerned immediately after completion for security or strategic reasons. The contractor is paid for its total investment plus a reasonable rate of return through amortization payments (footnote 1).

Only one project was implemented under the 1990 BOT Law—a public market-cum-commercial complex in Mandaluyong City, called the "marketplace."

**In 1991**, the Local Government Code (LGC) was passed, which institutionalized the decentralization of PPPs from the national government to LGUs and encouraged the participation of the private sector in local governance, particularly in the delivery of basic services.

**In 1993**, the BOT Law was amended to what is presently known as the Republic Act 7718 or the *Amended BOT Law and its Implementing Rules and Regulations.* The government, through Memorandum Order 166, directed the Coordinating Council of the Philippine Assistance Center (CCPAP) of the Office of the President to establish a BOT Center with the CCPAP Chairman as the BOT Action Officer.

Under the Amended BOT Law and its IRR, seven more schemes for contracting between the public and the private sector were introduced: (i) build–transfer–operate (BTO), (ii) build–own–operate (BOO), (iii) build–lease–transfer (BLT), (iv) contract–add–operate (CAO), (v) develop–operate–transfer (DOT), (vi) rehabilitate–operate–transfer (ROT), and (vii) rehabilitate–own–operate (ROO). It is only the BOO projects that need the approval of the President of the Philippines upon the recommendation of NEDA Board's Investment Coordination Committee (ICC). Under the Amended BOT Law and its IRR, other variations similar to the modalities enumerated in it are also allowed with the approval of the President of the Philippines. One such variant is a concession which is usually given for an existing facility in sectors that are natural monopolies, such as water supply and distribution, power transmission and distribution, and roads and railways. Another contractual mode recognized by the Amended BOT Law and its IRR are management contracts (footnote 1).

The Amended BOT Law and its IRR also introduced a new section on unsolicited proposals. Unsolicited proposals for projects may be accepted, subject to negotiations, if all the following conditions are met: (i) the project involves a new concept or technology and/or is not included in the list of priority projects; (ii) no direct government guarantee, subsidy, or equity is required; and (iii) no other proposal has been received for a period of 60 working days after publishing the invitation for comparative or competitive proposals, for 3 consecutive weeks in a newspaper of general circulation. If another proponent submits a lower price proposal, the original proponent has the right to match that price within 30 working days (footnote 1).

Additional incentives were offered to private sector proponents. Up to 50% of the project cost may be financed by direct government appropriations and/or from Official Development Assistance (ODA) of foreign governments or institutions, with the balance to be provided by the project proponent, for projects with difficulty in sourcing funds.[7] P rojects costing more than ₱1 billion were entitled to the incentives provided by the Omnibus Investment Code, upon registration with the Board of Investments. In addition to these financial incentives, in order to support the private sector, the government also attempted to create an investor-friendly business climate with minimum government regulations and procedures (footnote 1).

While the 1990 BOT Law only referred to infrastructure projects, the Amended BOT Law and its IRR also included development projects, which were otherwise financed or operated by the public sector.

**During 1998–2001**, the CCPAP BOT Center was reorganized into the Coordinating Council for Private Sector Participation (CCPSP) through Administrative Order 67. This has expanded the coverage of the BOT Program to other forms of private sector participation, and the BOT Program was renamed as Private Sector Participation (PSP) Program. The CCPSP also formalized its provision of technical assistance support through technical assistance agreements with NGAs and LGUs.[8]

7 Project cost is defined in the Implementing Rules and Regulations (IRRs) of the BOT Law as the total cost expended by the proponent to plan, develop, and construct the project to completion stage including, but not limited to, such costs as feasibility study, detailed engineering and design, construction, equipment, land, and right of way.

8 Public–Private Partnership Center. Historical Background. https://ppp.gov.ph/ppp-program/historical-background/#:~:text=The%20Root%20of%20PPPs%20in,also%20enacted%20Presidential%20Proclamation%20No.

**In 2002**, Executive Order 144 was signed, which converted the CCPSP into the BOT Center and lodged it under the Department of Trade and Industry's Industry and Investment Group. Its task was to promote and market BOT projects, and to make public–private partnerships as the cornerstone of the national infrastructure development plan. During this period, the PSP Program was renamed as the BOT Program.

**In 2010**, Executive Order 8 titled *Reorganizing and Renaming the Build-Operate-and-Transfer (BOT) Center to the Public–Private Partnership (PPP) Center of the Philippines and Transferring its Attachment from the Department of Trade and Industry to the National Economic and Development Authority and for Other Purposes* was signed.[9] PPPs were tagged as a powerful machinery to help push forward the country's development. The BOT Center was renamed as the PPP Center.

**In 2013**, Executive Order 136 was issued mandating the creation of the PPP Governing Board chaired by the Socioeconomic Planning Secretary, with the Finance Secretary as the co-chair. The Secretaries of Budget and Management, Justice, and Trade and Industry; the Executive Secretary; and the Private Sector co-chair of the National Competitiveness Council were appointed as members of the Board. The PPP Governing Board is the overall policy-making body for all PPP-related matters, including the Project Development and Monitoring Facility. It sets the strategic direction of the Philippine PPP Program while creating an enabling policy and institutional environment for PPPs in the Philippines (footnote 8).

**In 2016**, the government laid out a 10-point socioeconomic agenda, which includes accelerating annual infrastructure spending to account for 5% of gross domestic product as a critical objective, with public–private partnerships playing a key role. The government also envisioned to implement more infrastructure projects around the country to generate more employment opportunities and boost economic activities to attain inclusive growth in every region (footnote 8).

**Presently**, the PPP Center of the Philippines facilitates and coordinates the country's PPP program. The PPP Center manages a revolving fund called the Project Development and Monitoring Facility. It provides implementing agencies technical advisory support in project development and management and monitors the implementation of PPP priority projects. It is also tasked to formulate policy guidelines for PPP transactions, and develop and manage a central database of all PPP programs and projects.[10] The PPP Center aims to optimize PPP processes by drawing lessons from previous procurement bottlenecks, adopting best practices, and standardizing the good lessons learned.

In line with the government's socioeconomic agenda, and to help address the challenges in the country's infrastructure development, the PPP Center along with its partners and stakeholders continues to strengthen the PPP program through pipeline development, policy reforms, and process improvement. It aims to work closely with implementing agencies, strengthen its collaboration with development and private partners, and gain more support for PPPs in the Philippines from local and international organizations (footnote 10).

9 Official Gazette. Republic Act No. 9497. https://www.officialgazette.gov.ph/2008/03/04/republic-act-no-9497/.

10 Public–Private Partnership Center. Historical Background. https://ppp.gov.ph/about-the-ppp-center/#:~:text=136%20series%20of%20 2013%2C%20the,PPP%20projects%20in%20the%20Philippines.

## Public–Private Partnership Regulatory Framework in the Philippines

The existing legal and regulatory framework governing PPPs presently includes:

- The Philippine (Amended) BOT Law and its Revised Implementing Rules and Regulations (Republic Act 7718);
- Presidential Executive Order 136, Series of 2013; and
- Presidential Executive Order 8, Series of 2010.

## Other Supporting Laws and Regulations Governing Public–Private Partnerships

In addition to the Philippine (Amended) BOT Law and its Revised Implementing Rules and Regulations, the legal and regulatory framework governing PPPs in the Philippines also has supporting laws and regulations enabling the development of the PPP projects (Table 2).

### Table 2: Supporting Laws and Regulations for Public–Private Partnerships

| Type of Laws and Regulations | Description |
|---|---|
| **Pertinent Laws and Regulations** | • **Republic Act 10752:** An act facilitating the acquisition of right-of-way site or location for national government infrastructure projects<br>• **Republic Act 8975:** An act to ensure the expeditious implementation and completion of government infrastructure projects by prohibiting lower courts from issuing temporary restraining orders, preliminary injunctions or preliminary mandatory injunctions, providing penalties for violations thereof, and for other purposes<br>• **Republic Act 7160:** Local Government Code of the Philippines |
| **Administrative Orders** | • **Administrative Order 8:** Rationalizing the Composition of National Economic Development Authority (NEDA Board, the NEDA Board Executive Committee, and the Investment Coordination Committee) |
| **Circulars** | • **Department of the Interior and Local Government (DILG)—PPP Center Joint Memorandum Circular 2019-01:** Supplemental Guidelines for the Implementation of Public–Private Partnership for the People Initiative for Local Governments (LGU P4)<br>• **Joint Memorandum Circular 2018-01:** Reporting of PPP Project Spending and Contingent Liabilities<br>• **Joint Circular 2017-01:** Joint Memorandum Circular of National Economic and Development Authority, Department of Finance, and Department of Budget and Management on Implementation Guidelines for the Establishment of the Project Facilitation, Monitoring, and Innovation (PFMI) Task Force<br>• **DILG Memorandum Circular 2016-120:** Guidelines for the Implementation of Public–Private Partnership for the People Initiative for Local Governments (LGU P4)<br>• **DILG Memorandum Circular 2012-107:** Attendance to the Region-wide Public–Private Partnership (PPP) Orientation-Workshop<br>• **Department of Budget and Management (DBM) National Budget Circular 538:** Guidelines in the Submission of the Agency's Budgetary Proposal to be Funded from the Public–Private Partnership Support Fund (PPPSF) and Project Development and Monitoring Facility (PDMF)<br>• **DILG Memorandum Circular 2011-16:** Establishment of Public–Private Partnership (PPP) Sub-Committee in Local Development Councils (LDCs) of LGUs<br>• **Joint Circular 03-01:** Guidelines in the Processing of Receipt Arising from BOT Transactions and its Variant Schemes<br>• **Office of the Court Administrator Circular 232-2015:** Application of Republic Act 8974 |

*continued on next page*

*continued from previous page*

| Type of Laws and Regulations | Description |
|---|---|
| **Executive Orders** | • **Executive Order 78:** Mandating the inclusion of provisions of the use of alternative dispute resolution mechanisms in all contracts involving public–private partnership projects, build–operate and transfer projects, joint venture agreements between the government and private entities and those entered into by local government units |
| **Guidelines** | • PPP Governing Board (PPPGB) Guidelines and Issuances<br>– PPP Governing Board Resolution 2019-07-02: Suggested Guidelines on Managing Greenfield Solicited Hybrid PPP Projects<br>– PPP Governing Board Resolution 2018-12-02—Safeguards in PPP: Mainstreaming Environmental, Displacement, Social and Gender Concerns<br>– Guidelines on Managing Unsolicited Proposals under Republic Act 6957 as Amended by Republic Act 7718<br>– PPP Governing Board Resolution 2018-03-05: Framework on PPP Center's Assistance on Joint Venture Agreements<br>– PPP Governing Board Resolution 2018-03-03: Guidelines on Appointment of Probity Advisors for PPP Procurement<br>– PPP Governing Board Resolution 2017-12-06: Guidelines on Setting Financial Bid Parameters for the Selection of Project Proponent in PPP Projects<br>– Code of Conduct for the PPP Governing Board<br>– Policy Circular 05B-2017: Appointment of Probity Advisors for PPP Procurement<br>– PPP Governing Board Resolution 2016-06-02: Guidelines on Public Consultation and Engagement for PPP Projects<br>– PPP Governing Board Resolution 2016-06-05: Guidelines on Assessing Value for Money in PPP Projects<br>– PPP Governing Board Resolution 2016-06-04: Guidelines on Managing Government Employees Affected by PPP Projects<br>– Guidelines on Assessing Value for Money in PPP Projects<br>– Policy Circular 08-2016: Managing Government Employees Affected by PPP Projects<br>– Policy Circular 05A-2016-Appointment of Probity Advisors for PPP Procurement<br>– PPP Governing Board Resolution 2015-09-01: Guidelines on PPP Monitoring Framework and Monitoring Protocols<br>– Termination Payment for PPP Projects<br>– Policy Circular 05-2015: Appointment of Probity Advisors for PPP Procurement<br>– Guidelines on Viability Gap Funding<br>– Institutionalization of Best Practices in the Public–Private Partnership Processes<br>– Guidelines on the Identification, Selection and Prioritization of Public–Private Partnership (PPP) Projects<br>• Implementing Guidelines for the Special Provision on the Use of Un-programmed Appropriations for the Risk Management Program of 2017 General Appropriations Act<br>• Guidelines on the Preparation, Review and Approval and Implementation of ICT Projects Proposed for Financing Under BOT Law |
| **Other Issuances** | • Philippine Stock Exchange's Supplemental Listing and Disclosure Rules Applicable to a PPP Company<br>• Generic Preferred Risks Allocation Matrix<br>• Memorandum of Agreement between Board of Investments (BOI) and PPP Center on BOI Registration and Evaluation Process for PPP Projects<br>• TIEZA Joint Venture Guidelines<br>• PPP Center Local PPP Strategy |

BOT = build–operate–transfer, NEDA = National Economic and Development Authority, DILG = Department of the Interior and Local Government, LGU = local government unit, TIEZA = Tourism Infrastructure and Enterprise Zone Authority.

Sources: Public–Private Partnership Center. Other Pertinent Laws and Issuances. https://ppp.gov.ph/other-pertinent-laws/; NEDA. Joint Memorandum Circular No. 1 Series of 2016. http://blgf.gov.ph/wp-content/uploads/2017/10/JMC-No.-1-DILG-DBM-DOF-BLGF-NEDA.pdf; Public–Private Partnership Center. Historical Background. https://ppp.gov.ph/about-the-ppp-center/#:~:text=136%20series%20of%202013%2C%20the,PPP%20projects%20in%20the%20Philippines.

## 2. Types of Public–Private Partnerships

In the Philippines, the two most commonly used forms of PPPs are availability- and concession-based PPPs. These two forms are distinguished from each other based on the rights, obligations, and risks assumed by the public and the private parties in the PPP.

- **Availability-based PPP**

  In an availability-based PPP, the public authority contracts with a private sector entity to provide at a constant capacity to the implementing agency a public good, service or product for a given fee (capacity fee) and a separate charge for usage of the public good, product or service (usage fee). Fees or tariffs, regulated by a contract, provide for the recovery of debt service, fixed costs of operation, and a return on equity.[11]

  An example of an availability-based PPP is the Public–Private Partnership for School Infrastructure Project (PSIP) Phase I wherein the private sector is responsible for building classrooms (involving design, financing, construction, and maintenance) for a contract fee from the Department of Education (footnote 11).

- **Concession-based PPP**

  In a concession-based PPP, the public authority grants a private sector entity the right to build, operate, and charge public users of the public good, infrastructure or service, with a fee or tariff which is regulated by public entities and by a concession contract. Tariffs are structured to provide for the recovery of debt service, fixed costs of operation, and a return on equity (footnote 11).

  An example of a concession-based PPP is the Ninoy Aquino International Airport (NAIA) Expressway (Phase II) wherein the Department of Public Works and Highways (DPWH) granted a private sector entity the right to build and operate the expressway. Under a contract, the private sector entity was given the right to collect a toll (user charge) from the users of the expressway (footnote 11).

The Philippine BOT Law provides for nine specific types of PPP contractual arrangements or schemes that the public sector and private sector can enter into, to implement an infrastructure or development project. The arrangements represent several options for allocation functions between the implementing agency and the private firm (Table 3).[12]

### Table 3: Possible Contractual Arrangements between Public and Private Entities

| Scheme | Definition | Role of Private Proponent | Role of Public Proponent |
|---|---|---|---|
| **Build-Operate-and- Transfer (BOT)** | A contractual arrangement whereby the project proponent undertakes the construction, including financing, of a given infrastructure facility, and the operation maintenance thereof. The project proponent operates the facility over a fixed term during which it is allowed to charge facility users appropriate tolls, fees, rentals, and charges not exceeding those proposed in its bid or as negotiated and incorporated in the contract to enable the project proponent to recover its investment, and operating and maintenance expenses in the project. | • Undertakes financing, construction, operation and maintenance of facility for a fixed term<br>• Collects tolls, fees and other charges to recover investment plus profit | • Provides concession and regulates activities of BOT contractor<br>• Acquires ownership of facility at the end of BOT term<br>• May opt to share in the profits of the BOT proponent |

*continued on next page*

[11] Public–Private Partnership Center. What is PPP? https://ppp.gov.ph/ppp-program/what-is-ppp/.

[12] Government of the Philippines. 2012. *The Philippine Amended BOT Law Republic Act 7718 and its Revised Implementing Rules and Regulations*. Manila. https://ppp.gov.ph/wp-content/uploads/2017/04/BOT-IRR-2012_2017-printing.pdf.

*continued from previous page*

| Scheme | Definition | Role of Private Proponent | Role of Public Proponent |
|---|---|---|---|
| | The project proponent transfers the facility to the government agency or local government unit concerned at the end of the fixed term which shall not exceed fifty (50) years—provided, that in case of an infrastructure or development facility whose operation requires a public utility franchise, the proponent must be Filipino or, if a corporation, must be duly registered with the Securities and Exchange Commission and owned up to at least sixty percent (60%) by Filipinos.<br>The BOT may also include a supply-and-operate modality, which is a contractual arrangement whereby the supplier of equipment and machinery for a given infrastructure facility, if the interest of the government so requires, operates the facility providing in the process technology transfer and training to Filipino nationals. | • Transfer ownership of facility after BOT term to government entity<br>• May assign operation and maintenance to a facility operator | |
| **Build-and-Transfer** | A contractual arrangement whereby the project proponent undertakes the financing and construction of a given infrastructure or development facility and after its completion turns it over to the government agency or local government unit concerned, which shall pay the proponent on an agreed schedule its total investments expended on the project, plus a reasonable rate of return thereon. This arrangement may be employed in the construction of any infrastructure or development project, including critical facilities which, for security or strategic reasons, must be operated directly by the government. | • Finances and constructs infrastructure or development facility<br>• Turns over ownership of facility to government after project completion | • Acquires ownership of facility after construction<br>• Compensates project proponent at agreed amortization schedule |
| **Build-Own-and-Operate (BOO)** | A contractual arrangement whereby a project proponent is authorized to finance, construct, own, operate and maintain an infrastructure or development facility from which the proponent is allowed to recover its total investment, operating and maintenance costs plus a reasonable return thereon by collecting tolls, fees, rentals or other charges from facility users: Provided, that all such projects, upon recommendation of the Investment Coordination Committee (ICC) of the National Economic and Development Authority (NEDA), shall be approved by the President of the Philippines. Under this project, the proponent which owns the assets of the facility may assign its operation and maintenance to a facility operator. | • Finances, constructs, owns, operates and maintains facility in perpetuity<br>• Collects tolls, fees, rentals, and other charges to recover investments and profits<br>• May assign operation and maintenance to a facility operator | • Provides authorization and assistance in securing approval of BOO contract<br>• Can opt to buy the output/ service provided by the BOO operator |
| **Build-Lease-and-Transfer** | A contractual arrangement whereby a project proponent is authorized to finance and construct an infrastructure or development facility and upon its completion turns it over to the government | • Finances and constructs facility<br>• Turns over project to government after | • Compensates proponent for lease of facility at agreed term and schedule |

*continued on next page*

*continued from previous page*

| Scheme | Definition | Role of Private Proponent | Role of Public Proponent |
|---|---|---|---|
| | agency or local government unit concerned on a lease arrangement for a fixed period after which ownership of the facility is automatically transferred to the government agency or local government unit concerned. | completion under lease arrangement<br>• Turns over ownership of facility to government after lease period | • Acquires ownership of facility after lease period |
| **Build-Transfer-and-Operate** | A contractual arrangement whereby the public sector contracts out the building of an infrastructure facility to a private entity such that the contractor builds the facility on a turn-key basis, assuming cost overrun, delay and specified performance risks.<br><br>Once the facility is commissioned satisfactorily, title is transferred to the implementing agency/LGU. The private entity, however, operates the facility on behalf of the implementing agency/LGU under an agreement. | • Finances and constructs facility on a turn-key basis (assumes cost overrun, delay, specified performance risks)<br>• Transfers title of facility to implementing agency after commissioning<br>• Operates the facility for implementing agency under an agreement<br>• May assign operation and maintenance to a facility operator | • Assumes ownership of facility after commissioning<br>• Allows private proponent to receive compensation for the proponent's investment costs and reasonable return, and the operating charges |
| **Contract-Add-and-Operate** | A contractual arrangement whereby the project proponent adds to an existing infrastructure facility which it is renting from the government. It operates the expanded project over an agreed franchise period. There may, or may not be, a transfer arrangement in regard to the facility. | • Adds to an existing facility which the proponent is renting and operates expanded project for an agreed franchise period<br>• May assign operation and maintenance to a facility operator | • Collects rental payment from private proponent under agreed terms and schedule<br>• Re-acquires control over rented property/ facility at the end of lease term normally including improvements thereon |
| **Develop-Operate-and-Transfer** | A contractual arrangement whereby favorable conditions external to a new infrastructure project which is to be built by a private project proponent are integrated into the arrangement by giving that entity the right to develop adjoining property, and thus, enjoy some of the benefits the investment creates such as higher property or rent values. | • Has the right to develop adjoining property of an infrastructure to enjoy external benefits that the primary investment creates (such as higher property values | • May opt to share in the financial benefits of the investment<br>• Re-acquires ownership of properties turned over to investor after concession period |

*continued on next page*

*continued from previous page*

| Scheme | Definition | Role of Private Proponent | Role of Public Proponent |
|---|---|---|---|
| | | or commercial development rights)<br>• May assign operation and maintenance to a facility operator | |
| **Rehabilitate-Operate-and-Transfer (ROT)** | A contractual arrangement whereby an existing facility is turned over to the private sector to refurbish, operate and maintain for a franchise period, at the expiry of which the legal title to the facility is turned over to the government. The term is also used to describe the purchase of an existing facility from abroad, importing, refurbishing, erecting, and consuming it within the host country. | • Takes over operation and maintenance of an existing facility for a franchise period and/or imports existing facility for refurbishing, erecting and maintaining it within the host country<br>• Transfers ownership of a facility or equipment to government after franchise period<br>• May assign operation and maintenance to a facility operator | • Provides franchise to ROT company<br>• May opt to share in the profits of the ROT company<br>• Re-acquires ownership of facility equipment after franchise period |
| **Rehabilitate-Own-and-Operate (ROO)** | A contractual arrangement whereby an existing facility is turned over to the private sector to refurbish and operate with no time limitation imposed on ownership. As long as the operator is not in violation of its franchise, it can continue to operate the facility in perpetuity. | • Takes over an existing facility to refurbish and operate with no time limitation imposed on ownership | • Turns over existing facility to ROO proponent, with franchise to operate<br>• May opt to share in the income of ROO company |
| | | • Can continue to operate the facility in perpetuity<br>• May assign operation and maintenance to a facility operator | |

BOT = build-operate-transfer, BOO = build-own-operate, LGU = local government unit, ROT = rehabilitate-operate-transfer, ROO = rehabilitate-own-operate.

Sources: Public-Private Partnership Center. 2015. PPP Contractual Arrangementshttps://ppp.gov.ph/wp-content/uploads/2015/01/List-of-PPP-Modality.pdf; COA. Service Concession Arrangements: Grantor. https://www.coa.gov.ph/phocadownload/userupload/ABC-Help/GAM_B/sc1.2.htm; Government of the Philippines. 2012. *The Philippine Amended BOT Law Republic Act 7718 and its Revised Implementing Rules and Regulations.* Manila. https://ppp.gov.ph/wp-content/uploads/2017/04/BOT-IRR-2012_2017-printing.pdf

The above enumeration of contractual arrangements in the BOT Law is not exhaustive. Other forms of contractual arrangements may qualify as a PPP under the BOT Law, provided that such arrangement is approved by the President. Other contractual modes recognized as PPPs are concession and management contracts.

## 3. Eligible Sectors for Public–Private Partnerships

The Revised IRR of the BOT Law enumerates the list of sectors (Table 4) in which infrastructure and development projects could be undertaken under any of the recognized and valid BOT contractual arrangements (PPP modalities).[13]

### Table 4: Eligible Sectors and Subsectors for Public–Private Partnerships

| Sectors | Subsectors |
|---|---|
| 1. Transportation infrastructure | • Railways or rail-based projects that may or may not be packaged with commercial development opportunities<br>• Non-rail-based mass transit facilities<br>• Navigable inland waterways and related facilities<br>• Port infrastructures like piers, wharves, quays, storage, handling, ferry services, dredging, and related facilities<br>• Airports, air navigation, and related facilities<br>• Public fish ports and fishponds, including storage and processing facilities<br>• Warehouses |
| 2. Road infrastructure | • Highways, including expressways, roads, bridges, interchanges, tunnels, and related facilities |
| 3. Water resources and irrigation infrastructure | • Irrigation and related facilities |
| 4. Water supply infrastructure | • Water and related facilities |
| 5. Infrastructure for centralized water waste management systems | • Unavailable |
| 6. Infrastructure for local water waste management system | • Sewerage<br>• Drainage and related facilities |
| 7. Infrastructure for waste management system | • Collection equipment<br>• Composting plants<br>• Landfill<br>• Tidal barriers |
| 8. Telecommunication and informatics infrastructure | • Telecommunications, backbone network, terrestrial and satellite facilities, and related service facilities<br>• Information technology and database infrastructure, including modernization of IT, geospatial resource mapping, and cadastral survey for resource accounting and planning |
| 9. Energy and electricity infrastructure including renewable energy | • Power generation<br>• Transmission, sub-transmission<br>• Distribution<br>• Other related facilities |
| 10. Energy conservation infrastructure | • Unavailable |
| 11. Urban facilities infrastructure | • Land reclamation, dredging, and other related development facilities<br>• Government buildings<br>• Markets<br>• Slaughterhouses and related facilities |
| 12. Zone infrastructure | • Industrial infrastructure |

*continued on next page*

13 The oil and gas sector is not expressly included in the enumeration in the BOT Law. Nevertheless, the BOT Law provides that other infrastructure and development projects may also be proposed if authorized by the appropriate agency.

*continued from previous page*

| Sectors | Subsectors |
|---|---|
| 13. Tourism infrastructure (e.g., tourism information center) | • Tourism estates or townships, including ecotourism projects such as terrestrial and coastal/marine nature parks and related infrastructure facilities and utilities |
| 14. Education facilities, research and development infrastructure | • Education infrastructure |
| 15. Health infrastructure | • Healthcare facilities |
| 16. Public housing infrastructure | • Housing infrastructure |

Source: Public–Private Partnership Center. What is PPP? https://ppp.gov.ph/ppp-program/what-is-ppp/.

All concerned government agencies, including government-owned and controlled corporations and local government units, incorporate in their development programs the priority projects that may be financed, constructed, operated, and maintained by the private sector under the provisions of the BOT Law and its IRR. Concerned government agencies widely publicize all projects eligible for financing under the BOT Law, such as through national and international newspapers once every 6 months, and provide official notification of the project proponents registered with them.

The list of all such national projects must be part of the development programs of the agencies concerned. The list of projects costing up to ₱300 million ($6 million as of April 2020) are approved by NEDA-ICC and projects costing more than ₱300 million by the NEDA Board. The list of projects submitted to ICC of the NEDA Board are acted upon within 30 working days.

The list of local projects costing up to ₱20 million ($394,800 as of April 2020) to be implemented by the local government units concerned is submitted, for confirmation, to the municipal development council. Those costing above ₱20 million up to ₱50 million ($1 million as of April 2020) are submitted to the provincial development council; those costing up to ₱50 million to the city development council; those above ₱50 million up to ₱200 million ($4 million as of April 2020) to the regional development councils; and those above ₱200 million to ICC of NEDA.

## 4. Public–Private Partnership Institutional Framework

As per the Philippine BOT Law and its IRR, the various institutions associated with the PPP Program in the Philippines are the PPP Center, the PPP Governing Board, Department of the Interior and Local Government (DILG), Department of Finance (DOF), National Economic and Development Authority (NEDA), regional and local development councils, and the PPP subcommittees in local government units (Table 5).

| Parameter | |
|---|---|
| Does the country have a national PPP unit? | ✓ |
| What are the functions of the national PPP unit? | |
| • Supporting the design and operationalization of the National PPP Enabling Framework? | ✓ |
| • Helping develop a national PPP pipeline? | ✓ |
| • Supporting the arrangement of funding for project preparation (budgetary allocations, technical assistance funding from multilateral development agencies, operating a dedicated project preparation/ project development fund)? | ✓ |

*continued on next page*

*continued from previous page*

| Parameter | |
|---|---|
| • Guidance for project preparation to and coordination with the government agencies responsible for sponsoring the projects? | ✓ |
| • Making recommendations to the PPP Committee and/or other approving authorities to provide approvals associated with various stages of the PPP process? | ✓ |

✓ = Yes, × = No, NA = Not Applicable, UA = Unavailable

## Table 5: Principal Public Entities Supporting Public–Private Partnerships in the Philippines

| Key Agencies/Facilities | Function(s) |
|---|---|
| PPP Center | • Conducts project facilitation and assistance to national implementing agencies, including government corporations and local government units (LGUs), in addressing impediments or bottlenecks in the implementation of PPP programs and projects<br>• Provides advisory services, technical assistance, training, and capacity development to agencies/LGUs in PPP project preparation and development<br>• Recommends plans, policies, and implementation guidelines related to PPP in consultation with appropriate oversight committees, implementing agencies, LGUs, and the private sector<br>• Manages and administers a revolving fund, known as the Project Development and Monitoring Facility, for the preparation of business case, pre-feasibility and feasibility studies, and tender documents of PPP programs and projects<br>• Monitors and facilitates the implementation of priority PPP programs and projects designed by agencies/LGUs in coordination with the NEDA Secretariat<br>• Establishes and manages a central database system of PPP programs and projects<br>• Recommends improvements to timelines in processing PPP program and project proposals, and monitor compliance of all agencies/LGUs<br>• Prepares reports on the implementation of PPP programs and projects of the government for submission to the President by the end of each year<br>• Performs other functions which may be critical in expediting and implementing effectively the government's PPP programs and projects<br>• Acts as the Secretariat of the PPP Governing Board |
| PPP Governing Board (PPPGB) | • Undertakes the overall policymaking for all PPP-related matters, including the Project Development and Monitoring Facility<br>• Sets the strategic direction of the Philippines' PPP program and creates an enabling policy and institutional environment for PPPs |
| National Economic and Development Authority (NEDA) | • Functions as the independent planning agency of the government and implements integrated and coordinated programs and policies for national development, in consultation with the appropriate public agencies, the private sector, and LGUs |
| Investment Coordination Committee (ICC) | • Evaluates the fiscal, monetary, and balance of payments implications of major national projects and recommends to the President the implementation timetable of these projects on a regular basis<br>• Recommends to the President a domestic and foreign borrowing program which is updated each year, and subsequently submits to the President a status of the fiscal, monetary, and balance of payments implications of major national projects<br>• Reviews national BOT projects costing up to ₱300 million ($6 million as of April 2020) submitted for ICC approval; projects costing more than ₱300 million for NEDA Board approval; and LGU PPP projects costing more than ₱200 million ($4 million as of April 2020), submitted for ICC confirmation |
| Department of the Interior and Local Government (DILG) | • Coordinates the PPP programs and projects at the local government level<br>• Organizes capacity building, training, and technical assistance programs for LGUs and their key officials, in coordination with the PPP Center |

*continued on next page*

*continued from previous page*

| Key Agencies/Facilities | Function(s) |
|---|---|
| | • Assists the PPP Center in gathering reports on the implementation of PPP programs and projects of LGUs and in addressing impediments or bottlenecks<br>• Provides inputs for and assists in disseminating the PPP resource materials to LGUs |
| Department of Finance (DOF)–Municipal Development Fund Office (MDFO) | • Administers the Municipal Development Fund (MDF) which forms a critical component of the LGU Financing Framework. The MDF is a revolving fund created and capitalized by foreign loans and grants made available as loans to LGUs for projects specified in the agreements with international financial institutions and foreign governments. |
| | • Administers the PPP Fund (with a corpus of approximately ₱1 billion ($20 million as of April 2020) to provide funding support to LGUs that are already implementing or planning to implement PPP projects. The MDFO coordinates with the PPP Center in identifying LGUs that already have project proposals and feasibility studies and that may be interested in availing the PPP Fund.<br>• Administers the Project Technical Assistance and Contingency Fund which LGUs can access to fund the feasibility study or detailed engineering design of projects that can be implemented under BOT or similar schemes or through bond flotations or loans from private financing institutions, government financial institutions, or the MDFO itself |
| Regional and local development councils | • Serves as the counterpart of the NEDA Board in respective regions, provinces, cities, and municipal jurisdictions. These regional and local development councils are comprised of local government officials, regional heads of departments and other offices, and representatives from the private sector within the region. They have been set up to facilitate administrative decentralization, strengthen local autonomy, and accelerate economic and social development in the regions.<br>• Serves as a forum where development planners, government implementing agencies, and the private sector can identify the priority programs and projects that support the objectives and thrusts of the region. These are then packaged into investment programs for endorsement to implementing agencies and institutions as well as to the private sector.<br>• With the private sector's representation in these regional and local development councils, their interests and concerns are articulated and used as input in formulating the development and investment plan of the region<br>• Identifies measures to attract private investment in the region<br>• Reviews and endorses, as appropriate, projects that have an impact on the region |
| PPP subcommittees in local government units | • Assists the Local Development Council in formulating action plans and strategies related to the LGU's implementation of PPP programs and projects |

BOT = build-operate-transfer, ICC = Investment Coordination Committee, LGU = local government unit, MDF = Municipal Development Fund, MDFO = Municipal Development Fund Office, NEDA = National Economic and Development Authority.

Sources: Public–Private Partnership Center. What is PPP? https://ppp.gov.ph/ppp-program/what-is-ppp/; Public–Private Partnership Center. Mandate, Vision and Mission. https://ppp.gov.ph/about-the-ppp-center/; ADB. 2016. *Philippines: Public–Private Partnerships by Local Government Units*. Manila.

## Entities Responsible for Public–Private Partnership Project Identification, Approval, and Oversight

The PPP Center manages and updates a PPP project pipeline, which is available online. Implementing agencies and LGUs are required to prepare infrastructure or development programs and identify specific priority projects that may be financed, constructed, operated, and maintained by the private sector through the PPP contractual arrangements or schemes authorized under the BOT Law and its IRR. They are also required to submit a list of priority projects to the National Economic and Development Authority (NEDA) Board or to the Investment Coordination Committee (ICC) for approval. The list of priority projects should be consistent with the Philippines' Development Plan and Provincial Development and Physical Framework Plan.

| Parameter | |
|---|---|
| Who is responsible for identifying, preparing, and procuring the PPP projects? | Respective implementing agency and LGUs with the support of the PPP Center |
| Is there a PPP Committee for providing approvals at various stages of PPP projects? | ✓ |
| Who are the approving authorities other than the PPP Committee for the PPP projects? | • For National PPPs – ICC and NEDA Board<br>• For Local PPPs – Municipal, provincial, city, and regional development councils; ICC; and local *Sanggunians* (consultative body)<br>• For BOO projects, and projects using PPP scheme that is not under the BOT Law – President of the Philippines |
| Does the country have an independent think tank for various PPP planning, budgeting, and policy decisions? | ✓<br>PPP Governing Board for the PPP Program<br>NEDA for programs and policies for national development |
| Is there a legislature for the PPP program oversight? | × |

✓ = Yes, × = No, NA = Not Applicable, UA = Unavailable

In 2015, the PPP Governing Board (PPPGB) issued Policy Circular 02-2015 for implementing agencies to use Multi-Criteria Analysis (MCA) to identify and prioritize PPP projects from the list of priority projects. Figure 10 shows the flowchart for identifying and preparing PPP projects as per Policy Circular 02-2015.

**Figure 10: Flowchart for Identifying and Preparing Public–Private Partnership Projects**

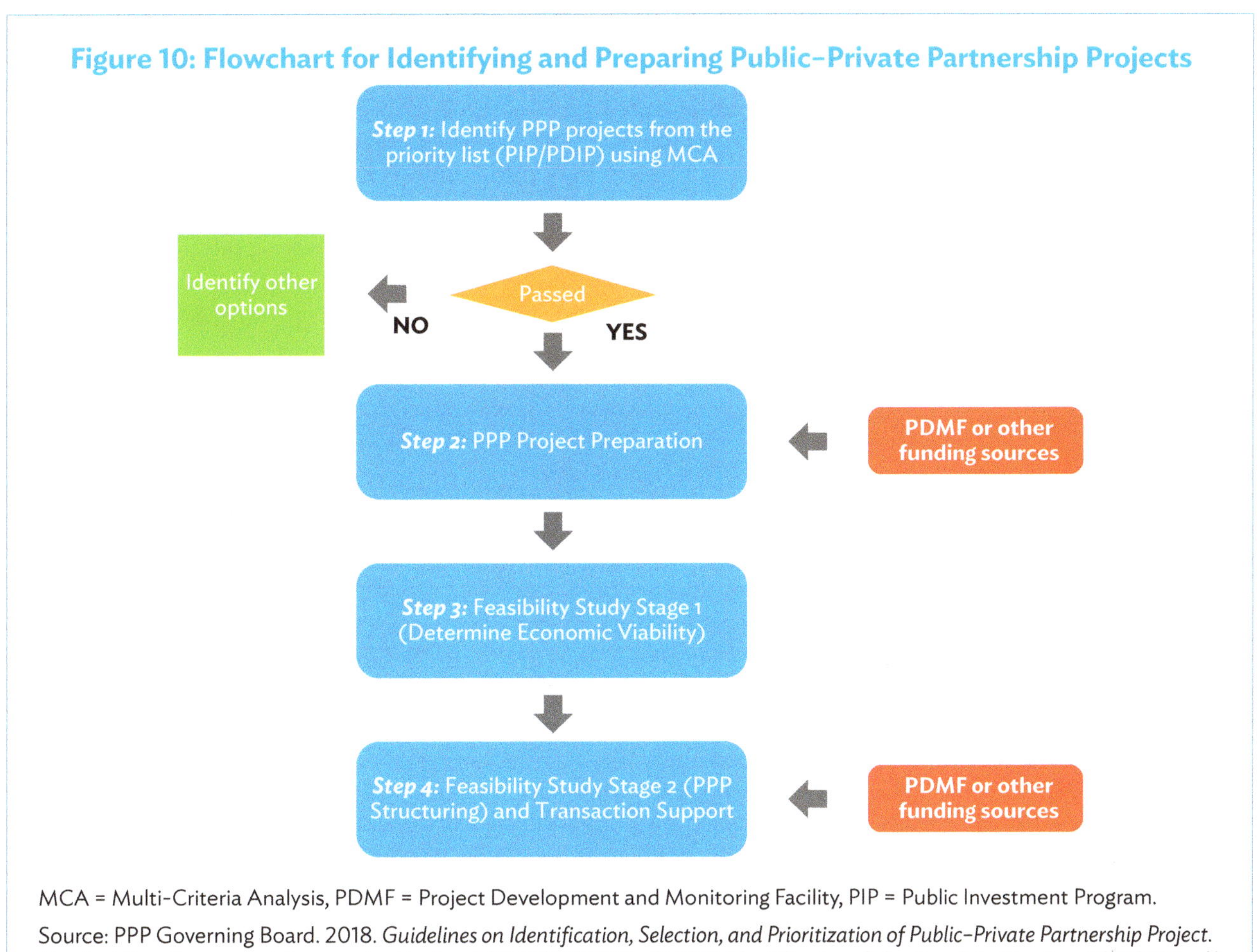


MCA = Multi-Criteria Analysis, PDMF = Project Development and Monitoring Facility, PIP = Public Investment Program.

Source: PPP Governing Board. 2018. *Guidelines on Identification, Selection, and Prioritization of Public–Private Partnership Project*. Manila. https://ppp.gov.ph/wp-content/uploads/2018/07/PPPC_GUIDE-Identification-Selection-Prioritization-20150325.pdf.

The approving authorities for the national PPP projects are the following (footnote 12):

- ICC for projects costing up to ₱300 million ($6 million as of April 2020)
- NEDA Board, upon the recommendation of ICC, for projects costing more than ₱300 million
- NEDA Board, upon the recommendation of ICC, for negotiated projects regardless of the amount

The approving authorities for the local PPP projects are:

- Municipal development council for projects costing up to ₱20 million ($0.39 million as of April 2020)
- Provincial development council for projects costing more than ₱20 million but less than ₱50 million ($1 million as of April 2020)
- City development council for projects costing up to ₱50 million
- Regional development council for projects costing more than ₱50 million up to ₱200 million ($4 million as of April 2020); for Metro Manila projects, the Regional Development Council for Metropolitan Manila acts as the approving authority.
- ICC for projects costing more than ₱200 million

The final approval of local PPP projects classified in the first four points immediately above is vested on the local *Sanggunians* (consultative bodies) as per the provisions of the Local Government Code.

Projects undertaken through the build-own-and-operate (BOO) scheme or through contractual arrangements or schemes other than those defined in the BOT Law and its IRR require the approval of the President. For this purpose, the head of implementing agency/LGU submits the proposed project to the NEDA Board through the ICC which evaluates the proposal and forwards its recommendations to the President. Such projects are deemed to have been approved by the President when approved at a NEDA Board meeting presided over by the President (footnote 15).

## Entities Responsible for Public–Private Partnership Project Monitoring

| Parameter | |
|---|---|
| Is there an entity for monitoring of PPP Projects post Commercial Close? | ✓ |
| Is there an entity for monitoring and management of fiscal risks and liabilities from PPP projects for the Ministry of Finance (MOF)? | ✓ |

✓ = Yes, × = No, NA = Not Applicable, UA = Unavailable

Source: Government of the Philippines. 2012. The Philippine Amended BOT Law Republic Act 7718 and its Revised Implementing Rules and Regulations. Manila. https://ppp.gov.ph/wp-content/uploads/2017/04/BOT-IRR-2012_2017-printing.pdf.

The PPP Center is responsible for the coordination and monitoring of projects implemented under various PPP contractual arrangements or schemes authorized under the BOT Law and its IRR. For this purpose, concerned implementing agencies/LGUs should periodically submit information on the status of projects to the PPP Center. At the end of every calendar year, the PPP Center reports to the ICC, the President, and the Congress on the progress of all projects implemented under the BOT Law and its IRR. The PPP Center submits a report on pipeline, awarded, ongoing, and completed projects to the Department of Budget and Management for inclusion in the Budget of Expenditures and Sources of Financing.

A Project Monitoring Committee (PMC) has been constituted to (i) review the assessment of the authorized representatives of the implementing agency/LGU and the PPP Center on the deliverables, completion of milestones, and contract variation proposals with cost implication, for probity advisory services; and (ii) recommend the appropriate action to the PPP Center's Executive Director or his/her duly authorized representative.[14]

The PPP Center is also responsible for compliance by the LGUs implementing PPP projects under the provisions of the amended BOT Law and its IRR. Given its PPP program monitoring and evaluation function, the PPP Center guides LGUs through the PPP project cycle: (i) project preparation, (ii) project review and approval, (iii) preparation of bid documents, (iv) prequalification and bid evaluation, and (v) contract award and implementation.

Each concerned implementing agency/LGU may create a PPP unit headed by a senior official of the implementing agency/LGU and may designate a senior official as PPP project development officer, who would be responsible for planning, overseeing, and monitoring the projects of implementing agencies/LGUs authorized under the BOT Law and its IRR. Such PPP unit may also include as members technical and legal personnel who are knowledgeable on the technical and legal aspects of the PPP projects.

In 2015, the PPPGB issued Resolution 2015-09-01 on PPP Project Monitoring Framework and Protocols to be followed by implementing agencies and LGUs.[15] The PPP Project Monitoring Framework and Protocols aims to:

- identify the roles and responsibilities of key parties involved in monitoring the implementation of PPP projects;
- define the protocols for generating, processing, and sharing information on monitoring the implementation of PPP projects;
- document lessons learned and best practices during project implementation that can be used in planning, evaluating, and implementing future PPP projects; and
- enable the national government to effectively manage the fiscal risks arising from PPPs. The PPP Center and the Department of Budget and Management formulated the Joint Memorandum Circular 2018-01 to standardize the reporting and monitoring of public and private sector spending on PPPs, including contingent liabilities arising from PPPs.[16]

## 5. The Public–Private Partnership Process

As per the BOT Law and its IRR, the overall PPP process in the Philippines includes the following stages:

- **Development** includes project identification, preparation, and structuring.
- **Approval** includes assessment and approval of the project by various approving entities.
- **Competition/procurement** includes bid documentation and bid process management up to award of the PPP project to the identified private developer.
- **Cooperation** includes activities from commercial close up to hand back/transfer of the project by the private developer to the implementing agency/LGU at the end of the PPP contract period.

---

14 Public–Private Partnership Center. 2001. *The Project Development and Monitoring Facility*. Manila. https://ppp.gov.ph/wp-content/uploads/2020/01/PDMFS_20190128_REP_Revised-Guidelines-January-2020.pdf.

15 Public–Private Partnership Center. 2018. *Public–Private Partnership Projects Monitoring Framework and Protocols*. Manila. https://ppp.gov.ph/wp-content/uploads/2018/07/PPPC_GUIDE_Monitoring-Framework-Protocols-20150825.pdf.

16 Public–Private Partnership Center. 2019. *Reporting of PPP Project Spending and Contingent Liabilities*. Manila. https://ppp.gov.ph/wp-content/uploads/2019/10/PPPC_POL_JMC-Reporting-of-PPP-Project-Spending.pdf.

| Parameter | |
|---|---|
| Does the PPP legal and regulatory framework provide for a PPP implementation process covering the entire PPP lifecycle? | ✓ |
| Does the Feasibility Assessment Stage cover— | |
| • Technical feasibility? | ✓ |
| • Socioeconomic feasibility? | ✓ |
| • Environmental sustainability? | ✓ |
| • Financial feasibility? | ✓ |
| • Fiscal affordability assessment? | ✓ |
| • Legal assessment? | ✓ |
| • Risk assessment and PPP project structuring? | ✓ |
| • Value for Money assessment? | ✓ |
| • Market sounding with stakeholders? | ✓ |
| Is the PPP procurement plan required? | ✓ |
| Is there a need to set up a separate PPP procurement committee? | ✓ |
| Is competitive bidding the only method for selection of PPP private developer? | × |
| Is the prequalification stage necessary? Or does the PPP legal and regulatory framework allow flexibility to skip the prequalification stage? | Flexibility is allowed to skip prequalification |
| Does the PPP legal and regulatory process provide the option to the preferred bidder for contract negotiations? | ✓ Limited to unsolicited projects |
| Does the PPP Legal and Regulatory Framework allow unsuccessful bidders to challenge the award/submit complaints? | ✓ |
| What is the maximum time allowed for submitting a complaint/challenging the award by unsuccessful bidders from the announcement of the preferred bidder? | 15 days |
| Does the PPP legal and regulatory framework provide for transparency? | ✓ |
| Which of the following are required to be published? | |
| • Findings from the feasibility assessment? | × |
| • Procurement notice? | ✓ |
| • Outcome of stakeholder consultations from market sounding? | ✓ |
| • Clarifications to prequalification queries? | ✓ |
| • Prequalification results? | ✓ |
| • Clarifications to pre-bid queries? | ✓ |
| • Results for the bid stage and selection of preferred bidder? | ✓ |
| • Final concession agreement to be entered between the government agency and the preferred bidder? And other PPP project agreements executed between government agency and preferred bidder? | × |
| • Confidentiality | ✓ |

✓ = Yes, × = No, NA = Not Applicable, UA = Unavailable

Figure 11 depicts the overall PPP process for taking a PPP project from conceptualization to closure.[17]

**Figure 11: The Public–Private Partnership Process**

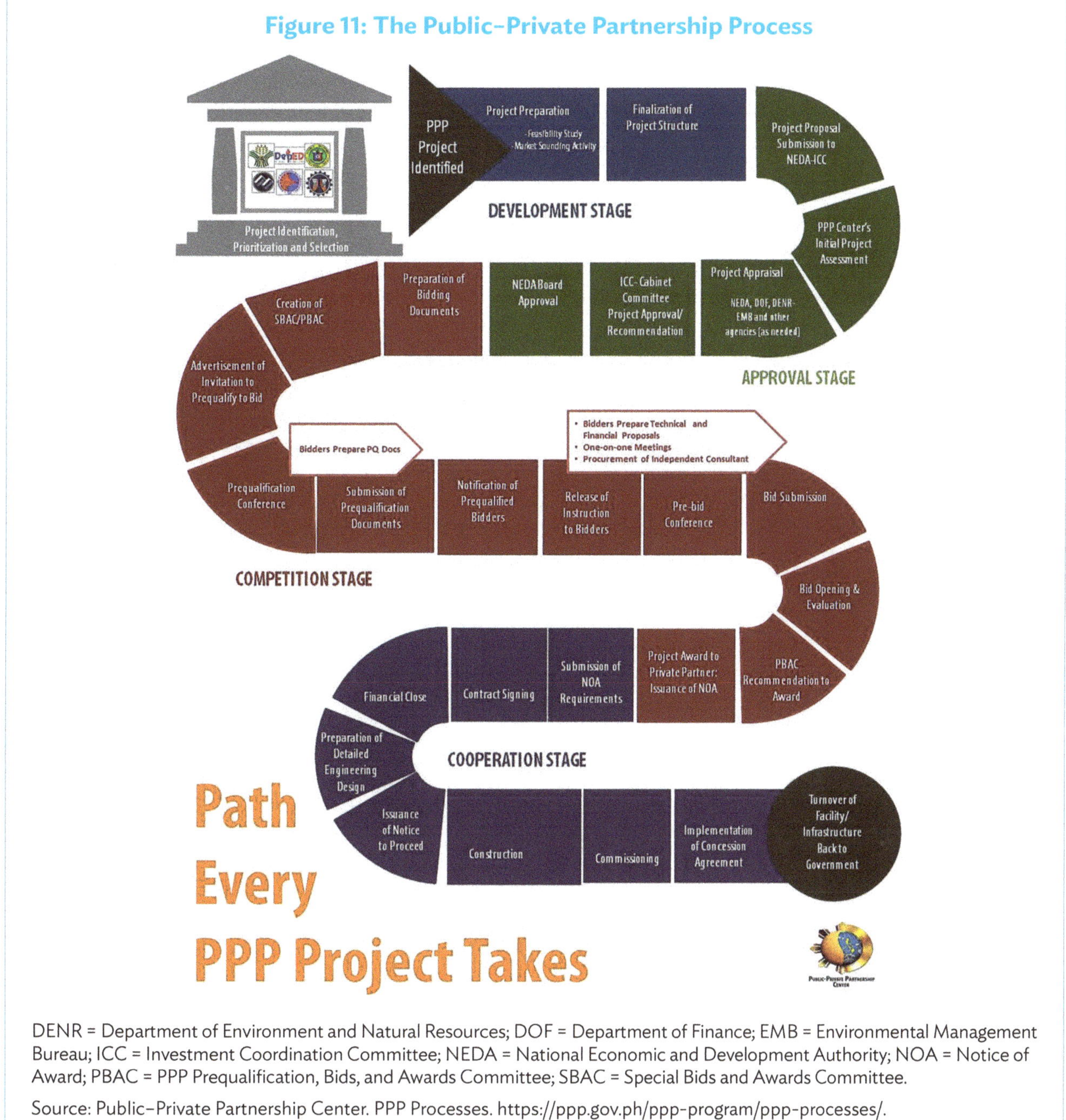


DENR = Department of Environment and Natural Resources; DOF = Department of Finance; EMB = Environmental Management Bureau; ICC = Investment Coordination Committee; NEDA = National Economic and Development Authority; NOA = Notice of Award; PBAC = PPP Prequalification, Bids, and Awards Committee; SBAC = Special Bids and Awards Committee.

Source: Public–Private Partnership Center. PPP Processes. https://ppp.gov.ph/ppp-program/ppp-processes/.

## Public–Private Partnership Development Process in the Philippines

According to the BOT Law and its IRR, the PPP development process in the Philippines consists of three stages: PPP project identification, preparation, and structuring.

17 Public–Private Partnership Center. PPP Processes. https://ppp.gov.ph/ppp-program/ppp-processes/.

### *Public–Private Partnership Project Identification*

Implementing agencies and LGUs are encouraged to use multivariate analysis (MVA) to identify projects that could be procured and implemented through the PPP route. The MVA methodology uses carefully selected variables designed to screen out those projects that do not appear to be commercially sustainable. Implementing agencies and LGUs may also combine the MVA with social cost–benefit analysis (SCBA) to identify PPP projects considered to be strategic for long-term sustainable economic development. Table 6 lists the MVA criteria that could be used by implementing agencies and LGUs to identify potential PPP projects.

**Table 6: Criteria for Identifying Potential Public–Private Partnership Projects**

| Criteria | Data/Information Needs |
|---|---|
| Socioeconomic benefits | Economic Internal Rate of Return (EIRR), if available from studies, or brief description of social and economic rationale and benefits; factors such as employment, poverty alleviation, and investment in human resource development should also be taken into account |
| Likely financial viability | Use of a simple and objective financial model, otherwise use available information from public sources |
| Land acquisition | Indication of the degree of complexity of land acquisition |
| Environmental impacts | Indication of the degree of positive impact on environment as opposed to negative or complex aspects |
| Social safeguards | Indication of the degree of complexity related to resettlement; impact on indigenous, poverty-stricken, and/or other vulnerable groups |
| Risks | The number and gravity of the risks |
| Demand | Growth trends, total volume, and demand/capacity ratios |
| Regional development | Regional impact and contribution to the regional economy |
| Stakeholder support | Indication of consultation with and the degree of support from various stakeholders |
| Sector strategy and plan | Importance of project in subsector strategy and plan |
| Safety aspects | Specific safety objectives being sought: Are they complicated and costly (negative), or simple and conventional (positive)? |

Sources: Government of the Philippines. 2012. *The Philippine Amended BOT Law Republic Act 7718 and its Revised Implementing Rules and Regulations*. Manila. https://ppp.gov.ph/wp-content/uploads/2017/04/BOT-IRR-2012_2017-printing.pdf; PPP Manual for LGUs–Developing PPP Projects for Local Government Units.

The projects are screened and prioritized using a scoring and ranking procedure, which uses a mix of subjective and objective assessment of selected criteria to provide a score for each attribute. These scores are then added, and projects are then ranked by their total score (Table 7). It should be noted that the MVA does not justify the viability of a PPP project, but only indicates which projects should be developed further.

**Table 7: Indicative Guidelines for Scoring and Ranking of Projects**

| Criteria | High Score (7–10 points) | Medium Score (4–6 points) | Low Score (1–3 points) |
|---|---|---|---|
| Socioeconomic benefits | Economic IRR (EIRR) > 20% | 20% > EIRR > 10% | EIRR < 10% (FAIL) |
| Likely financial viability | Project/Financial Internal Rate of Return (FIRR) > 20% | 20% > FIRR > 14% | FIRR < 14% (FAIL) |
| Land acquisition | No land acquisition involved, or some but not complex | Medium complexity owing to amount and issues | Very complex and problematic owing to a number and seriousness of issues (FAIL) |
| Environmental impacts | No impacts, or some, but issues are not complex | Medium complexity impacts are few and not serious | Many issues/severe impacts (FAIL) |

*continued on next page*

*continued from previous page*

| Criteria | High Score (7–10 points) | Medium Score (4–6 points) | Low Score (1–3 points) |
|---|---|---|---|
| Social safeguards | None, or few affected but not seriously | Medium complexity because of number of issues involved | Large number of people affected and/or seriousness of issues (FAIL) |
| Risks | Few issues/risks | Some issues/risks exist but can be managed | Many issues/risks which are not easily managed |
| Demand | Growth >15%; Total volume >5 million ($98,700 as of April 2020),<br>or<br>equivalent demand capacity ratio >1.2 | Growth is 5% to 15%; Total volume = 2.5 million ($49,350 as of April 2020),<br>or<br>equivalent demand capacity ratio 0.8–1.2 | Growth <5%; Total volume <2 million ($39,480 as of April 2020),<br>or<br>equivalent demand capacity ratio <0.8 |
| Regional development | Impact on low Gross Regional Domestic Product (GRDP) states and/or high poverty alleviation focus | Impact on medium GRDP states and/or medium poverty alleviation focus | Impact on high GRDP provinces and/or low poverty alleviation focus |
| Stakeholder support | Evidence of strong support from all/most stakeholders | Mixed support from all/most stakeholders | Low level of support or lack of support from most stakeholders |
| Sector strategy and plan | Forms integral part of, and already included in plans | Part of subsector plan | Ad hoc project but not in conflict with sector plan |
| Safety aspects | High safety focus | Moderate safety focus and impacts | Low safety focus and impacts |

Source: Government of the Philippines. 2012. *The Philippine Amended BOT Law Republic Act 7718 and its Revised Implementing Rules and Regulations*. Manila. https://ppp.gov.ph/wp-content/uploads/2017/04/BOT-IRR-2012_2017-printing.pdf; PPP Manual for LGUs – Developing PPP Projects for Local Government Units.

## *Public–Private Partnership Project Preparation*

The project preparation stage consists of the following main components (footnote 12).

- A **technical assessment study** involves a preliminary design with sufficient technical ground surveys to prepare a capital cost estimate of ±20%. This design process identifies and records the relevant design standards, together with primary design criteria that are compatible with the project's objectives and location. The outline design moderates alternative sites and alternative layouts at each site, so that several feasible options that would provide the basic operational requirements for the PPP project could be identified. This process also identifies physical limitations on available sites that could restrict the design layout. A cost is prepared for each development alternative that clearly identifies all major elements including engineering works, environmental mitigation works, service diversion costs, accommodation works, land costs, and resettlement costs. The operational and maintenance costs are determined for each element of the alternative technical solutions. Some maintenance costs are routine in nature and others are estimated on a periodic basis. The preliminary cost estimate is also accompanied by an outline implementation program reflecting the timing and interrelationships of all of the major project components. The technical specification must conform to the least cost solution to meet the projected demand for the service (phased if necessary) and other objectives. A preliminary technical evaluation is usually initiated as soon as a project is identified and selected for PPP implementation. The data gathered at this stage need to (i) arrive at a 'least cost' solution for implementation, and (ii) complete a social cost–benefit analysis (SCBA). SCBA explores the different technical configurations of a project to determine which option yields the greatest economic benefit (footnote 1).

- A **demand/market study** involves demand forecasts for the product or service the project would deliver. Forecasts should be derived for short-, medium-, and long-term (5, 10, 15 plus years) and should provide for different growth scenarios (footnote 1).
- A **social cost–benefit analysis (SCBA)** sets forth the rationale for undertaking the project based on economic benefits to the community. The economic viability indicators used are economic internal rate of return (EIRR), economic net present value (ENPV), and present value (PV) of economic benefits/PV of economic cost (B/C ratio) (footnote 1).
- An **environment, social and gender impact analysis** identifies all social impacts and resettlement activities, and the proposed mitigation and their related costs. This analysis is undertaken as a next step in the process. Social studies should conform to Philippine social impact regulations including those that relate to indigenous peoples, when relevant. The environmental impact assessment defines and addresses all major impacts, the proposed mitigation, and the broad estimate of mitigation costs. The assessment draws inputs from environmental studies and consultations to inform the preparation and formulation of environmental impact statements, management and mitigation plans, and other activities, particularly disaster risk mitigation and climate change adaptation. Environmental studies should conform to Philippine environmental regulations (footnote 1).
- A **financial analysis** tests the viability, stability, and profitability of a project by looking at financial indicators such as financial internal rate of return (FIRR), financial net present value (FNPV), payback period (cost of project/projected annual cash flow), and debt service coverage ratio (DSCR). It is carried out as a next step in the process. Various financial scenarios are simulated using a financial model to determine tariff structure, tariff path and escalation, extent of cost recovery, debt–equity options, debt service options, and requisite government support, among others. The financial model is also used to undertake a sensitivity analysis and outline a financial structure that shows funding sources for each project component. The financial analysis includes a technical description and a project implementation plan that identifies all relevant engineering and non-engineering components. It also includes a preliminary outline design, containing technical specifications such as location, technology, right of way requirements, and initial capacity. The preliminary output design includes a construction schedule, standard of project outputs, and performance standards which provide the basis of the minimum technical requirements to be included in the request for proposals (footnote 1).
- A **market sounding process** is carried out toward the end of the financial analysis when there is sufficient data that permits a substantive discussion with the private sector, including both potential contractors and investors. The output from the market sounding is integrated into the final project structure (footnote 1).

### *Public–Private Partnership Project Structuring*

As the next step in the process, a detailed risk assessment using the Generic Preferred Risks Allocation Matrix (GPRAM) is undertaken, identifying all the risks associated with the project and their most optimal allocation among the parties to arrive at the most optimal PPP structure.

The feasibility assessment, the risk assessment, and the PPP structuring follow an iterative process to ensure that the overall project viability is optimized. One of the nine eligible PPP types as prescribed by the BOT Law and its IRR is selected based on the most optimal project viability and risk allocation.

## Public–Private Partnership Procurement Process in the Philippines

The procurement of solicited PPP projects may involve one of two options, as provided for under RA 7718. The procurement process under option 1 has four distinct steps and is distinguished from the abridged process of option 2, with the inclusion of prequalification as a distinct step. The different steps are prequalification, tendering, submission, and receipt and opening of bids (footnote 12).

In option 1, prequalification is undertaken prior to the issuance of request for proposals while in option 2, it is incorporated in the tendering step and followed by submission, receipt, and opening of bids. In short, in option 2, the qualification documents are simultaneously submitted together with the technical and financial proposals (Figure 12). Moreover, the procurement of unsolicited PPP projects is different from the typical procurement process for solicited PPP projects, and is composed 14 steps (Figure 13 and Table 8).

**Figure 12: Procurement Process for Solicited Public–Private Partnership Projects**

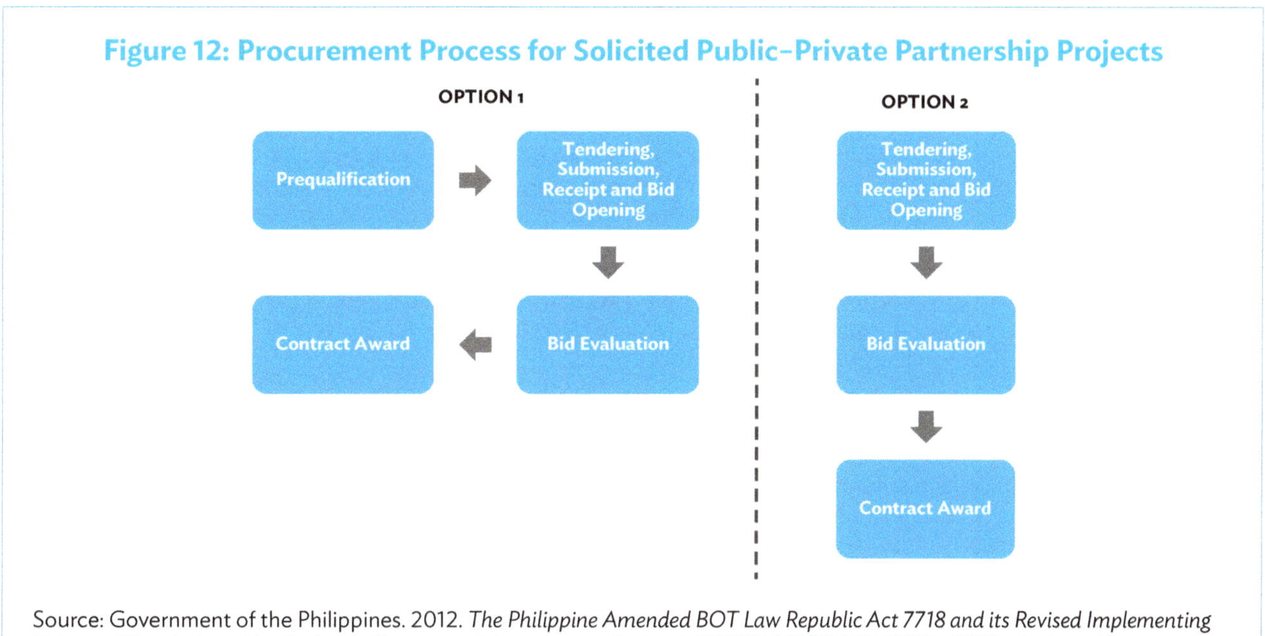


Source: Government of the Philippines. 2012. *The Philippine Amended BOT Law Republic Act 7718 and its Revised Implementing Rules and Regulations*. Manila. https://ppp.gov.ph/wp-content/uploads/2017/04/BOT-IRR-2012_2017-printing.pdf.

**Figure 13: Procurement Process for Unsolicited Public–Private Partnership Projects**

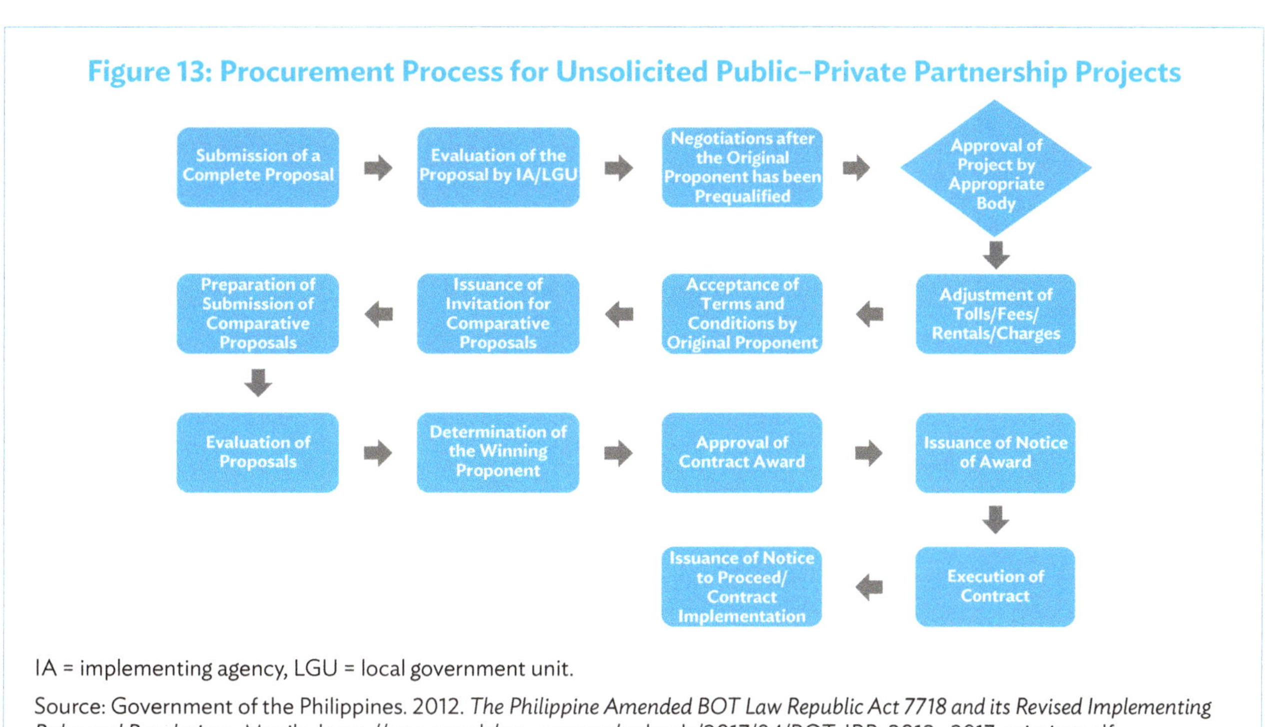


IA = implementing agency, LGU = local government unit.

Source: Government of the Philippines. 2012. *The Philippine Amended BOT Law Republic Act 7718 and its Revised Implementing Rules and Regulations*. Manila. https://ppp.gov.ph/wp-content/uploads/2017/04/BOT-IRR-2012_2017-printing.pdf

## Table 8: Description of the Procurement Process for Unsolicited Public–Private Partnership Projects

| Parameter | Description |
|---|---|
| Responsible agency | Implementing agency or LGU refers to any department, bureau, office, commission, authority, or agency of the national government, including government-owned and/or -controlled corporations, government financial institutions, and state universities and colleges authorized by law or their respective charters to contract for or undertake infrastructure or development projects.<br><br>Following project and contract approval, the implementing agency/LGU must set up a Prequalification, Bids, and Awards Committee consisting of at least a third-ranking regular official of the host agency as chairperson, a legal officer, a technical officer knowledgeable of the technical aspects of the project, a finance officer, a management/operations officer, two representatives from the private sector (one from recognized contractor associations and the other from either facility users or recognized accounting associations), a representative from the Commission on Audit, a PPP Center for national projects representative, and a local government office representative (for LGU projects only). The committee is responsible for all aspects of the pre-bidding and bidding processes. |
| Project announcement | Announcement of a project's invitation to tender or request for proposal is organized by the responsible agency—both on its website and in local newspapers. For project values of at least ₱500 million ($10 million as of April 2020), publication on at least one international newspaper is required. After obtaining approval for the project, a project announcement must be made once every week for 3 consecutive weeks, in at least two newspapers of general circulation, and in at least one local newspaper of general circulation in the region, province, city, or municipality in which the project is to be implemented. |
| Prequalification invitation documentation (optional, at Selection Committee's discretion) | Investors are guided by the following information:<br>• General requirements for the investors<br>• Requirements on investors' qualifications and experience regarding project implementation and financial-commercial capability<br><br>In the exigence of service, the host agency may opt to do a simultaneous qualification, instead of a prequalification of proponents. In this case, the bidders are asked to submit their proposal in three envelopes: the qualification documents corresponding to the requirements, the technical proposal, and the financial proposal. The period for the preparation of the qualification documents are subsumed under the time allotted for bid preparation. |
| Prequalification evaluation criteria | Legal requirement (local/foreign-owned entity), experience or track record in terms of the firm's experience, key personnel experience, and financial capability in terms of debt and equity. |
| Prequalification evaluation method | The prequalification evaluation method is not defined. |
| Shortlist (Results of the prequalification stage) | Shortlist is announced.<br><br>In case only one investor registers and satisfies the requirements of the invitation for prequalification or only one investor passes the prequalification, direct negotiation is possible. |
| Request for proposal (RFP) document | The typical contents of an RFP document include:<br>• Instructions to bidders, including<br>  – general project description and objectives<br>  – contractual arrangements<br>  – bid submission procedures and requirements<br>  – investment incentives and government undertakings<br>  – bid security and bid security validity period<br>  – milestones<br>  – evaluation methods and criteria |

*continued on next page*

*continued from previous page*

| Parameter | Description |
|---|---|
| | – minimum equity amount<br>– formula and appropriate indices to be used in the adjustments of tolls/fees/rentals/charges, when applicable<br>– requirements and timelines/milestones of concerned agencies in granting of franchise, if applicable<br>– requirements of concerned regulatory bodies<br>– current rules and regulations of the Bangko Sentral ng Pilipinas<br>– revenue-sharing arrangements<br>– expected commissioning date<br>– national and ownership requirements<br>• Minimum design, performance specifications, and economic parameters<br>• Draft contract<br>• Bid forms<br>• Forms of bid and performance securities<br>• Other documents as may be deemed necessary by the implementing agency/LGU concerned |
| Methods of interactions with the bidders | • Extension and award notices in writing<br>• Bid conferences |
| Evaluation of technical proposals | • *Technical soundness (preliminary engineering design).* The basic engineering design of the project should conform to the minimum design and performance standards and specifications set by the relevant agency/LGU as prescribed in the bidding documents. The engineering surveys, plans, and estimates should be undertaken within ±20% of the final quantities. The construction methods and schedules should also be presented and shown to be feasible or "doable."<br>• *Operational feasibility.* The proposed organization, methods, and procedures for operating and maintaining the completed facility must be well defined, should conform to the prescribed performance standards, and should be shown to be workable. Where feasible, it should provide for the transfer of technology used in every phase of the project.<br>• *Environmental standards.* The proposed design and the project technology to be used must be in accordance with the environmental standards set forth by the Department of Environment and Natural Resources, as indicated in the bid documents. Any adverse effects on the environment as a consequence of the project, as proposed by the prospective project proponent, must be properly identified, including the corresponding corrective/mitigating measures to be adopted.<br>• *Project financing.* The proposed financing plan should positively show that the financing could adequately meet the construction cost as well as the operating and maintenance costs requirements of the project. Relevant agency/LGU would assess the financing proposals of the bidders whether they match and adequately meet the cost requirements of the project under bidding. |
| Evaluation of financial proposals | Evaluation of financial proposals is carried out only for investors who satisfy the above technical requirements. Evaluation can be done based on any one or more of the following methods:<br>• Lowest proposed toll, fee, rental, or charge at the start of project operation, if a pre-agreed parametric tariff adjustment formula is prescribed in the bid document<br>• Lowest present value of the government subsidy to be provided for the period covered by the contract<br>• Highest present value of proposed payments to the government, such as concession fees, lease/rental payments, fixed/guaranteed payments, and/or variable payments/percentage shares of revenue for the period covered by the contract<br>• Any other appropriate financial bid parameter as may be approved by the approving body<br>In the case of build–transfer and build–lease–transfer schemes, a Filipino project proponent who submits an equally advantageous bid with exactly the same price and technical specifications as that of a foreign project proponent is given preference. |
| Investor selection | Investor is selected. |

*continued on next page*

*continued from previous page*

| Parameter | Description |
|---|---|
| Contract negotiation | • Negotiated contracts are allowed under direct negotiation when there is only one complying bidder or when there are unsolicited proposals<br>• For negotiated projects for solicited proposals, a reasonable rate of return are determined prior to negotiation.<br>• When applicable, the same rules provided for the evaluation of the technical and financial aspects of bid proposals are applied in the evaluation of negotiated contracts. |
| Contract signing (Commercial close) | Upon the head of agency/LGU's approval of the recommendation to award to the winning bidder, and within 5 days of the receipt by the winning bidder of the notice from the agency/LGU that all conditions stated in the Notice of Award have been complied to, the winning bidder and the head of agency/LGU would execute and sign the contract for the project. |

Sources: ADB. 2019. *Public–Private Partnership Monitor Second Edition*. Manila. https://www.adb.org/sites/default/files/publication/509426/ppp-monitor-second-edition.pdf; Government of the Philippines. 2012. *The Philippine Amended BOT Law Republic Act 7718 and its Revised Implementing Rules and Regulations*. Manila. https://ppp.gov.ph/wp-content/uploads/2017/04/BOT-IRR-2012_2017-printing.pdf

## 6. Public–Private Partnership Standard Operating Procedures, Toolkits, Templates, and Model Bid Documents

| Parameter | |
|---|---|
| Does the country have PPP Guidelines/PPP Guidance Manual? | ✓ |
| Does the PPP Guidelines/PPP Guidance Manual adequately cover the process, entities involved, roles and responsibilities of various entities, approvals required at various stages, and the timelines for the various stages of the PPP project lifecycle? | ✓ |
| What are the templates and checklists available in the PPP Guidelines/PPP Guidance Manual?<br>• Project Needs Assessment and Options Analysis checklist?<br>• Project Due Diligence checklist?<br>• Technical Assessment checklist?<br>• Environmental Assessment checklist?<br>• PPP Procurement Plan template? | <br>✓<br>✓<br>✓<br>✓<br>✓ |
| Does the country have standardized/model bidding documents for PPPs?<br>• Model Request for Qualification (RFQ) document?<br>• Model Request for Proposal (RFP) document?<br>• Model PPP/Concession Agreement?<br>• State Support Agreement?<br>• VGF Agreement?<br>• Guarantee Agreement?<br>• Power Purchase Agreement?<br>• Capacity Take-or-Pay Contract?<br>• Fuel Supply Agreement?<br>• Transmission and Use of System Agreement?<br>• Performance-based Operations and Maintenance Contract?<br>• Engineering, Procurement and Construction Contract? | <br>×<br>×<br>×<br>×<br>×<br>×<br>×<br>×<br>×<br>×<br>×<br>×<br>Only for LGU PPP Projects Model RFQ, RFP, and PPP Agreement are available |
| Does the country have standardized PPP agreement terms? | ×[a]<br>Except for LGU PPP Projects |

*continued on next page*

*continued from previous page*

| Parameter | |
|---|---|
| Does the country have standardized/model toolkits to facilitate identification, preparation, procurement, and management of PPP projects? | |
| • PPP Family Indicator? | × |
| • PPP Mode Validity Indicator? | |
| • PPP Suitability Filter? | × |
| • PPP Screening Tool? | × |
| • Financial Viability Indicator Model? | × |
| • Economic Viability Indicator Model? | × |
| • VFM Indicator Tool? | × |
| • Readiness Filter? | × |
| Is there a framework for monitoring fiscal risks from PPPs including the following? | |
| • Process for assessing fiscal commitments? | ✓ |
| • Process for approving fiscal commitments? | ✓ |
| • Process for monitoring fiscal commitments? | ✓ |
| • Process for reporting fiscal commitments? | ✓ |
| • Process for budgeting fiscal commitments? | ✓ |
| Are there fiscal prudence norms/thresholds to limit fiscal exposure to PPPs? | ✓ |
| Is there a process for assessing and budgeting contingent liabilities from PPPs? | ✓ |

✓ = Yes, × = No, NA = Not Applicable, UA = Unavailable

LGU = local government unit, PPP = public–private partnership, RFQ = request for qualification, RFP = request for proposal, VFM = value for money.

[a] It was previously understood that the PPP Center is currently developing a standard PPP concession agreement. As of April 2020, there has been no update on this.

Sources: Public–Private Partnership Center. PPPGB Guidelines and Issuances. https://ppp.gov.ph/guidelines-and-issuances/; Government of the Philippines. 2012. *PPP Manual for LGUs – Volume 3: Utilizing LGU PPP Project Templates and Bid Documents.* Manila. https://ppp.gov.ph/wp-content/uploads/2012/03/Volume-3-LGU-PPP-Manual.pdf; Law Business Research. 2015. *The Public–Private Partnership Law Review.* London. https://www.syciplaw.com/Documents/LegalResources/2015/PPP%20Law%20Review%20-%20Philippines%202015.pdf

PPPs implemented under the framework of the BOT Law and its IRR must comply with its requirements, processes, and procedures. However, for PPPs involving public utilities, the Philippine Constitution requires that:[18]

- the franchise, certificate, or authorization to operate public utilities be held by Filipino citizens, or corporations or associations organized under the Philippine law with at least 60% of its capital owned by Filipino citizens;
- the participation of foreign investors in the governing body of any public utility enterprise should be limited to their proportionate share in its capital; and
- all the executive and managing officers of such corporation or association must be citizens of the Philippines.

Moreover, such franchise, certificate or authorization for operation of a public utility is limited to a period of 50 years. While there are no value thresholds for PPP contracts, additional registration requirements or approvals are imposed on certain contractual schemes, such as presidential approval for BOO projects and contract arrangements other than those listed in Section 2 of the BOT Law (footnote 18).

18 Law Business Research. 2015. *The Public–Private Partnership Law Review.* London. https://www.syciplaw.com/Documents/LegalResources/2015/PPP%20Law%20Review%20-%20Philippines%202015.pdf.

## *Key clauses related to Public–Private Partnership Agreement*

- **Payments.** To facilitate payments under PPP contracts, the BOT Regulations prescribe specific payment schemes for particular contractual arrangements (Table 9).

### Table 9: Payment Schemes for Various Contractual Arrangements

| Contractual Arrangement | Typical Payment Scheme |
|---|---|
| Build–Operate–Transfer, Design–Operate–Transfer, and Rehabilitate–Operate–Transfer | Collection of reasonable tolls, fees, and charges for a fixed term, which shall not exceed 50 years |
| Build–Own–Operate and Rehabilitate–Own–Operate | Collection of reasonable tolls, fees, and charges for a fixed term Upon renewal of its franchise or contract with the implementing agency or LGU, the proponent is allowed to continue collecting tolls, fees, charges, and rentals for the operation of the facility or the provision of the service. |
| Build–Transfer–Operate | Option 1: Appropriate amortization and collection of reasonable tolls, rentals, and charges while operating the facility on behalf of the implementing agency or LGU, which may be directly applied to the amortization. Moreover, the facility operator may be repaid by the implementing agency or LGU through a management fee provided in the management contract.<br>Option 2: Directly collect tolls, rentals, and charges for a fixed term |
| Build–Transfer and Build–Lease–Transfer | Repayment through amortization |
| NEDA Board approved/ authorized contractual arrangements/schemes not enumerated under Section 2 of the BOT Law | Repayment through any of the schemes recommended by the ICC and approved by the NEDA Board |
| **Note:** Where applicable, the proponent may likewise be paid in the form of revenue sharing or other non-monetary payments (i.e., grant of commercial development rights, grant of a portion or percentage of the reclaimed land, subject to constitutional requirements or any other non-monetary payments). | |

BOT = build-operate-transfer, ICC = Investment Coordination Committee, LGU = local government unit, NEDA = National Economic and Development Authority.

Source: Law Business Research. 2015. *The Public–Private Partnership Law Review*. London. https://www.syciplaw.com/Documents/LegalResources/2015/PPP%20Law%20Review%20-%20Philippines%202015.pdf

- **Distribution of risk.** In the Philippines, PPP projects follow the risk allocation principle that the risk should be assigned to the party that is best able to control or influence the occurrence or manage the consequences of the risks. Thus, commercial risks (e.g., demand risk, supply risk, operational risk, and financing risk) are typically allocated to the private sector while legal, political or regulatory risk are allocated to the government (e.g., approval of rates or tariff adjustments, change in law, and material adverse government action). In some instances, the parties may agree to share certain risks. For instance, PPP agreements may provide that the government would only be liable for certain risks (e.g., force majeure risk) after a particular monetary threshold has been reached (footnote 18).

  In December 2010, the ICC–Cabinet Committee adopted the Generic Preferred Risk Allocation Matrix. It is intended to be recommendatory and is envisioned to serve as reference of the ICC and the proponent agencies in the ICC review of PPP projects. It is also based on the same principles and identifies the party that could best handle the risk involved in undertaking a PPP project, including some proposed mitigating strategies and contractual provision for each risk.[19]

[19] Government of the Philippines. 2016. *Generic Preferred Risk Allocation Matrix*. Manila. https://ppp.gov.ph/wp-content/uploads/2017/02/GPRAM_2Aug2016.pdf.

- **Lenders' security and step-in rights.** Security over the shares of a PPP project company and the possibility of a direct agreement between the government and project lenders are not explicitly stated in the regulations; however, it is possible on a contract case-by-case basis. Domestically owned companies can get security over land on a case-by-case basis (footnote 1).

| Parameter | |
|---|---|
| Does the law specifically enable lenders the following rights: | |
| Security over the project assets | ✓[a] |
| Security over the land on which they are built (land use right) | ✓ |
| Security over the shares of a PPP project company | ✓ |
| Can there be a direct agreement between the government and lenders? | ✓ |
| Do lenders get priority in the case of insolvency? | × |
| Can lenders be given step-in rights? | ✓ |

✓ = Yes, × = No, NA = Not Applicable, UA = Unavailable

[a] On a case-by-case basis

- **Government support/state guarantees.** These details are already covered in the subsequent subsection (Section 1.2.2).
- **Ownership of project assets.** Generally, the government would obtain ownership of the underlying assets; however, the time of the transfer of ownership would depend on the contractual agreement between the parties. For example, in a build–transfer–operate or build–and–transfer scheme, transfer of ownership of the assets to the government occurs immediately after completion of the project, subject to later payments to the private party comprising its investment plus a reasonable rate of return. In contrast, in a BOT or BLT scheme, transfer will occur only after an agreed period, during which the private entity will be allowed to operate or lease the facility and charge its users the appropriate rentals, fees, or tolls (footnote 18).
- **Termination and compensation.** The PPPGB Policy Circular 06-2015 on Termination Payment for PPP Projects has introduced a regulation of events that trigger termination and compensation payment. Force majeure and private sector default were also among these. Until then, regulations have been allowing a compensation payable to the private sector only in case of adverse public sector actions or public sector defaults.[20]

  The government compensates the proponent for the actual expenses incurred in the project as of termination, including a reasonable rate of return, in cases wherein: (i) the implementing agency or LGU terminates, cancels or revokes the contract through no-fault of the project proponent; (ii) the parties terminate the contract by mutual agreement; or (iii) a court revokes or cancels the contract by final judgment through no-fault of the proponent, thereon not exceeding those stated in the contract and subject to such reliefs available to it under the insurance provision of the contract (footnote 18).

  When the government defaults on certain major obligations in the PPP contract and such failure is not remediable or, it should not be remedied for an unreasonable length of time, if remediable, in this case, the proponent is reasonably compensated by the government for the equivalent or proportionate cost as defined in the contract, subject to the reliefs available to the government under the insurance provision of the contract (footnote 18).

20 PPPGB. 2015. *Termination Payment for Public–Private Partnership Projects.* Manila. https://ppp.gov.ph/wp-content/uploads/2018/07/PPPC_GUIDE_TP-PPP-Projects-20150325.pdf.

In both instances, the compensation is determined by an independent appraiser, mutually acceptable to the implementing agency or LGU and the proponent. The compensation is paid by the implementing agency or LGU concerned within 90 calendar days from the independent appraiser's advice of such determination, unless the parties agree on a different payment period, subject to the enactment of a law or ordinance, as the case may be, appropriating such amount, if required (footnote 18).

Lastly, the implementing agency or LGU concerned may rescind the contract when the proponent: (i) refuses or fails to perform any of the provisions of the technical and performance standards in the approved contract; (ii) fails to satisfy any of the contract provisions including compliance with the prescribed or agreed milestone activities; or (iii) commits any substantial breach of the approved contract. In such cases, an implementing agency or LGU may either take over the facility or allow the proponent's lenders, creditors, and banks to exercise their rights and interests under the loan and collateral documents with respect to the project, aside from forfeiting the proponent's performance bond (footnote 18).

| Parameter | |
|---|---|
| Does the law specifically enable compensation payment to the private partner in case of early termination due to: | |
| • Public sector default or termination for reasons of public interest | ✓ |
| • Private sector default | ✓ |
| • Force majeure | ✓ |
| • Does the law enable the concept of economic/financial equilibrium? | ✓ |
| Does the law enable compensation payment to the private partner due to: | |
| • Material adverse government action | ✓ |
| • Force majeure | ✓ |
| • Change in law | ✓ |

✓ = Yes, × = No, NA = Not Applicable, UA = Unavailable

- **Adjustment and revision to the PPP contract.** Changes to the PPP contract may be allowed before the submission of the bids provided the head of the relevant implementing agency or LGU secures the approval of the approving body.[21] Changes after the bid submission and before the execution of the contract are not allowed except for changes to contract terms affected or decided by the winning bidder's bid (footnote 18).

  During the implementation of the PPP contract, a contract may be varied upon approval by the head of the implementing agency or LGU provided that: (i) there is no impact on the basic parameters and terms of the contract as approved by the approving body; (ii) there is no reduction in the scope of works or performance standards, or fundamental change in the contractual arrangement nor extension in the contract term, except in cases of breach on the part of the implementing agency or LGU of its obligations under the contract; (iii) there is no increase in the agreed fees, tolls, and charges or a decrease in the implementing agency or the LGU's revenue or profit share derived from the project, except as may be allowed under a parametric formula in the contract itself; or (iv) there is no additional government undertaking, or increase in the financial exposure of the government under the project. For contract variations that do not meet these requirements, approval by the approving body is required. Failure to observe this rule renders the contract variation void (footnote 18).

[21] Approval must be sought for the following: (i) changes that reduce the service levels to the public; (ii) changes that reduce the economic internal rate of return below the hurdle rate used in the original analysis of the project; (iii) changes that increase the total government subsidy to a project by at least 5% of the total project cost; and (iv) changes in the risk profile that are detrimental to the best interest of the government. See BOT Regulations. Section 2.8, Rule 2.

## 7. Unsolicited Public–Private Partnership Proposals

| Parameter | |
|---|---|
| Does the PPP legal and regulatory framework allow submission and acceptance of unsolicited proposals? | ✓ |
| What are the advantages provided to the project proponent for an unsolicited bid?<br>• Competitive advantage at bid evaluation?<br>• Swiss Challenge?<br>• Compensation of the project development costs?<br>• Government support for land acquisition and resettlement cost?<br>• Government support in the form of viability gap funding and guarantees? | <br>×<br>✓[a]<br>×<br>×<br>× |

✓ = Yes, × = No, NA = Not Applicable, UA = Unavailable

[a] There are LGU PPP Codes (i.e., Quezon City, Cebu City) that allow losing parties to recoup compensation for project development costs in the case of the Swiss Challenge

Source: PPPGB. 2018. *Guidelines on Managing Unsolicited Proposals under RA 6957, as amended by RA 7718.* Manila.

Unsolicited proposals are generally accepted on a negotiated basis, provided certain conditions are met (footnote 12):

- The project involves new concept or technology and/or is not part of the list of priority projects.
- No direct government guarantee, subsidy, or equity is required.
- The implementing agency/LGUs have invited, by publication in a newspaper of general circulation for 3 consecutive weeks, comparative or competitive proposals; and no other proposal is received for a period of 60 working days. In the event another proponent submits a lower price proposal, the original proponent has the right to match that price within 30 working days. If the original proponent fails to match the price proposal of the comparative proponent within the specified period, the contract is awarded to the comparative proponent. On the other hand, if the original proponent matches the price proposal of the comparative proponent within the specified period, the project is immediately awarded to the original proponent (footnote 12).

## 8. Foreign Investor Participation Restrictions

| Parameter | |
|---|---|
| Is there any restriction for foreign investors on: | |
| • Land use/ownership rights as opposed to similar rights of local investors | ✓ |
| • Currency conversion | × |
| • PPP projects with foreign sponsor participation (number) | 39 |

✓ = Yes, × = No, NA = Not Applicable, UA = Unavailable

In case an infrastructure facility's operation requires a public utility franchise, the facility operator must be a Filipino, or if a corporation, it must be duly registered with the Securities and Exchange Commission and owned up to at least 60% by Filipinos. In the case of foreign contractors, Filipino labor are employed or hired in the different phases of construction where Filipino skills are available (footnote 1).

## 9. Dispute Resolution

| Parameter | |
|---|---|
| Does the country have a dispute resolution tribunal (DRT)? | ✓ |
| Does the country have an institutional arbitration mechanism? | ✓ |
| Can a foreign law be chosen to govern PPP contracts? | × |
| What dispute resolution mechanisms are available for PPP agreements? | |
| • Court litigation | ✓ |
| • Local arbitration | ✓ |
| • International arbitration | ✓ |
| Has the country signed the New York Convention on the Recognition and Enforcement of Foreign Arbitral Awards? | ✓ |

✓ = Yes, × = No, NA = Not Applicable, UA = Unavailable

Despite its transparency, the dispute resolution mechanism is still considered as inefficient and time-consuming, and involves costly court processes. Typically, the resolution of disputes is left to the discretion of parties, including the use of alternative dispute resolution with agreements citing international arbitration as a mechanism of choice. Executive Order 78 of 6 July 2012 mandates alternative dispute resolutions on all PPP contracts (footnote 1).

In the Philippines, the Alternative Dispute Resolution Act (Republic Act 9285) provides that international commercial arbitration shall be governed by the UN Commission on International Trade Law Model Law (chapter 4, section 19) and contains provisions on international commercial arbitration (sections 19–31). Domestic arbitration is governed by the Arbitration Law (Republic Act 876), and by certain provisions of the UN Commission Model Law (footnote 1).

The Philippines ratified the New York Convention with the reservation that it does so on the basis of reciprocity. It applies the convention to the recognition and enforcement of awards made only in the territory of another contracting state, and only to differences arising out of legal relationships, whether contractual or not, which are considered as commercial under the national law of the state making such a declaration (footnote 1).

Neither online alternative dispute resolution nor fast-track arbitration is currently available in the Philippines.

Strictly speaking, there is no consolidated law encompassing all aspects of commercial mediation or conciliation in the Philippines. Commercial mediation in the Philippines generally consists of two kinds: (i) voluntary mediation and (ii) compulsory or court-annexed mediation.[22]

The Philippine Dispute Resolution Center, Inc. (PDRCI) was incorporated in 1996 out of the Arbitration Committee of the Philippine Chamber of Commerce and Industry (PCCI). As an arbitral institution, it does not itself resolve disputes. PDRCI promotes and encourages the use of arbitration, mediation, and other modes of avoiding or settling commercial disputes such as dispute boards. It also provides alternative dispute resolution (ADR) services to the business community.[23]

22 ICLG. Practice Areas. Litigation and Disputes. https://iclg.com/practice-areas/litigation-and-dispute-resolution-laws-and-regulations/philippines; ADB. 2019. *Public–Private Partnership Monitor Second Edition.* Manila. https://www.adb.org/sites/default/files/publication/509426/ppp-monitor-second-edition.pdf; https://ppp.gov.ph/wp-content/uploads/2015/03/EO-78-s-2012-ADR-Mechanisms-in-PPP-BOT-Contracts-and-JV-Agreements.pdf.

23 Philippine Dispute Resolution Center, Inc. News. www.pdrci.org.

## 10. Environmental and Social Issues

| Parameter | |
|---|---|
| Is there a local regulation establishing a process for environmental impact assessment? | ✓ |
| Is there a legal mechanism for the private partner to limit environmental liability for what is outside of its control or caused by third parties? | ✓ |
| Is there a local regulation establishing a process for social impact assessment? | ✓ |
| Is there involuntary land clearance for PPP projects? | ✓ |

✓ = Yes, × = No, NA = Not Applicable, UA = Unavailable

Project implementation is subject to the implementing rules and regulations of Presidential Decree 1586, also known as the Philippine Environmental Impact Statement System. It requires a project proponent to conduct an environmental impact assessment (EIA) to ensure that all possible environmental effects of the project are addressed, in line with the country's overall goal of sustainable development. The Environmental Management Bureau of the Department of Environment and Natural Resources (DENR) is responsible for conducting a review of the EIA, the environmental risk analysis, and the proposed mitigation measures. The review also covers the integration of climate change adaptation measures and disaster risk reduction, if there are any, as well as environmental monitoring and management plan for the project. The DENR then issues the Environmental Clearance Certificate, which is necessary to obtain before the commencement of project construction (footnote 1).

The process for social compliance is regulated by a number of regulations, such as the Right-Of-Way Act 10752 (2016) and PPPGB Policy Circular 10-2016 on public consultations and engagement for PPP projects (footnote 1).

The land can be expropriated. The property owner is given 30 days to decide whether to accept the offer as payment for the property. Upon refusal or failure of the property owner to accept such an offer, expropriation proceedings can be initiated (footnote 1).

In December 2018, the PPPGB Resolution 2018-12-02 was passed for mainstreaming environmental, displacement, social, and gender concerns associated with PPP projects.[24] The objective of this resolution is to prevent delays associated with safeguard concerns in the PPP process due to the lack of capacity and resources of implementing agencies to review all safeguards-related laws and regulations that have an impact on various stages of a PPP project delivery. This resolution provides guidelines for the implementing agency during each of the following phases:

- **Project development phase.** Identify all the applicable requirements in laws, decrees, orders, issuances, rules and regulations, and the corresponding required studies, outputs, or standards for a particular PPP project, and ensure that safeguards are considered in the project's feasibility study and design.
- **Review and approval phase.** Ensure that the approved terms of the project consider various safeguard concerns identified during the project development phase, including their mitigation measures.
- **Procurement phase.** Ensure that the safeguard considerations are integrated in the PPP contract, including their mitigation measures.
- **Implementation phase.** Identify specific monitoring, evaluation, and feedback mechanisms to ensure that safeguard measures embedded in the PPP contract are complied with, and to provide the implementing agency with the necessary mechanisms to manage unforeseen safeguard concerns.

24 PPPGB. 2018. *Safeguards in PPPs: Mainstreaming Environmental, Displacement, Social, and Gender Concerns*. Manila. https://ppp.gov.ph/wp-content/uploads/2019/01/PPPC_PPPGB_Reso-Safeguards-in-PPP.pdf.

## 11. Land Rights

| Parameter | |
|---|---|
| Which of the following is permitted to the private partner: | |
| • Transfer land lease/use/ownership rights to third party | ✓ |
| • Use leased/owned land as collateral | ✓ |
| • Mortgage leased/owned land | ✓ |
| Is there a legal mechanism for granting wayleave rights, for example, laying water pipes or fiber cables over land occupied by persons other than the government or the private partner? | ✓ |
| Is there a land registry/cadastre with public information on land plots? | ✓ |
| Which of the following information on land plots is available to the private partner: | ✓ |
| • Appraisal of land value | ✓ |
| • Landowners | ✓ |
| • Land boundaries | ✓ |
| • Utility connections | × |
| • Immovable property on land | ✓ |
| • Plots classification | ✓ |

✓ = Yes, × = No, NA = Not Applicable, UA = Unavailable

Republic Act 8974 (2000) and Republic Act 10752 (2016) facilitate the acquisition of right-of-way, site, or location for national government infrastructure projects. For PPP projects, the private sector might be requested to either finance the right-of-way cost which can be recovered partly or fully by the investor from the tolls, fees, or tariffs to be charged to the users of the completed project, or advance the funds covering the cost of the right-of-way which would be reimbursed later by the implementing agency, with the exception of unsolicited proposal.[25]

According to the 1987 Constitution, private ownership of land is only allowed for corporations which are at least 60% owned by Filipino citizens. Public land cannot be owned irrespective of company ownership structure and can only be leased from the government (footnote 25).

## Government Support for Public–Private Partnership Projects

| Parameter | |
|---|---|
| Project Funding Support | |
| Is there a dedicated government financial support mechanism for PPP projects? | ×[a] |
| What are the instruments of government financial support available under this government financial support mechanism? | |
| • Capital grant | ✓ |
| • Operations grant | ✓ |

*continued on next page*

[25] ADB. 2019. *Public–Private Partnership Monitor Second Edition.* Manila. https://www.adb.org/sites/default/files/publication/509426/ppp-monitor-second-edition.pdf; Public–Private Partnership Center. 2016. *Right of Way Act, Philippines.* https://ppp.gov.ph/wp-content/uploads/2016/03/Right-of-Way-Act-RA10752.pdf; Public–Private Partnership Center. 2015. *Republic Act 8974, Philippines.* https://ppp.gov.ph/wp-content/uploads/2015/01/Republic-Act-8974.pdf.

*continued from previous page*

| Parameter | |
|---|---|
| • Annuity/availability payments | ✓ |
| • Guarantees to cover<br>– Currency inconvertibility and transfer risk<br>– Foreign exchange risk<br>– War and civil disturbance risk<br>– Breach of contract risk<br>– Regulatory risk<br>– Expropriation risk<br>– Government payment obligation risk<br>– Credit risk<br>– Minimum demand/revenue risk<br>– Risk of making annuity/availability payments in a timely manner | <br>×<br>×<br>×<br>✓<br>×<br>×<br>✓<br>✓<br>×<br>× |
| What are the caps/ceilings for the government financial support under each of the abovementioned government financial support instruments? | 50% of project cost |
| Is there a minimum PPP project size (investment) for a PPP project to be eligible for receiving government financial support? | × |
| Are there minimum financial commitment requirements for the private developer equity before the government support could be drawn? | × |
| Is the government financial support required, and is there an allowed bid parameter for PPP projects? | ✓ |
| Are unsolicited PPP proposals eligible to receive government financial support? | × |
| Are there standard operating procedures for providing government financial support to PPP projects?<br>• Appraisal and approval process<br>• Budgeting process<br>• Disbursement process<br>• Monitoring process<br>• Accounting, auditing, and reporting process | <br>✓<br>✓<br>✓<br>✓<br>✓ |
| Who are the signatories to the Government Financial Support Agreement? | Head of implementing agency, but DOF and DBM must approve of any financial support |
| Who is responsible for monitoring the performance of PPP projects availing government financial support?<br>• Independent engineer?<br>• Government agency?<br>• Ministry of Finance? | <br>✓[b]<br>✓<br>✓ |
| What are the other forms of government support available for PPP projects? | |
| • Land acquisition funding support? | ×[c] |
| • Funding support for resettlement and rehabilitation of affected parties? | ✓ |
| • Tax holidays/exemptions? | ✓ |
| • Real estate development rights? | ✓[d] |
| • Advertising and marketing rights? | ✓ |
| • Interest rate/cost of debt subventions? | × |
| • Other subsidies and subventions? | ✓ |

*continued on next page*

*continued from previous page*

| Parameter | |
|---|---|
| Can the other forms of government support be availed over and above the government financial support through various instruments listed above? | ✓ |

✓ = Yes, × = No, NA = Not Applicable, UA = Unavailable

[a] There is no dedicated financial support mechanism. Financial support is decided and set up on a per project basis.

[b] Independent engineer, implementing agency, and PPP Center.

[c] Where land is required, the project is usually on government land or on land acquired by the government.

[d] Though such rights are granted, the government does not provide financial support for real estate development.

The various types of government support mechanisms for providing project funding support to PPPs in the Philippines are described below:

- **Capital grant/cost sharing.** As per the Amended BOT Law Republic Act 7718 and its Revised Implementing Rules and Regulations (IRR) 2012, the concerned contacting agency could fund a portion of capital expenses associated with the establishment of an infrastructure development facility. This may include access infrastructure; right-of-way; transfer of ownership, usufruct, or possession of land; or a building or any real or personal property for direct use in the project and/or any partial financing of the project, or components of the project. The provided support does not exceed 50% of the project cost, and the balance to be provided by the project proponent. Such government share may be financed from direct government appropriations and/or from official development assistance (ODA) of foreign government or institutions. No direct government guarantee, subsidy or equity would be provided for unsolicited proposals. PPP Governing Board Policy Circular 04-2015 on VGF[26] highlights that the implementing agency or the approval body has the flexibility to determine the amount of VGF, if required (subject to the BOT Law).[27]
- **Operations and maintenance support.** As per the Amended BOT Law and its IRR, the implementing agency can pay for or shoulder a portion of the project cost or the expenses and costs in operating or maintaining the project and contribute any property or assets to the project (footnote 27).
- **Availability and performance-based payment schemes** are allowed under the build–transfer–operate arrangement and have been implemented in practice in Investment Priorities Plan projects. Many of the bulk water supply systems were awarded on availability- and performance-based payment schemes (footnote 23).
- **Credit enhancements/government guarantees** refers to the support to a development facility by the project proponent and/or implementing agency/LGU concerned. The provision of these guarantees is contingent upon the occurrence of certain events and/or risks, as stipulated in the contract. Credit enhancements are allocated to the party that is best able to manage and assume the consequences of the risk involved. Credit enhancements may include, but are not limited to, government guarantees on the performance, or the obligation of the implementing agency/LGU under its contract with the project proponent. Few past Investment Priorities Plan contracts also received tariff rate guarantees (footnote 27).
- **Direct government subsidy** refers to an agreement whereby the government, or any of its implementing agencies/LGUs would (i) defray, pay for, or shoulder a portion of the project cost or the expenses and

[26] PPPGB. 2015. *Policy on Viability Gap Funding (VGF) for Public–Private Partnership (PPP) Projects.* Manila. https://ppp.gov.ph/wp-content/uploads/2015/04/PPP-Governing-Board-Policy-Circular-No-04-2015.pdf.

[27] Government of the Philippines. Commission on Audit. Downloads. https://www.coa.gov.ph/phocadownload/userupload/ABC-Help/BOT_LAW/BOT/Section13.3.htm.

costs in operating or maintaining the project; (ii) in the case of LGUs, waive or grant special rates on real property taxes on the project during the term of the contractual arrangement; (iii) contribute any property or assets to the project; and/or (iv) waive charges or fees relative to business permits or licenses that are to be obtained for the construction of the project, all without receiving payment or value from the project proponent and/or facility operator for such payment, contribution or support (footnote 27).

- **Direct government equity** refers to the subscription by the government or any of its agencies or LGUs of shares of stock or other securities convertible to shares of stock of the project company. This applies irrespective of whether such subscription will be paid by the money or assets (footnote 27).
- **Land acquisition and resettlement support.** Support for land acquisition and resettlement cost could be provided by the implementing agency/local government unit on a case-by-case basis only for solicited projects (footnote 1).
- **Tax incentives.** Among other incentives, for projects in excess of ₱1 billion ($20 million as of April 2020), there are investment incentives established under Omnibus Investment Code of 1987[28], subject to the compliance of the project to the criteria set by the Board of Investment (footnote 1).
- **Performance undertaking** refers to an undertaking of a department, bureau, office, commission, authority, agency, GOCC, or LGU in assuming responsibility for the performance of the implementing agency/LGU's obligations under the contractual arrangement, including the payment of monetary obligations, in case of default. These undertakings may be subject to payment of risk premium to the government or LGU, or any other authorized agency (footnote 27).
- **Legal assistance** refers to the extension of representation by government lawyers to a project proponent but only in cases, hearings, or inquiries where the implementing agency/LGU and project proponent are party defendants/respondents. It also includes the adoption by such government lawyers of positions and strategies consistent with upholding the validity of the approved contractual arrangement (footnote 27).
- **Security assistance** refers to the deployment of government security forces, either from the Philippine National Police (PNP) or the Armed Forces of the Philippines (AFP) in the vicinity of the project site to provide security during the implementation of the project up to its completion (footnote 27).
- Renewable energy projects receive special incentives under Republic Act 9513, also known as the Renewable Energy Act of 2008, and Republic Act 7156, also known as the Mini-Hydroelectric Power Incentives Act (footnote 1).

Mactan–Cebu Airport PPP project received land acquisition support, while the Tarlac–La Union Toll Expressway and Daang Hari–South Luzon Expressway Link Road projects received VGF. The projects that received government guarantees are all energy generation projects, with the exception of the Metro Rail Transit (MRT) Line 3 project.

The implementing agency/LGU may offer any one or more forms of government support for a project, which would be pre-cleared in principle, in writing, by the department, bureau, office, commission, authority, agency, GOCC, or LGU or any other government entity that would grant the support as mandated by law, provided that the total government support does not exceed 50% of the total project cost.

The government support should be based on the approved risk allocation matrix issued by the approving body/ICC (footnote 12).

28 Government of the Philippines. 2018. *The Omnibus Investments Code.* Manila. http://boi.gov.ph/wp-content/uploads/2018/02/EO-226-omnibus-investments-code.pdf.

| Parameter | |
|---|---|
| **Project Development Funding** | |
| What are the various sources of funds for PPP project preparation? | |
| • Budgetary allocations | ✓ |
| • Dedicated project preparation/project development fund | ✓ |
| • Technical assistance from multilateral, bilateral, and donor agencies? | ✓ |
| • Recovery of project preparation funding from the preferred bidder? | ✓ |
| At what stage of the PPP project can the project preparation/development funding be availed by the government agency? | |
| • Pre-feasibility stage | ✓ |
| • Detailed feasibility stage | ✓ |
| • Transaction stage | ✓ |
| Is there a list of project preparation/project development activities toward which the project development funding can be utilized? | ✓ |
| Can the project development funding be utilized to appoint transaction advisors for PPP projects? | ✓ |
| Is there a specific process to be followed by government agencies to appoint transaction advisors? | ✓ |
| What are the payment mechanisms for making payments to transaction advisors? | |
| • Timesheet based | ✓ |
| • Milestone based | ✓ |
| Are there standard agreements and documents to avail project development funding? | ✓[a] |
| Who are the signatories to the project development funding agreements? | PPP Center head and implementing agency head [b] |

✓ = Yes, × = No, NA = Not Applicable, UA = Unavailable

[a] The forms are available at PPP Center. PDMF Guidelines. https://ppp.gov.ph/pdmf-guidelines/

[b] Source: Public–Private Partnership Center. 2020. *The Project Development and Monitoring Facility Guidelines*. Manila. https://ppp.gov.ph/wp-content/uploads/2020/01/PDMFS_200190128_REP_Revised-Guidelines-January-2020.pdf

The Project Development and Monitoring Facility (PDMF) is a revolving fund established by Executive Order 144, with assistance from development partners, Australian Department of Foreign Affairs and Trade, and Asian Development Bank.[29] Managed by the PDMF committee (National Economic and Development Authority, Department of Finance, Department of Budget and Management, and PPP Center), the Facility aims to develop a robust pipeline of properly prepared and well-structured PPP projects. The PDMF was created with an initial seed capital of ₱300 million ($6 million as of April 2020) from the Government of the Philippines. Appropriated funds under the BOT Center's Project Development Facility (PDF) were also added to this seed capital pursuant to Executive Order 8.

The PDMF is a funding mechanism available to implementing agencies/LGUs for developing bankable PPP projects and ensuring effective monitoring of project implementation. The PDMF can be used to engage consultants for any or a combination of the following services:

29 Public–Private Partnership Center. 2020. *The Project Development and Monitoring Facility Guidelines*. Manila. https://ppp.gov.ph/wp-content/uploads/2020/01/PDMFS_200190128_REP_Revised-Guidelines-January-2020.pdf.

- Project preparation and assistance in managing the bidding process for solicited projects
- Assistance in evaluation of unsolicited proposals submitted to implementing agencies or LGUs
- Assistance in contract negotiations between the implementing agencies/LGUs and the private sector proponent for unsolicited proposals
- Assistance in management of the competitive bidding process for unsolicited proposals
- Assistance up to financial close
- Assistance in probity advisory
- Assistance in monitoring of project implementation

As a revolving fund, reimbursement of the PDMF support is a condition precedent for contract award to the winning project proponent. Figure 14 provides the details on the PDMF oversight and management, and Figure 15 shows the PDMF application process.

**Figure 14: Oversight and Management of the Project Development and Monitoring Facility**

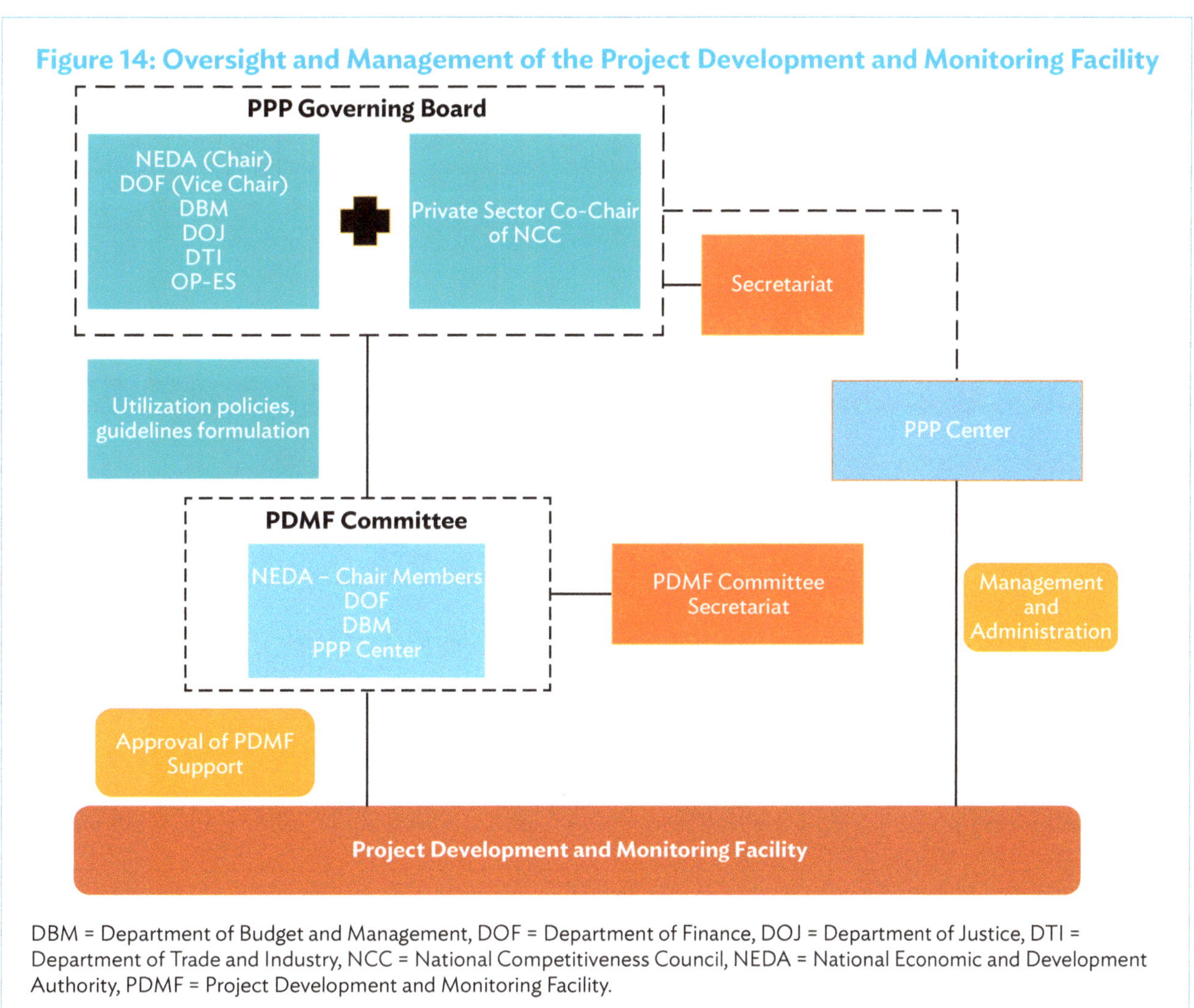


DBM = Department of Budget and Management, DOF = Department of Finance, DOJ = Department of Justice, DTI = Department of Trade and Industry, NCC = National Competitiveness Council, NEDA = National Economic and Development Authority, PDMF = Project Development and Monitoring Facility.

Source: Public–Private Partnership Center. PDMF. Oversight and Management. https://ppp.gov.ph/pdmf/oversight-and-management/.

**Figure 15: Application Process for the Project Development and Monitoring Facility**

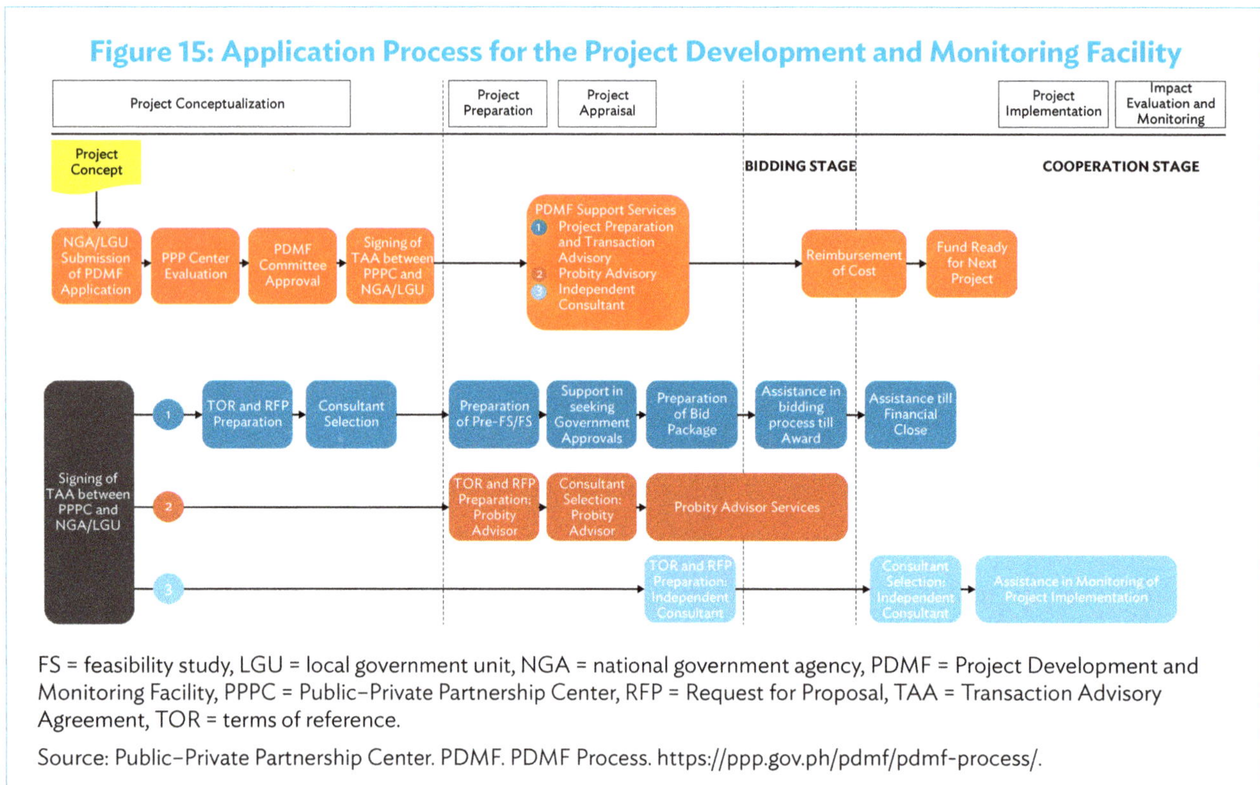


FS = feasibility study, LGU = local government unit, NGA = national government agency, PDMF = Project Development and Monitoring Facility, PPPC = Public–Private Partnership Center, RFP = Request for Proposal, TAA = Transaction Advisory Agreement, TOR = terms of reference.

Source: Public–Private Partnership Center. PDMF. PDMF Process. https://ppp.gov.ph/pdmf/pdmf-process/.

## Maturity of the Public–Private Partnership Market

| Parameter | |
|---|---|
| **PPP Project Statistics** | |
| Is there a National PPP database for the country? | ✓[a] |
| Is the distribution of PPP projects across infrastructure sectors available? | ✓ |
| Is the distribution of PPP projects across various stages of the PPP lifecycle available? | ✓ |

✓ = Yes, × = No, NA = Not Applicable, UA = Unavailable

[a] Source: Public–Private Partnership Center. Projects Database. https://ppp.gov.ph/project-database/.

The PPP Center maintains a project database listing the names, size, and status of the projects, and distribution of projects across sectors.

| Parameter | |
|---|---|
| Does the country publish a national PPP project pipeline? | ✓ |
| At what frequency is the national PPP project pipeline published? | As updates arise |
| Is the national PPP project pipeline based on the National Infrastructure Plan for the country? | ✓ |

✓ = Yes, × = No, NA = Not Applicable, UA = Unavailable

The priority projects identified across various sectors (roads, railways, airports, energy, social infrastructure, water and sanitation) for the PPP mode of implementation based on NEDA's *Revised List of Infrastructure Flagship Projects* (published on 17 February 2020) guides implementing agencies and the PPP Center in developing a pipeline of PPP projects.

| Parameter | Yes/No |
|---|---|
| **Sources of PPP Financing** | |
| Who are the typical entities financing PPP projects in the country? | |
| • Private developers | ✓ |
| • Construction contractors | ✓ |
| • Institutional/financial/private equity investors | ✓ |
| • Pension funds | ×[a] |
| • Insurance companies | ×[b] |
| • Banks | ✓ |
| • Non-banking financial corporation/financial institutions | ×[c] |
| • Donor agencies | ✓ |
| • Government agencies and state-owned enterprises | ✓ |
| What is the distribution of financing among these entities financing PPP projects? | Mainly financed through bank loans and equity |
| Does the country have the history/track record of issuing bonds by infrastructure projects? | × |
| How many infrastructure projects/private developers for infrastructure projects have raised funding through bond issuances? | UA |
| What is the value of funding raised through capital markets by PPPs? | UA |
| Does the country have a matured derivatives market to hedge certain risks associated with PPPs? | ✓ |
| Does the country have a national development bank? | ✓ |
| Does the country have credit rating agencies to rate infrastructure projects? | ✓ |
| Typically, what are the credit ratings achieved/received by infrastructure projects? | UA |
| Is there a threshold credit rating for infrastructure PPPs below which institutional investors, pension funds, and insurance companies would not invest in infrastructure PPPs? | UA |
| What is the typical funding model for infrastructure PPPs—corporate finance or project finance? | Both models are used |
| Are there regulatory limits/restrictions for the maximum exposure that can be taken by banks to infrastructure projects? | ✓ |

✓ = Yes, × = No, NA = Not Applicable, UA = Unavailable

[a] Government pension funds (SSS and GSIS) do not participate in financing. However, GSIS insurance coverage is a requirement in some projects.

[b] Insurance companies typically do not participate as a financier, but they provide insurance coverage instead.

[c] Except for captive financial institutions of large conglomerate groups, which may participate as financiers in some cases.

The government has been looking into the Philippine bond market as another alternative source of financing for PPP projects (Table 10). In 2016, ADB provided support for the issuance of the Philippines' first peso-denominated green project bond for the refinancing of the Tiwi and Makiling–Banahaw (Tiwi–MakBan) geothermal facilities. It is noteworthy that the SEC approved the listing of PPP projects on the Philippine Stock Exchange in November 2016 (footnote 1).

Moreover, Special Purpose Vehicles (SPV), with project cost of at least ₱5 billion ($99 million as of April 2020), are permitted to list in the Philippine Dealing and Exchange Corporation (PDEX) as per the SEC approved Public–Private Partnership Listing Rules (9 November 2016).[30] However, until 2019, no SPV has been listed.

## Table 10: Key Infrastructure Financing Sources in the Philippines

| | Non/ Limited Recourse Loan | Non/ Limited Recourse Local Currency Loan | Project Financing, Local Public Sector Banks | Interest Rate Swaps | Currency Swaps | Project Financing through Project Bond Issuance |
|---|---|---|---|---|---|---|
| Maximum Tenor (in years) | 15–20 | Up to 15 | 7–8 | 20 | 5-9 | UA |
| Up-front arrangement fee (bps) | 100–300 | 100–150 | | | | |
| Floor rate | London Interbank Offered Rate (LIBOR) | PHP BVAL Reference Rates | | | | |
| Margin rate (bps) | 100–500 | 100-300 | | | | |
| Percentage of foreign debt out of total debt for project financing | UA | UA | UA | UA | UA | UA |
| Percentage of project bonds out of total debt for project financing | UA | UA | UA | UA | UA | UA |
| Typical debt to equity ratio | 70:30 (In some cases, it can be 80:20) | | | | | |
| Timeline to financial close (month) | 6-12 | | | | | |
| Minimum DSCR covenant levels (x) | 1.25x-1.3x | | | | | |
| Nominal interest rates | UA | | | | | |
| Real interest rates | UA | | | | | |
| Security package | UA | | | | | |

✓ = Yes, × = No, NA = Not Applicable, UA = Unavailable

BPS = Basis Points, DSCR = debt service coverage ratio, LIBOR = London Inter-Bank Offered Rate, PDST = Philippine Dealing System Treasury.

The project financing scenario in the Philippines is monopolized by local banks that have strong relationships with local conglomerates. The requirement for loans to be in local currency provides the local banks a distinct advantage over foreign loans in terms of pricing. Furthermore, domestic banks do not require any political risk guarantee, unlike the international lenders, and offer terms which are light on covenants (footnote 1).

In late 2016, the Bangko Sentral ng Pilipinas (Central Bank of the Philippines) announced an end to the temporary single borrowing limit relief which had been available to companies involved in PPP projects. This relief was originally established in 2010 to facilitate lending on PPP projects (footnote 1).

Nevertheless, in 2018, the central bank decided to review the single borrowing limit to provide leeway for infrastructure financing. The single borrower limits were relaxed to accommodate bank lending for Special

[30] Securities and Exchange Commission. Uploads. https://www.sec.gov.ph/wp-content/uploads/2020/01/2016_PressReleases_SECApproved PublicPrivatePartnershipListingRules.pdf.

Purpose Vehicles holding big-ticket projects (footnote 1). A cap of 25% was made available for exposure to a single Special Purpose Vehicle.

Table 11 provides the list of banks actively participating in project finance in the Philippines in the last 24 months.

**Table 11: Banks in Project Finance in the Philippines in 24 Months Preceding December 2019**

| Name | Total Project Financing ($ million) | (₱ billion) | Transactions |
|---|---|---|---|
| ING Group (ING) | 275 | 138.52 | 2 |
| Australia and New Zealand Banking Group (ANZ) | 200 | 100.74 | 1 |
| Banco de Oro Unibank | 91 | 45.84 | 1 |
| Land Bank of the Philippines | 91 | 45.84 | 1 |
| Security Bank Corporation | 91 | 45.84 | 1 |
| Bank of the Philippine Islands | 91 | 45.84 | 1 |
| DBS Bank | 20 | 10.07 | 1 |
| Standard Chartered Bank PLC | 20 | 10.07 | 1 |
| Mitsubishi UFJ Financial Group (MUFG and BTMU) | 20 | 10.07 | 1 |
| Mizuho Bank | 20 | 10.07 | 1 |
| Fubon Financial | 16.50 | 8.31 | 1 |
| Bank of China (BOC) | 16.50 | 8.31 | 1 |

ANZ = Australia and New Zealand Banking Group, BOC = Bank of China, BTMU = Bank of Tokyo-Mitsubishi, DBS = Development Bank of Singapore Limited, ING = Internationale Nederlanden Groep, MUFG = Mitsubishi UFJ Financial Group, UFJ = United Financial of Japan.

Source: Inframation Deals. Country Fact Books. Philippines. Debt and Equity. https://www.inframationnews.com/country-factbook/1414947/philippines.thtm (accessed 28 August 2020).

## The Development Bank of the Philippines

The Development Bank of the Philippines (DBP) was established in 1958 to take over and expand the functions of the Rehabilitation Finance Corporation that had been created in 1947 to finance the reconstruction of properties damaged by World War II. DBP is authorized to give loans to LGUs for the purchase of machineries, or rehabilitation or construction of public markets, slaughterhouses, irrigation, waterworks, toll bridges, and other income-producing services.[31]

## The Land Bank of the Philippines

The Land Bank of the Philippines (LBP) was created in 1963 to provide financial support for the Agricultural Land Reform Program. The first ODA-funded financing facility offered by LBP to LGUs was the LGU Support Credit Program for social infrastructure and environmental projects, funded by the Japan International Cooperation Agency. Cost recovery is very slow in this case. The financing facility covers low-cost housing projects, hospitals or health centers, water supply, wastewater treatment, solid waste management, flood control, community-based forestry management, and project preparation activities (footnote 31).

31 ADB. 2014. *Philippines: Public–Private Partnerships by Local Government Units*. Philippines. https://www.adb.org/sites/default/files/publication/213606/philippines-ppp-lgus.pdf.

The second ODA-funded facility offered by LBP to LGUs was the World Bank-funded Water District Development Project, originally intended for water districts to implement sewerage projects. When LGU commitments made prior to loan negotiations fell through after loan approval, the project was restructured in May 1999 to offer loans to LGUs for water supply, sanitation, sewerage, or drainage projects. Water user associations were formed and registered with the SEC to operate and maintain the water system with fees collected from the water users (footnote 31).

The third ODA-funded facility offered by LBP to LGUs was the LGU Private Infrastructure Project Development Facility (PIPDF) supported by ADB. It sought to facilitate private sector participation in local infrastructure by providing loans for the conduct of feasibility studies (footnote 31).

Taking off from the Water District Development Project, the Strategic Support for Local Development and Investment Project, funded by the World Bank, is one of the latest ODA-funded facilities offered by LBP to LGUs and their private sector partners. It offers a wide menu of infrastructure projects including water supply, drainage and flood control, solid waste management, and public markets (footnote 31).

## Philippine Guarantee Corporation

The Philippine Guarantee Corporation is a government-owned and controlled corporation attached to the Department of Finance. It serves as the principal agency for State Guarantee Finance of the Philippines. It offers credit guarantees for affordable housing and micro, small, and medium enterprises and agriculture programs.

Table 12 provides the list of project sponsors actively participating in PPPs in the Philippines in the last 24 months.

**Table 12: Active Project Sponsors in the Philippines in 24 Months Preceding December 2019**

| Private Sponsor | Country of Origin | Total Investment | | Number of PPP Projects |
|---|---|---|---|---|
| | | ($ million) | (₱ billion) | |
| Metro Pacific Investments | Philippines | 1,478 | 74.45 | 2 |
| D.M. Consunji | Philippines | 1,100 | 55.41 | 1 |
| Tollways Management Co. (Philippines) | Philippines | 1,100 | 55.41 | 1 |
| Manila North Tollways Development Co. | Philippines | 1,100 | 55.41 | 1 |
| Aboitiz Power | Philippines | 573 | 28.86 | 1 |
| Udenna Corporation | Philippines | 400 | 20.15 | 1 |
| Kohlberg Kravis Roberts (KKR) | United States of America | 192 | 9.67 | 1 |
| Manila Electric Company (MERALCO) | Philippines | 120 | 6.04 | 2 |
| Kansai Electric Power Company | Japan | 120 | 6.04 | 1 |
| Marubeni | Japan | 120 | 6.04 | 1 |
| Chubu Electric Power Company | Japan | 120 | 6.04 | 1 |

Source: Inframation Deals. Country Fact Books. Philippines. Debt and Equity. https://www.inframationnews.com/country-factbook/1414947/philippines.thtm (accessed 28 August 2020).

## Credit Rating Agencies in the Philippines

The credit rating agencies involved in rating infrastructure projects are the Philippine Rating Services Corporation (PhilRatings) and the Credit Rating and Investors Services (CRISP) Inc.

# III. Sector-Specific Public–Private Partnership Landscape

## ROADS

| Parameter | Value | Unit |
|---|---|---|
| Length of the total road network | 200,037 | kilometers |
| Quality of road infrastructure | 3.70 | 1(low) – 7(high) |

✓ = Yes, × = No, NA = Not Applicable, UA = Unavailable

Sources: Trading Economics. Philippines-Road Total Network. https://tradingeconomics.com/philippines/roads-total-network-km-wb-data.html; The Global Economy. Compare Countries. https://www.theglobaleconomy.com/compare-countries/.

### 1. Contracting Agencies in the Road Sector

The Department of Public Works and Highways (DPWH) implements road projects and offers concessions for PPP projects. For the Metro Manila Skyway Stage 3 project, however, the Toll Regulatory Board (TRB) acted as the implementing agency.

The DPWH functions as the engineering and construction arm of the government and is tasked to continuously develop technology to ensure the safety of all infrastructure facilities and the highest efficiency and quality of construction for all public works and highways. It is currently responsible for the planning, design, construction, and maintenance of infrastructure, especially the national highways, flood control and water resources development system, and other public works in accordance with national development objectives.[32]

### 2. Road Sector Laws and Regulations

The TRB, created by the Toll Operation Decree (Presidential Decree 1112), acts as the main regulatory body for road sector PPP projects. It regulates the toll and publishes the toll rates on its website. As per the Limited Access Highway Act (Republic Act 2000), the Department of Public Works and Communications (now the DPWH) is authorized to design any limited access facility and to regulate, restrict, or prohibit access to best serve the traffic. The following are the key regulations that govern the road sector:

- Revised Philippine Highway Act (Presidential Decree 17, series of 1972),
- Limited Access Highway Act (Republic Act 2000),
- Right-of-Way Act (Republic Act 10752), and
- Prohibited Uses within the Right-of-Way of National Roads (Department Order 73, 2014, DPWH).

32 DPWH. About DPWH. https://www.dpwh.gov.ph/dpwh/content/about-dpwh.

## 2.1 Foreign Investment Restrictions in the Road Sector

The maximum equity investment allowed for foreign investors in greenfield projects is 40%.[33]

| Parameter | 2017 | 2018 | 2019 |
|---|---|---|---|
| Maximum allowed foreign ownership of equity in greenfield projects | 40% | 40% | 40% |

## 2.2 Standard Contracts in the Road Sector

There are no standard contacts for PPPs in the road sector.

| Type of contract | Availability |
|---|---|
| PPP/concession agreement | × |
| Performance-based operation and maintenance contract | × |
| Engineering procurement and construction contract | × |

✓ = Yes, × = No, NA = Not Applicable, UA = Unavailable

# 3. Road Sector Master Plan

In 2010, the DPWH and the Japan International Cooperation Agency (JICA) developed the Masterplan on High Standard Highway Network Development. The masterplan covered areas within 200-kilometer radius from Metro Manila, Metro Cebu, and Tagum–Davao–General Santos Corridor, totaling 3,460 kilometers of highways. In 2019, the DPWH partnered with JICA to prepare a new master plan for high standard highway network.[34] Table 13 shows the priority projects identified in the road sector for the PPP mode of implementation based on NEDA's *Revised List of Infrastructure Flagship Projects* (published on 17 February 2020).

### Table 13: Public–Private Partnership Priority Projects, 2020

| No. | Project | Implementing Agency | Estimated Project Cost ($ million) | Estimated Project Cost (₱ billion) | Status |
|---|---|---|---|---|---|
| 1. | Southeast Metro Manila Expressway Project | DPWH | 894 | 45.29 | Ongoing implementation |
| 2. | Metro Manila Skyway Stage 3 | DPWH | 739 | 37.43 | Ongoing implementation |
| 3. | NLEX-SLEX Connector Road | DPWH | 460 | 23.30 | Ongoing implementation |
| 4. | C5 Southlink Expressway Project | DPWH | 250 | 12.64 | Ongoing implementation |
| 5. | Southern Luzon Expressway Toll Road 4 | DPWH | 377 | 19.10 | Ongoing implementation |
| 6. | Quezon–Bicol Expressway | DPWH | 1,763 | 89.30 | Under preparation |
| 7. | Tarlac–Pangasinan–La Union Expressway Extension Project | DPWH | 473 | 23.95 | Under preparation – Advanced stages of government approval |
| 8. | Cavite–Tagaytay–Batangas Expressway Project | DPWH | 443 | 22.43 | Under preparation |

₱1 = $ 0.01974

DPWH = Department of Public Works and Highways, NLEX = North Luzon Expressway, SLEX = South Luzon Expressway

Source: NEDA. 2020. *Revised List of Infrastructure Flagship Projects*. Manila. https://www.neda.gov.ph/infrastructure-flagship-projects/.

---

[33] Government Procurement Policy Board. 1990. *Republic Act 7718. An Act Authorizing the Financing, Construction, Operation and Maintenance of Infrastructure Projects by the Private Sector, and for Other Purposes*. Manila. https://www.gppb.gov.ph/laws/laws/RA_6957.pdf.

[34] DPWH. News. https://www.dpwh.gov.ph/DPWH/news/15539.

## 3.1 Projects under Preparation and Procurement in the Road Sector

Figure 16 shows the number of PPP projects which are under preparation and procurement in the Philippines' road sector.

### Figure 16: Public–Private Partnership Roads under Preparation and Procurement

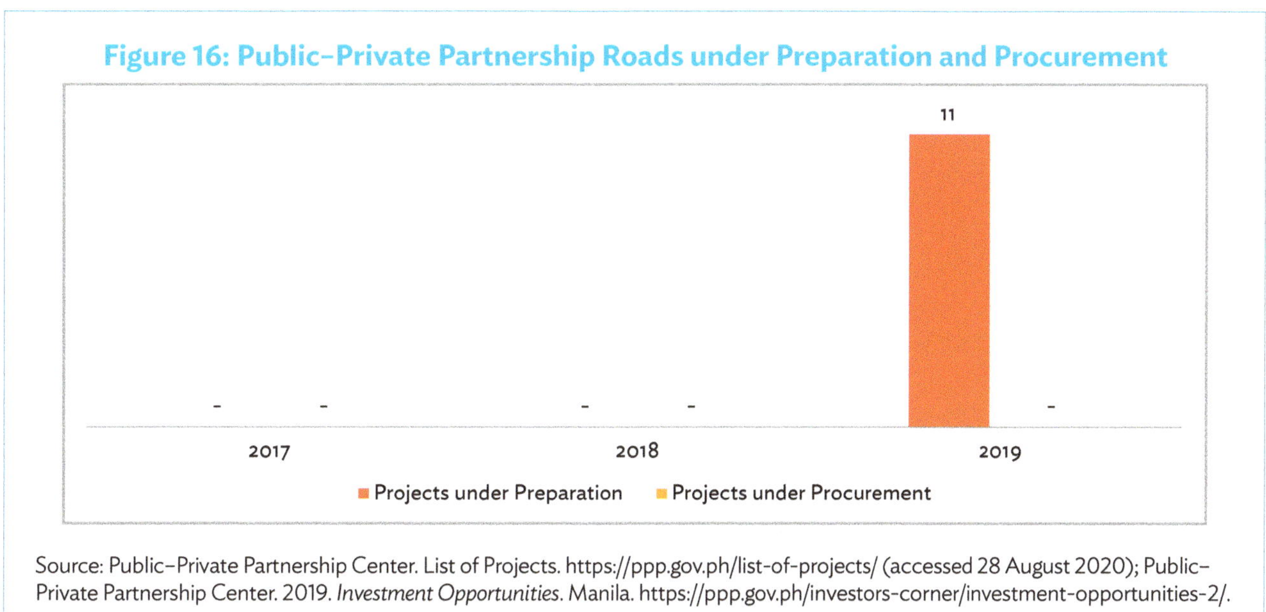


Source: Public–Private Partnership Center. List of Projects. https://ppp.gov.ph/list-of-projects/ (accessed 28 August 2020); Public–Private Partnership Center. 2019. *Investment Opportunities*. Manila. https://ppp.gov.ph/investors-corner/investment-opportunities-2/.

The PPP Center tracks the progress of a pipeline of PPP projects in the Philippines, which is updated regularly and published on the PPP Center website (Table 14).[35]

### Table 14: Public–Private Partnership Pipeline Projects in the Road Sector

| No. | Type of Contract | Length (km) | Estimated Project Cost ($ million) | Estimated Project Cost (₱ billion) |
|---|---|---|---|---|
| 1. | Central Luzon Link Expressway Phase II (Cabanatuan–San Jose, Nueva Ecija) | 35.7 | 249 | 12.61 |
| 2. | Tarlac–Pangasinan–La Union Expressway Extension | 59.4 | 473 | 23.94 |
| 3. | Quezon–Bicol Expressway | 220 | 1,763 | 89.3 |
| 4. | Davao–Digos Expressway | 60 | NA | NA |
| 5. | Metro Cebu Expressway (Cebu Circumferential Road) | 73.75 | 555 | 28.1 |
| 6. | Mindoro–Batangas Super Bridge (Floating Bridge) | 15 | TBD | TBD |
| 7. | North Luzon Expressway East, Phase II | 99.1 | 881 | 44.61 |
| 8. | Delpan–Pasig–Marikina Expressway | 25 | TBD | TBD |

*continued on next page*

[35] DPWH. PPP Menu. http://www.dpwh.gov.ph/dpwh/ppp/priority; Public–Private Partnership Center. List of Projects. https://ppp.gov.ph/list-of-projects/ (accessed 28 August 2020).

continued from previous page

| No. | Type of Contract | Length (km) | Estimated Project Cost | |
|---|---|---|---|---|
| | | | ($ million) | (₱ billion) |
| 9. | Operation, Maintenance and Improvement of Kennon Road and Marcos Highway | 33.7 | TBD | TBD |
| 10. | Cavite–Tagaytay–Batangas Expressway Project | 50 | 446 | 22.59 |
| 11. | Davao People Mover Project | 13 | 592 | 30 |

₱1 = $0.01974, TBD = To be decided

Sources: NEDA. 2020. *Revised List of Infrastructure Flagship Projects*. Manila; https://ppp.gov.ph/list-of-projects/; DPWH. List of Public–Private Partnership (PPP) Priority Projects. http://www.dpwh.gov.ph/dpwh/ppp/priority (accessed 28 August 2020); Public–Private Partnership Center. 2019. *Investment Opportunities*. Manila. https://ppp.gov.ph/investors-corner/investment-opportunities-2/.

## 4. Features of Past Public–Private Partnership Projects in the Road Sector

Figure 17 presents the number of PPP projects procured through various modes including direct appointment, unsolicited bids, and competitive bids in the Philippines' road sector.

Figure 17: Modes of Procurement for Public–Private Partnership Roads

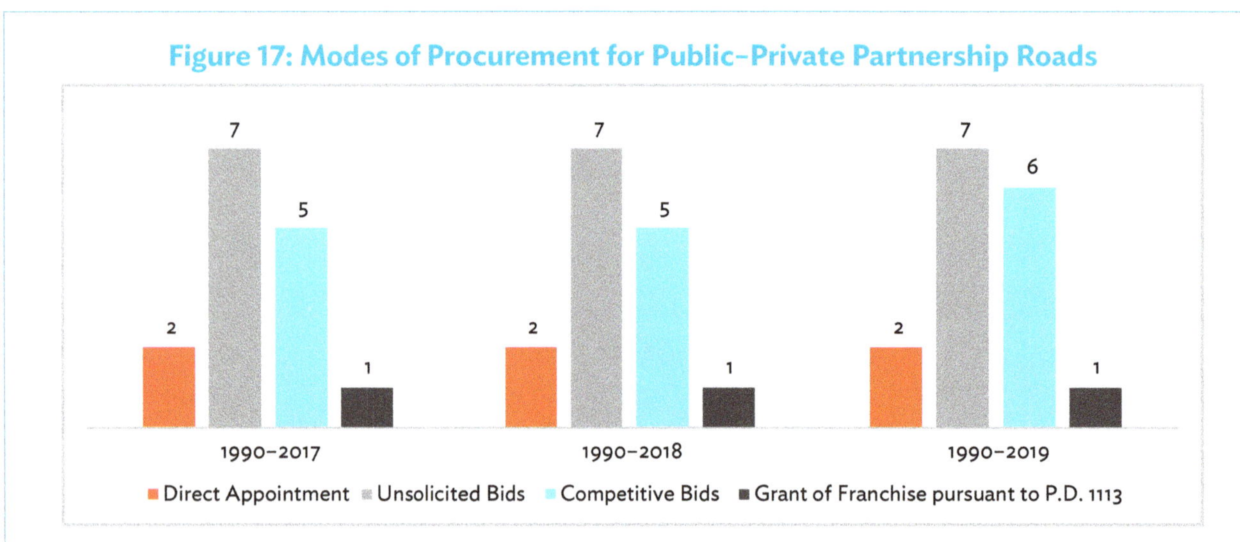


Note: Only active projects are considered in the above graph.

Source: ADB, World Bank. Infrastructure Finance, PPPs and Guarantees. Country Snapshots. Philippines. https://ppi.worldbank.org/en/snapshots/country/philippines (accessed 28 August 2020).

Figure 18 shows the number of PPP projects which have reached financial closure and the total value of those projects in the Philippines' road sector.

Figure 18: Public–Private Partnership Projects Reaching Financial Closure

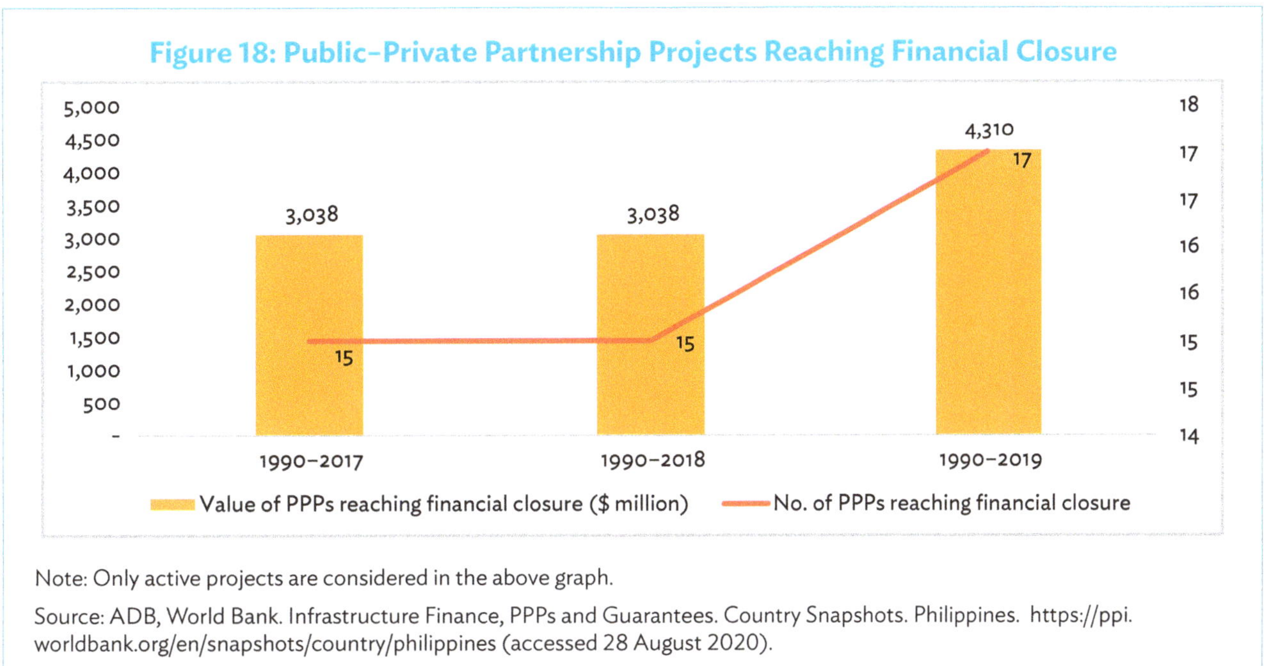


Note: Only active projects are considered in the above graph.

Source: ADB, World Bank. Infrastructure Finance, PPPs and Guarantees. Country Snapshots. Philippines. https://ppi.worldbank.org/en/snapshots/country/philippines (accessed 28 August 2020).

Figure 19 presents the number of PPP projects which have received foreign sponsor participation in the Philippines' road sector.

Figure 19: Public–Private Partnership Road Projects with Foreign Sponsor Participation

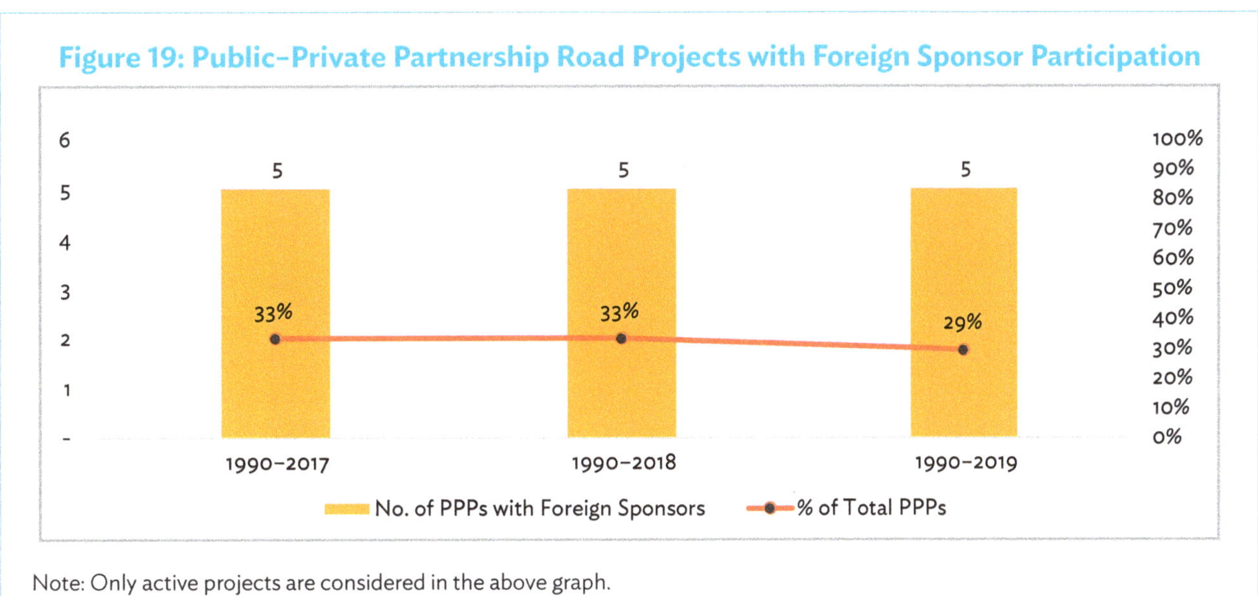


Note: Only active projects are considered in the above graph.

Source: ADB, World Bank. Infrastructure Finance, PPPs and Guarantees. Country Snapshots. Philippines. https://ppi.worldbank.org/en/snapshots/country/philippines (accessed 28 August 2020).

Figure 20 shows the number of PPP projects which have received government support including viability gap funding (VGF) mechanism, government guarantees, and availability/performance payment in the Philippines' road sector.

### Figure 20: Government Support to Public–Private Partnership Road Projects

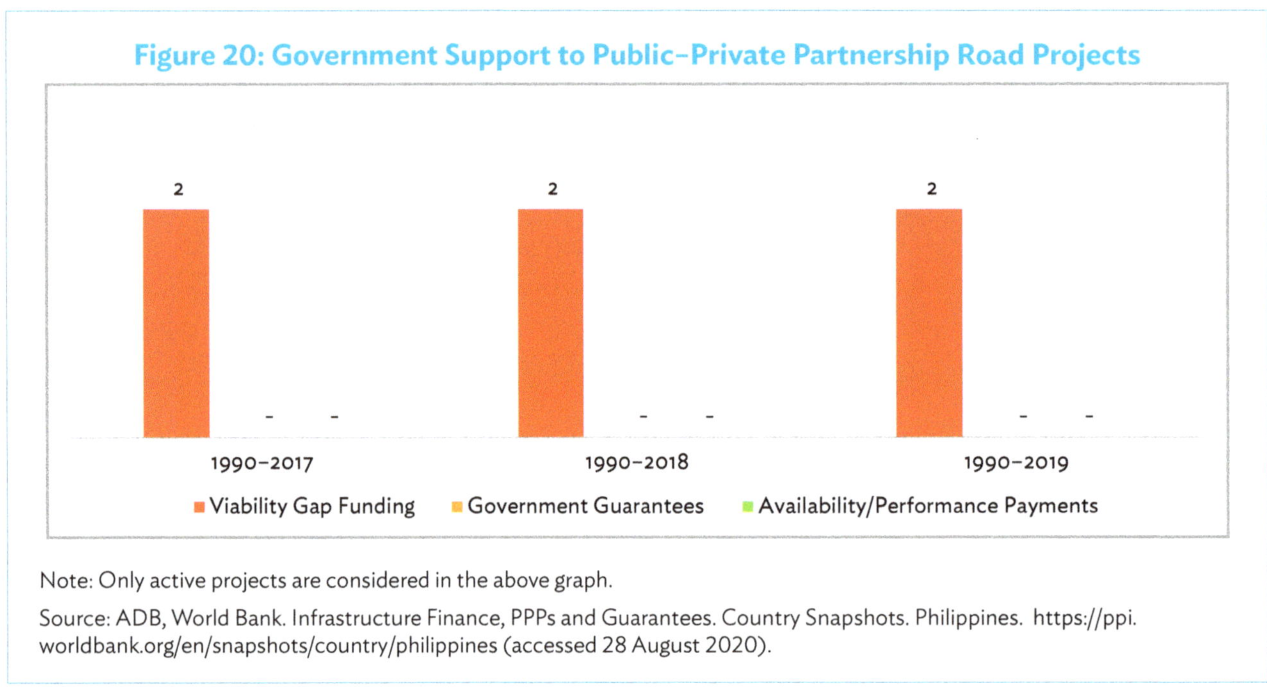


Note: Only active projects are considered in the above graph.

Source: ADB, World Bank. Infrastructure Finance, PPPs and Guarantees. Country Snapshots. Philippines. https://ppi.worldbank.org/en/snapshots/country/philippines (accessed 28 August 2020).

Figure 21 presents the number of PPP projects which have received payment in the form of user charges and government pay (off-take) in the Philippines' road sector.

### Figure 21: Payment Mechanisms for Public–Private Partnership Road Projects

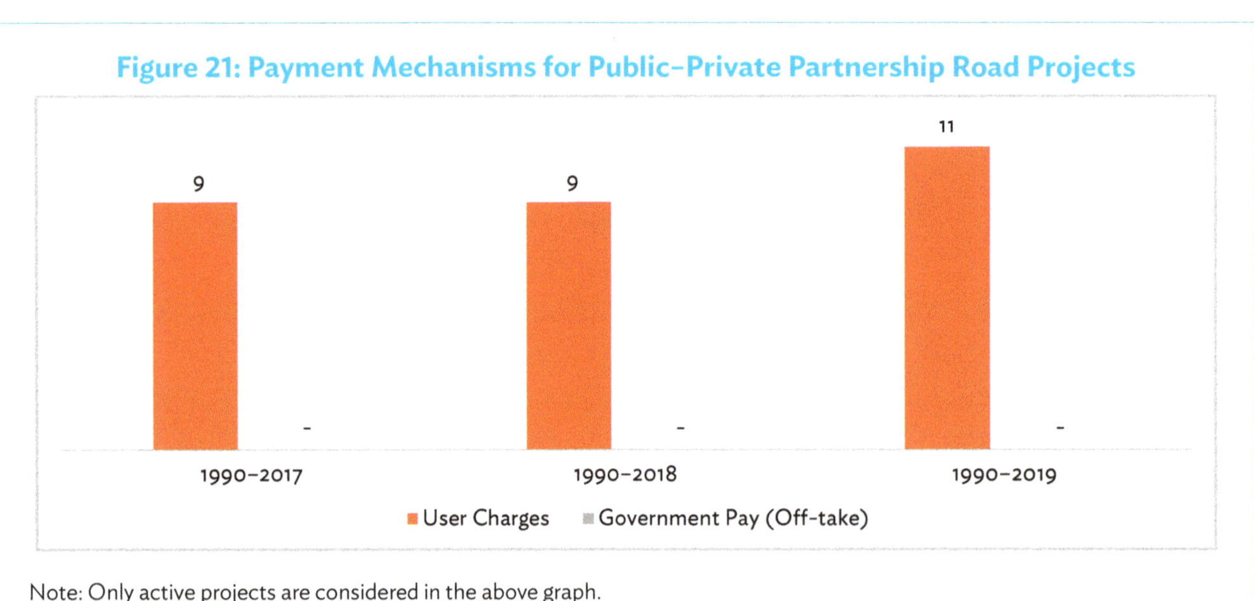


Note: Only active projects are considered in the above graph.

Source: ADB, World Bank. Infrastructure Finance, Public–Private Partnerships and Guarantees. Country Snapshots. Philippines. https://ppi.worldbank.org/en/snapshots/country/philippines (accessed 28 August 2020).

## 4.1 Tariffs in the Road Sector

The TRB sets the rates of tolls to be charged on national highways, roads, and bridges (Table 15). LGUs can set toll fees or charges to any regional public road, bridge, pier, waterway, ferry, or telecommunication system which they have funded and constructed (footnote 1).

For build–operate–transfer projects, contractors may charge and collect toll fees and charges. Such charges/fees must be based on the terms incorporated in the concession agreement and not exceed the charges proposed in the bid. These fees and charges are to be approved by LGUs. The LGU is responsible for the adjustment of the fees and charges over time, in response to macroeconomic variables (footnote 1).

However, evidence was found of an apparent uncertainty in how the regulatory boards (TRB and LGU) approve toll rate increases, which has caused delays to the approval of toll adjustments (footnote 1).

The tariffs for toll roads are published on the website of TRB.[36]

### Table 15: Tariffs for Toll Roads

| Road | Toll Type | Class 1: Cars, Jeepneys, Pickups, Vans (₱) | Class 2: Light Trucks, Tourist and School Buses, Class 1 > 7 feet in height (₱) | Class 3: Heavy and Multiaxle Trucks, Trailers (₱) |
|---|---|---|---|---|
| Subic–Clark–Tarlac Expressway | Close | 5–324 | 11–648 | 140–180 |
| Muntinlupa–Cavite Expressway | Open | 17 | 35 | 52 |
| North Luzon Expressway | Close | 6–485 | 11–1,113 | 18–1,455 |

Source: Toll Regulatory Board. http://trb.gov.ph./ (accessed 28 August 2020).

## 4.2 Typical Risk Allocation for Public–Private Partnership Road Projects

| Risk Type | Private | Public | Shared | Remarks |
|---|---|---|---|---|
| Traffic risk | ✓ | | | |
| Collection risk | ✓ | | | |
| Competition risk | ✓ | | | |
| Government payment risk | | | | There are no road sector projects that receive government payments |
| Environmental and social risk | ✓ (unsolicited) | | ✓ (solicited) | |
| Land acquisition risk | ✓ (unsolicited) | ✓ (solicited) | | |
| Permits | | | ✓ | |
| Geotechnical risk | ✓ | | | |

*continued on next page*

[36] Toll Regulatory Board. http://trb.gov.ph./ (accessed 4 July 2020).

*continued from previous page*

| Risk Type | Private | Public | Shared | Remarks |
|---|---|---|---|---|
| Brownfield risk: inventories studies, property boundaries, project scope | | | ✓ | |
| Political risk | | | ✓ | |
| Force majeure | | | ✓ | |
| Foreign exchange risk | ✓ | | | |
| Construction risk | ✓ | | | |

✓ = Yes, × = No, NA = Not Applicable, UA = Unavailable

## 4.3 Financing Details of Public–Private Partnerships in the Road Sector

| Parameter | 1990–2017 | 1990–2018 | 1990–2019 |
|---|---|---|---|
| PPP projects with foreign lending participation | 0 | 0 | 0 |
| PPP projects that received export credit agency/international financing institution support | 2 | 2 | 2 |
| Typical debt:equity ratio | 70:30 to 80:20 | | |
| Time for financial closure | 3 months after the issuance of Notice to Proceed | | |
| Typical concession period | 20–25 years | | |
| Typical Financial Internal Rate of Return | UA | | |

✓ = Yes, × = No, NA = Not Applicable, UA = Unavailable

Source: ADB, World Bank. Infrastructure Finance, PPPs and Guarantees. Country Snapshots. Philippines. https://ppi.worldbank.org/en/snapshots/country/philippines (accessed 28 August 2020).

# 5. Challenges in the Road Sector

- Restriction on foreign investments (capped at 40% for greenfield projects) limits the competition in the sector, as the controlling stake in the project company belongs to local companies. The government is taking steps to ease the restriction on foreign investment to attract international investors.
- Land acquisition delays have been a common challenge in road projects. Many projects had been awarded before the right-of-way was acquired. This led to tie and cost overruns.
- There have been several challenges in regard to procurement:
  - The tendering in the past had been subject to delays. Moreover, certain tenders did not give sufficient time for the developers to prepare the bids.
  - In the past, the government introduced changes in the project structure during tender process.
  - The private sector has limited opportunity to negotiate key terms of the contract, especially on risk allocation.

# RAILWAYS

| Parameter | Value | Unit |
|---|---|---|
| Length of total railway network | 995 | total route-km |
| Total number of passengers carried | 384.00 | Million passenger-km |
| Total volume of freight carried | UA | Million ton-km |
| Quality of railways infrastructure | 2.40 | 1(low) - 7(high) |

✓ = Yes, × = No, NA = Not Applicable, UA = Unavailable

Sources: The Economist Intelligence Unit. Philippines. https://infrascope.eiu.com/; The Global Economy. Railway Passengers—Country Rankings. https://www.theglobaleconomy.com/rankings/railway_passengers/; The Global Economy. Railway Transport of Goods—Country Rankings. https://www.theglobaleconomy.com/rankings/Railway_transport_of_goods/; The Global Economy. Railroad Infrastructure Quality—Country Rankings. https://www.theglobaleconomy.com/rankings/railroad_quality/

## 1. Contracting Agencies in the Railway Sector

Various government agencies and state-owned enterprises could act as concessionaires:

- The Light Rail Transit Authority (LRTA) is a wholly state-owned government corporation created under Executive Order 603. The LRTA is primarily responsible for the construction, operation, maintenance, and/or lease of light rail transit systems in the Philippines.
- The Department of Transportation (DOTr) is the primary policy, planning, programming, coordinating, implementing, and administrative entity of the government's executive branch on the promotion, development, and regulation of a dependable and coordinated network of transportation and communications systems.[37]
- The Philippine National Railways (PNR) was established by Republic Act 10638 in 2013. The Act extended the corporate life of the Philippine National Railways for another 50 years. It was further amended as the Republic Act 4156. It created the Philippine National Railways, prescribing its powers, functions and duties, and provided for the necessary funds for its operation.[38] The PNR operates the Metro South and North Commuter trains in Manila.

## 2. Railway Sector Laws and Regulations

The Land Transportation Franchising and Regulatory Board (an agency of DOTr) sets routes, regulates fares, and oversees licensing requirements for land-based transportation services.

### 2.1 Foreign Investment Restrictions in the Railway Sector

The maximum equity investment allowed for foreign investors in greenfield projects is 40% (footnote 33).

| Parameter | 2017 | 2018 | 2019 |
|---|---|---|---|
| Maximum allowed foreign ownership of equity in greenfield projects | 40% | 40% | 40% |

37 Department of Transportation and Communication. http://www.dotc.gov.ph/.

38 Boholanoko 100. Republic Acts of Philippines. https://boholanoko100.wordpress.com/.

## 2.2 Standard Contracts in the Railway Sector

| Type of Contract | Availability |
|---|---|
| PPP/concession agreement | × |
| Performance-based operation and maintenance contract | × |
| Engineering procurement and construction contract | × |

✓ = Yes, × = No, NA = Not Applicable, UA = Unavailable

# 3. Railway Sector Master Plan

There is no sector-specific masterplan for the railway sector. Table 16 outlines the priority projects identified in the railway sector for the PPP mode of implementation based on NEDA's *Revised List of Infrastructure Flagship Projects* (published on 17 February 2020).

### Table 16: Public–Private Partnership Priority Projects in the Railway Sector

| No. | Project | Implementing Agency | Estimated Cost ($ million) | Estimated Cost (₱ billion) | Status |
|---|---|---|---|---|---|
| 1. | Manila Metro Line 1 Cavite Extension (Baclaran–Niog, Bacoor) (LRT 1 Cavite Extension Project) | Department of Transportation | 1,281 | 64.9 | Under pre-construction |
| 2. | MRT 7 | Department of Transportation | 1,398 | 70.8 | Under preparation – under evaluation by relevant approving body |
| 3. | C5 MRT 10 Project | Department of Transportation | 1,608 | 81.47 | Under preparation – under evaluation by relevant approving body |
| 4. | Fort Bonifacio–Makati Sky Train | Department of Transportation | 69 | 3.52 | Under preparation – under evaluation by relevant approving body |
| 5. | MRT 11 | Department of Transportation | 1,404 | 71.11 | Under preparation – under evaluation by relevant approving body |
| 6. | LRT 6 Cavite Line N: Modified LRT 6 Project Phases 1 (Niog–Dasmarinas City) and 2 (Dasmarinas City–Tagaytay) | Department of Transportation | 995 | 50.38 | Under preparation – under evaluation by relevant approving body |
| 7. | Cebu Monorail System | Department of Transportation | 1,557 | 78.89 | Under preparation – under evaluation by relevant approving body |

₱1 = $ 0.01974

LRT = light rail transit, MRT = metro rail transit

Source: NEDA. 2020. *Revised List of Infrastructure Flagship Projects*. Manila. https://www.neda.gov.ph/infrastructure-flagship-projects/.

## 3.1 Projects under Preparation and Procurement in the Railway Sector

Figure 22 shows the number of PPP projects which are under preparation and procurement in the Philippines' railway sector.

### Figure 22: Public–Private Partnership Railway Projects under Preparation and Procurement

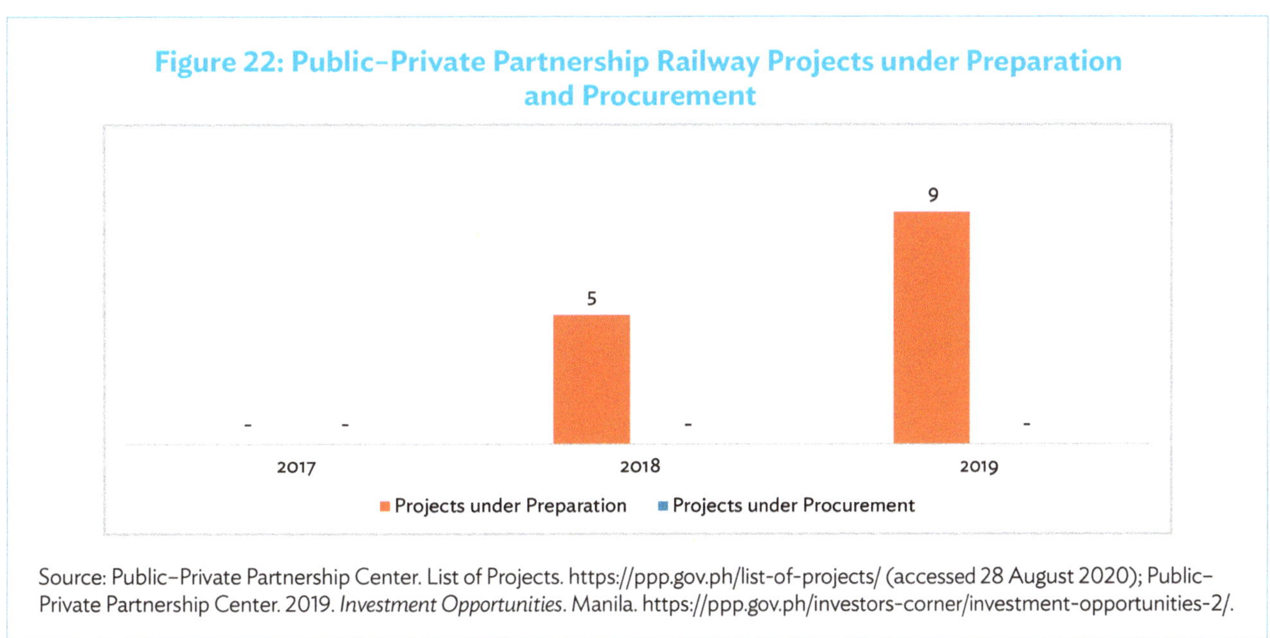


Source: Public–Private Partnership Center. List of Projects. https://ppp.gov.ph/list-of-projects/ (accessed 28 August 2020); Public–Private Partnership Center. 2019. *Investment Opportunities*. Manila. https://ppp.gov.ph/investors-corner/investment-opportunities-2/.

The PPP Center tracks the progress of a pipeline of PPP projects in the Philippines, which is updated regularly and published on the PPP Center website (Table 17).[39]

### Table 17: Pipeline of Public–Private Partnership Railway Projects

| No. | Project | Implementing Agency | Estimated Total Investment ($ million) | Estimated Total Investment (₱ billion) |
|---|---|---|---|---|
| 1. | C5 MRT 10 Project[a] | Department of Transportation | 1,583 | 80.17 |
| 2. | Cebu Monorail Transit System Project | Department of Transportation | 1,446 | 73.24 |
| 3. | East-West Rail Project[a] | Philippine National Railways | 1,095 | 55.46 |
| 4. | Fort Bonifacio–Makati Skytrain Project[a] | Department of Transportation | 69 | 3.52 |
| 5. | MRT-11 Project[a] | Department of Transportation | 1,404 | 71.1 |
| 6. | Modified Light Rail Transit (LRT)-6 Project (formerly LRT 6 Cavite Line A) | Department of Transportation | 1,111 | 56.27 |
| 7. | MRT 7 Airport Access–North Line | Philippine National Railways | 274 | 13.9 |
| 8. | MRT 7 Katipunan Spur Line | Philippine National Railways | 2,112 | 107 |
| 9. | Cavite LRT Line 6c and Sucat Line 6b Projects[b] | Department of Transportation | 3,100 | 157.02 |

₱1 = $ 0.01974

LRT = light rail transit, MRT = mass rail transit.

[a] The estimated investment values were given in *Investment Opportunities*, December 2019, published by the Public–Private Partnership Center of the Philippines.

[b] This project was mentioned in *Investment Opportunities*, December 2019, published by the Public–Private Partnership Center of the Philippines. Projects 1 to 8 were published by the Public–Private Partnership Center of the Philippines.

[39] PPP Center. List of Projects. https://ppp.gov.ph/list-of-projects/.

## 4. Features of Past Public–Private Partnership Projects in the Railway Sector

Figure 23 presents the number of PPP projects procured through various modes including direct appointment, unsolicited bids, and competitive bids in the Philippines' railway sector.

Figure 23: Modes of Procurement for Public–Private Partnership Railway Projects

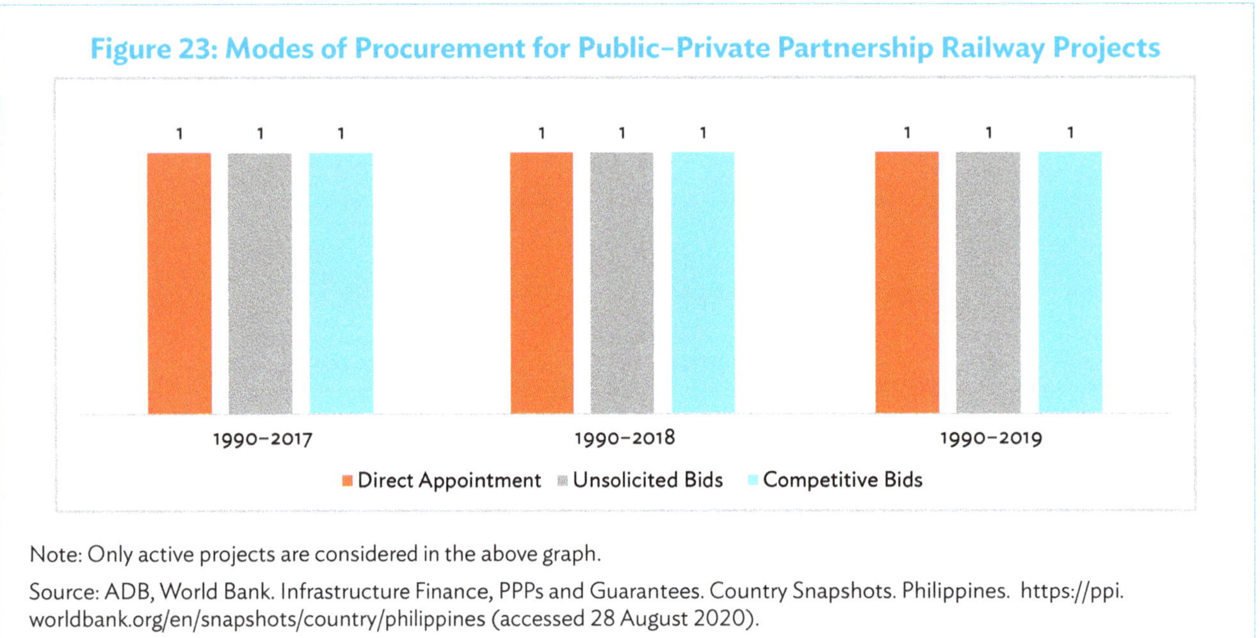


Note: Only active projects are considered in the above graph.

Source: ADB, World Bank. Infrastructure Finance, PPPs and Guarantees. Country Snapshots. Philippines. https://ppi.worldbank.org/en/snapshots/country/philippines (accessed 28 August 2020).

Figure 24 shows the number of PPP projects which have reached financial closure and the total value of those projects in the Philippines' railway sector.

Figure 24: Public–Private Partnership Railway Projects Reaching Financial Closure

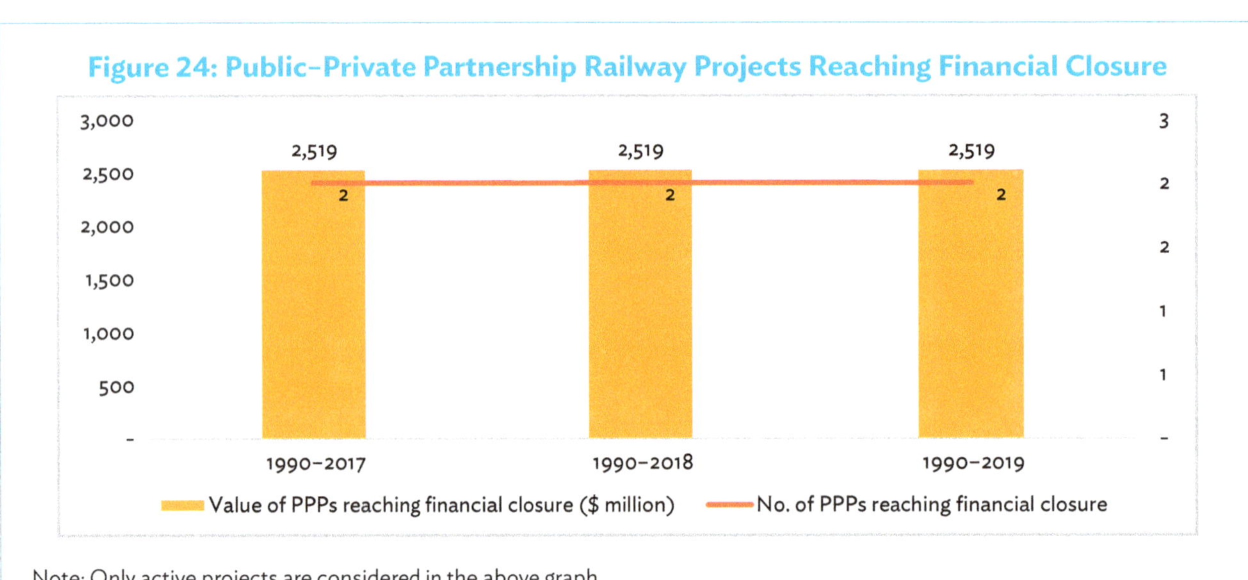


Note: Only active projects are considered in the above graph.

Source: ADB, World Bank. Infrastructure Finance, PPPs and Guarantees. Country Snapshots. Philippines. https://ppi.worldbank.org/en/snapshots/country/philippines (accessed 28 August 2020).

Figure 25 presents the number of PPP projects which have received foreign sponsor participation in the Philippines' railway sector.

Figure 25: Public–Private Partnership Railway Projects with Foreign Sponsor Participation

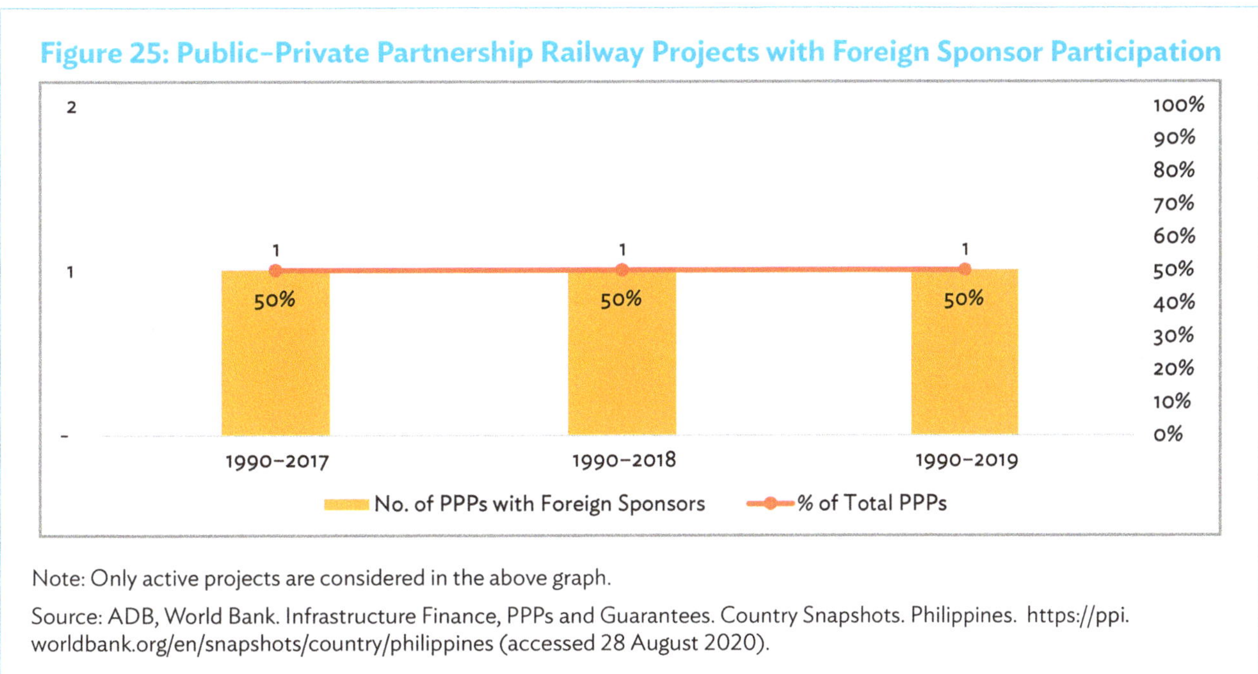


Note: Only active projects are considered in the above graph.

Source: ADB, World Bank. Infrastructure Finance, PPPs and Guarantees. Country Snapshots. Philippines. https://ppi.worldbank.org/en/snapshots/country/philippines (accessed 28 August 2020).

Figure 26 provides the number of PPP projects which have received government support including viability gap funding (VGF) mechanism, government guarantees, and availability/performance payment in the Philippines' railway sector.

Figure 26: Government Support to Public–Private Partnership Railway Projects

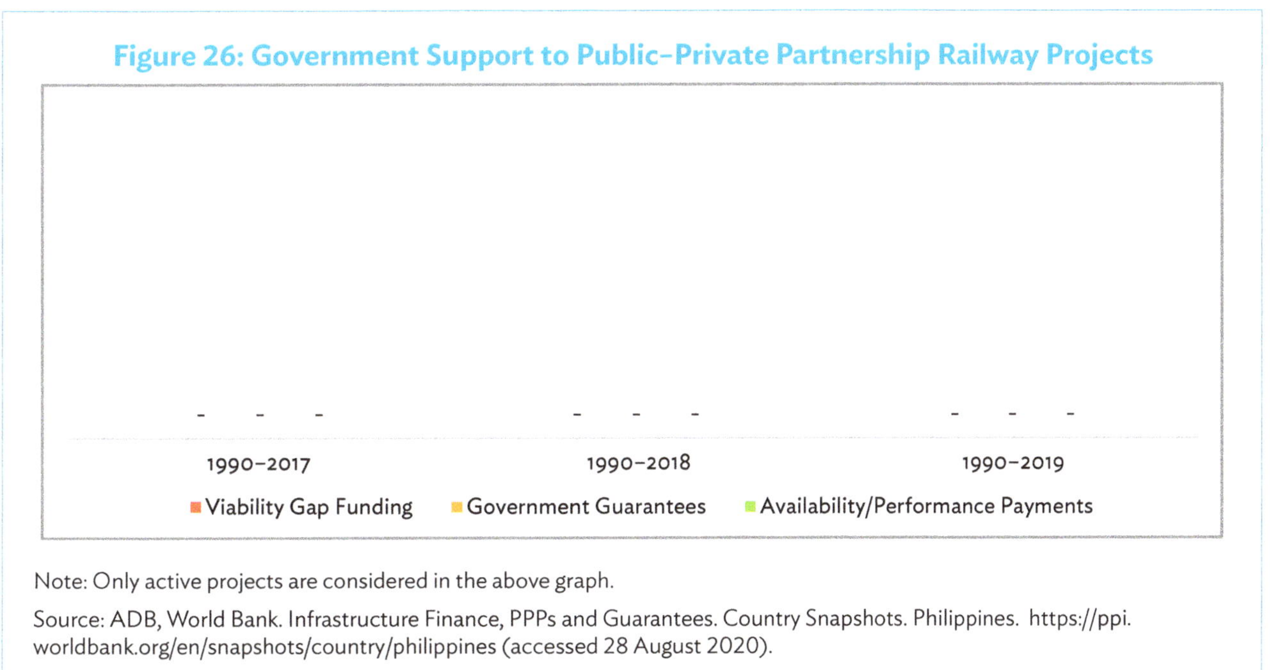


Note: Only active projects are considered in the above graph.

Source: ADB, World Bank. Infrastructure Finance, PPPs and Guarantees. Country Snapshots. Philippines. https://ppi.worldbank.org/en/snapshots/country/philippines (accessed 28 August 2020).

Figure 27 provides the number of PPP projects which have received payment in the form of user charges and government pay (off-take) in the Philippines' railway sector.

**Figure 27: Payment Mechanism for Public–Private Partnership Railway Projects**

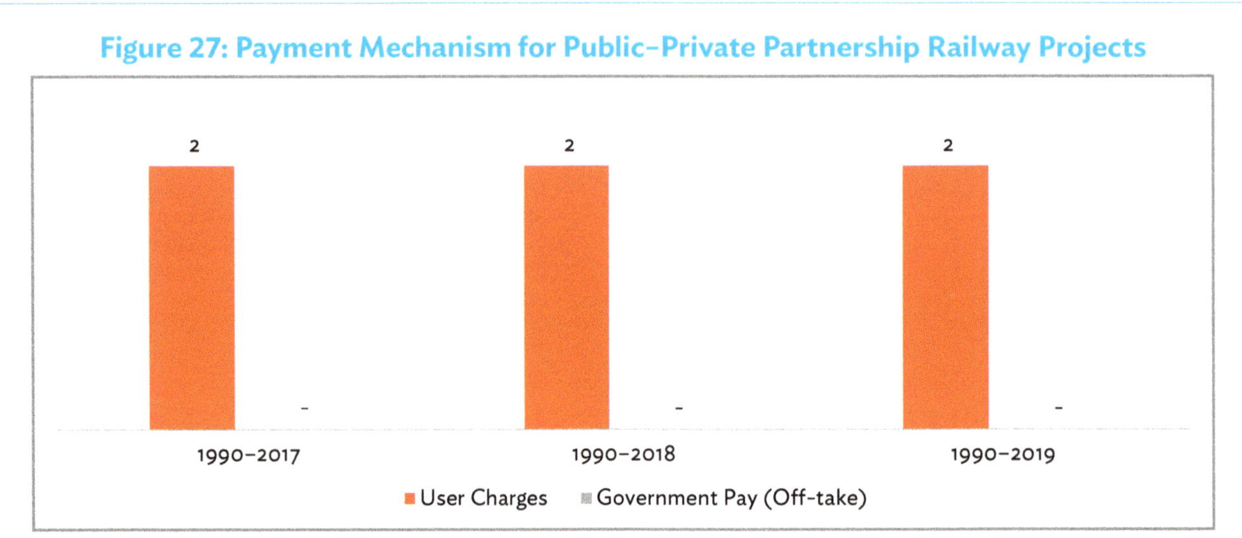


Note: Only active projects are considered in the above graph.

Source: ADB, World Bank. Infrastructure Finance, PPPs and Guarantees. Country Snapshots. Philippines. https://ppi.worldbank.org/en/snapshots/country/philippines (accessed 28 August 2020).

Light Rail Transit 1 (LRT-1) Cavite Extension and Manila Metro Rail Transit Line 7 (MRT-7) earn revenues from collecting user charges. Having additional revenue from land development rights and advertising is a common practice in the Philippines.

## 4.1 Tariffs in the Railway Sector

Currently, the MRT Line-3 employs distance-based fare structure, with fares ranging from ₱13 ($0.26 as of April 2020) to ₱28 ($0.55 as of April 2020), depending on the number of stations traveled. It is understood that tariffs are not being revised and escalated on a regular basis.

## 4.2 Typical Risk Allocation for Railway Public–Private Partnership Projects

| Risk Category | Private | Public | Shared | |
|---|---|---|---|---|
| Demand risk | ✓ | | | For MRT Line-3, the government assumes the risk; however, the preferred risk allocation is for the private entity. For LRT-1 extension, the private party bears the risk. |
| Revenue collection risk | ✓ | | | |
| Tariff risk | ✓ | | | |
| Government payment risk | ✓ | | | |

*continued on next page*

*continued from previous page*

| Risk Category | Private | Public | Shared | |
|---|---|---|---|---|
| Environmental and social risk | | | ✓ | |
| Land acquisition risk | | ✓ | | |
| Interface | | | ✓ | |
| Handover | | | ✓ | |
| Political risk | | | ✓ | |
| Foreign exchange risk | | ✓ | | For MRT Line-3, the government assumes the risk; however, the preferred risk allocation is for the private entity. |
| Early termination risk | | | ✓ | |

✓ = Yes, × = No, NA = Not Applicable, UA = Unavailable

## 4.3 Financing Details of Public–Private Partnerships in the Railway Sector

| Parameter | 1990–2017 | 1990–2018 | 1990–2019 |
|---|---|---|---|
| PPP projects with foreign lending participation | 0 | 0 | 1 |
| PPP projects that received export credit agency/international financing institution support | 0 | 0 | 0 |
| Typical debt:equity ratio | 70:30 | | |
| Time for financial closure | 18 months after commercial close | | |
| Typical concession period | 25–30 years[a] | | |
| Typical Financial Internal Rate of Return | UA | | |

✓ = Yes, × = No, NA = Not Applicable, UA = Unavailable

[a] Concession period for MRT 7 and LRT 1 was 25 and 30 years, respectively.

Source: ADB, World Bank. Infrastructure Finance, PPPs and Guarantees. Country Snapshots. Philippines. https://ppi.worldbank.org/en/snapshots/country/philippines (accessed 28 August 2020).

# 5. Challenges in the Railway Sector

- Restriction on foreign investments (capped at 40% for greenfield projects) limits the competition in the sector, as the controlling stake in the project company belongs to local companies. The government is taking steps to ease the restriction on foreign investment to attract international investors.
- Land acquisition remains a key challenge. San Miguel Corporation secured the mandate for LRT-7, which was delayed initially due to land acquisition issues. As the project had extended beyond prescribed deadlines, the project had to be taken back through government approval processes. San Miguel Corporation subsequently sought to restructure its consortium and financing (footnote 1).
- LRT-6 projects did not attract sufficient market interest due to project feasibility challenges. Feasibility and alignment studies are currently being revisited. These projects were reviewed by implementing agencies in January 2017 to evaluate various options to optimize their feasibilities (footnote 1).

- There have been several challenges in regard to procurement:
  - Tendering in the past had been subject to delays. Moreover, certain tenders did not give sufficient time for the developers to prepare the bids.
  - In the past, the government introduced changes in the project structure during the tender process.
  - The private sector has limited opportunity to negotiate key terms of the contract, especially on risk allocation.

# PORTS

| Parameter | Value | Unit |
|---|---|---|
| Total number of ports | 68.00 | No. |
| Total freight capacity of all ports | UA | MTPA |
| Total container traffic at ports | 86,37,520 | TEUs |
| Quality of port infrastructure | 2.90 | 1(low) – 7(high) |
| Quality of trade and transport-related infrastructure index | 2.60 | 1=low to 5=high |

✓ = Yes, × = No, NA = Not Applicable, UA = Unavailable

Sources: World Port Source. Ports. http://www.worldportsource.com/countries.php; The Global Economy. Port Traffic—Country Rankings. https://www.theglobaleconomy.com/rankings/Port_traffic/; https://infrascope.eiu.com/

## 1. Contracting Agencies in the Port Sector

The Department of Transport and the Philippine Ports Authority, a state-owned enterprise, are the key government contracting agencies in the port sector.

## 2. Port Sector Laws and Regulations

The Philippine Ports Authority (PPA) is a government-owned and controlled corporation (GOCC) attached to the Department of Transportation (DOTr). It is responsible for policy and program coordination. In October 2018, the PPA issued the Guidelines for the Selection and Award of Contract under the Port Terminal Management Regulatory Framework (Administrative Order 12).

The PPA was created on 11 July 1974 under Presidential Decree 505, which was revised into Presidential Decree 857 on 23 December 1975. The latter expanded the concept of port administration not only to focus on revenue collection, harbor maintenance, and cargo handling but also on the role of ports as key to spurring regional growth. Subsequent amendments further enhanced PPA's corporate powers to be more responsive in attaining optimum port utilization, development, and operation.[40] In Executive Order 159 (dated 13 April 1987), the corporate autonomy was reverted to the PPA to ensure the rapid development of the port system directly under it. Authority was granted to the PPA to execute port projects under its port program.[41]

40 Executive Order 513 dated 16 November 1978, Executive Order 546 dated 23 July 1979, and Letter of Instruction 1005-A dated 11 April 1980.

41 Philippines Ports Authority. https://www.ppa.com.ph/.

The PPA regulates private ports through issuance of permits to construct and operate ports, approval of increases in cargo handling rates, and collection of shares from port dues. Six independent port authorities, which operate outside the control of the Philippine Ports Authority, can set their own rates for port charges, but they would normally follow the lead of the state-run ports authority (footnote 1).

The Maritime Industry Authority, attached to the DOTr, was created in 1974. The government agency regulates domestic and overseas shipping, shipbuilding, ship repair, and the maritime workforce. The Maritime Industry Authority is not involved in ship operating activities (footnote 1). Table 18 shows the functions of key agencies in the Philippines' port sector.

### Table 18: Functions of the Maritime Industry Authority and the Philippine Ports Authority

| Agency | Function |
|---|---|
| Maritime Industry Authority | • Develop and formulate plans, policies, programs, projects, standards, specifications, and guidelines geared toward the promotion and development of the maritime industry, the growth and effective regulation of shipping enterprises, and the national security objectives of the country<br>• Establish, prescribe, and regulate routes, zones, and/or areas of operation of particular operators of public water services<br>• Issue certificates of public convenience for the operation of domestic and overseas water carriers<br>• Register vessels and issue certificates and licenses<br>• Undertake the safety regulatory functions pertaining to vessel construction and operation including the determination or manning levels and issuance of certificates of competency to seafarers<br>• Enforce laws and prescribe and enforce rules and regulations (including penalties for violations), govern water transportation and the Philippine merchant marine, and deputize the Philippine Coast Guard and other law enforcement agencies to effectively discharge these functions<br>• Undertake the issuance of license to qualified seafarers and harbour, bay, and river pilots<br>• Determine, fix, and/or prescribe charges and/or rates pertinent to the operation of public water transport utilities, facilities, and services except in cases where charges or rates are established by international bodies or associations of which the Philippines is a participating member, or by bodies or associations recognized by the Government of the Philippines as the proper arbiter of such charges or rates<br>• Accredit marine surveyors and maritime enterprises engaged in shipbuilding, ship repair, ship breaking, domestic and overseas shipping, and ship management<br>• Issue and register the continuous discharge book of Filipino seafarers<br>• Establish and prescribe rules and regulations and standards and procedures for the efficient and effective discharge of the above functions<br>• Perform such other functions as may now or hereafter be provided by law |
| Philippine Ports Authority | • Formulate, in coordination with the National Economic and Development Authority, a comprehensive and practicable port development for the state, program its implementation, and renew and update the same annually in coordination with other national agencies<br>• Supervise, control, regulate, construct, maintain, operate, and provide the facilities or services that are necessary in the ports vested in, or belonging to, the Philippine Ports Authority<br>• Prescribe rules and regulation, procedures, and guidelines governing the establishment, construction, maintenance, and operations of all other ports, including private ports in the country<br>• License, control, regulate, and supervise any construction or structure within any port district |

*continued on next page*

*continued from previous page*

| Agency | Function |
|---|---|
| | • Provide services (whether on its own, by contract, or otherwise) within the port district and the approaches thereof, including but not limited to berthing, towing, mooring, moving, slipping, or docking any vessel; loading or discharging any vessel; and sorting, weighing, measuring, warehousing, or otherwise handling goods<br>• Exercise control of or administer any foreshore rights or leases which may be vested in the Philippine Ports Authority from time to time<br>• Coordinate with the Bureau of Lands or any other government agency or corporation in the development of any foreshore area<br>• Control, regulate, and supervise pilotage and the conduct of pilots in any port district<br>• Provide or assist in the provision of training programs and training facilities for its staff of port operators and users for the efficient discharge of its functions, duties, and responsibilities |

Sources: Maritime Industry Authority. 2007. *Annual Report 2007*. Manila. https://marina.gov.ph/wp-content/uploads/2018/07/AR2017-1.pdf; Department of Transportation and Communications and the Philippine Ports Authority. 2015. Davao Sasa Port Modernization Project. *Information Memorandum*. Manila. http://dotr.gov.ph/images/PPP/2015/P17BDavaoSasaPortMP/filepart1.pdf; ADB. 2019. *Public–Private Partnership Monitor*. Second Edition. Manila. https://www.adb.org/sites/default/files/publication/509426/ppp-monitor-second-edition.pdf.

## 2.1 Foreign Investment Restrictions in the Port Sector

The maximum equity investment allowed for foreign investors in greenfield projects is 40% (footnote 33).

| Parameter | 2017 | 2018 | 2019 |
|---|---|---|---|
| Maximum allowed foreign ownership of equity in greenfield projects | 40% | 40% | 40% |

## 2.2 Standard Contracts in the Port Sector

| Type of Contract | Availability |
|---|---|
| PPP/concession agreement | × |
| Performance-based operation and maintenance contract | × |
| Engineering procurement and construction contract | × |

✓ = Yes, × = No, NA = Not Applicable, UA = Unavailable

# 3. Port Sector Master Plan

The ports sector does not have a sector specific masterplan. PPPs in the ports sector are not listed in NEDA's *Revised List of Infrastructure Flagship Projects* (published on 17 February 2020).

## 3.1 Projects under Preparation and Procurement in the Port Sector

Figure 28 presents the number of PPP projects which are under preparation and procurement in the Philippines' port sector.

Figure 28: Public–Private Partnership Port Projects under Preparation and Procurement

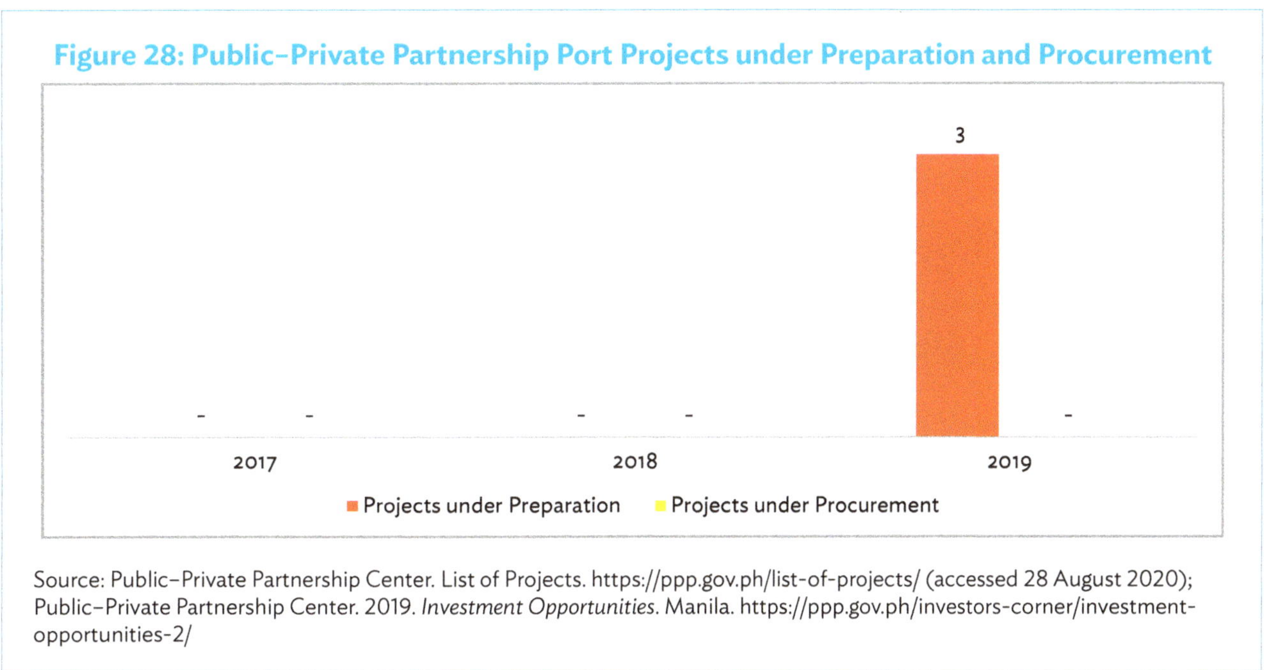


Source: Public–Private Partnership Center. List of Projects. https://ppp.gov.ph/list-of-projects/ (accessed 28 August 2020); Public–Private Partnership Center. 2019. *Investment Opportunities*. Manila. https://ppp.gov.ph/investors-corner/investment-opportunities-2/

The Public–Private Partnership Center tracks the progress of a pipeline of PPP projects in the Philippines, which is updated regularly and published on the PPP Center website (Table 19).

### Table 19: List of Port Projects (as of March 2020)

| No. | Project Name | Implementing Agency | Estimated Project Cost | |
|---|---|---|---|---|
| | | | ($ million) | (₱ billion) |
| 1. | Preservation and Development of Laguna de Bay Project | Laguna Lake Development Authority | 370 | 18.7 |
| 2. | San Ramon Newport Project | Zamboanga City Special Economic Zone Authority | TBD | TBD |
| 3. | Redevelopment of the Port of Irene | Cagayan Economic Zone Authority | 84 | 4,231 |

₱1 = $0.01974, TBD = to be decided

Source: Public–Private Partnership Center. 2019. *Investment Opportunities*. Manila. https://ppp.gov.ph/investors-corner/investment-opportunities-2/.

## 4. Features of Past Public–Private Partnership Projects in the Port Sector

Figure 29 shows the number of PPP projects procured through various modes including direct appointment, unsolicited bids, and competitive bids in the Philippines' port sector.

Figure 29: Modes of Procurement for Public–Private Partnership Port Projects

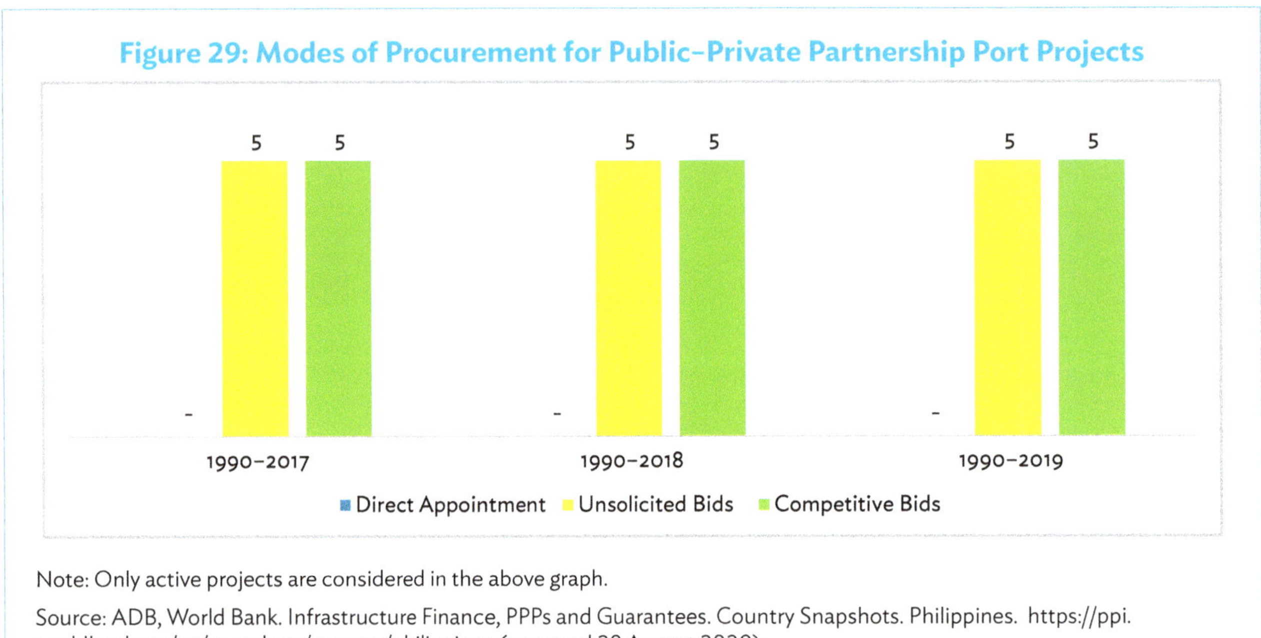


Note: Only active projects are considered in the above graph.

Source: ADB, World Bank. Infrastructure Finance, PPPs and Guarantees. Country Snapshots. Philippines. https://ppi.worldbank.org/en/snapshots/country/philippines (accessed 28 August 2020).

Figure 30 presents the number of PPP projects which have reached financial closure and the total value of those projects in the Philippines' port sector.

Figure 30: Public–Private Partnership Port Projects Reaching Financial Closure

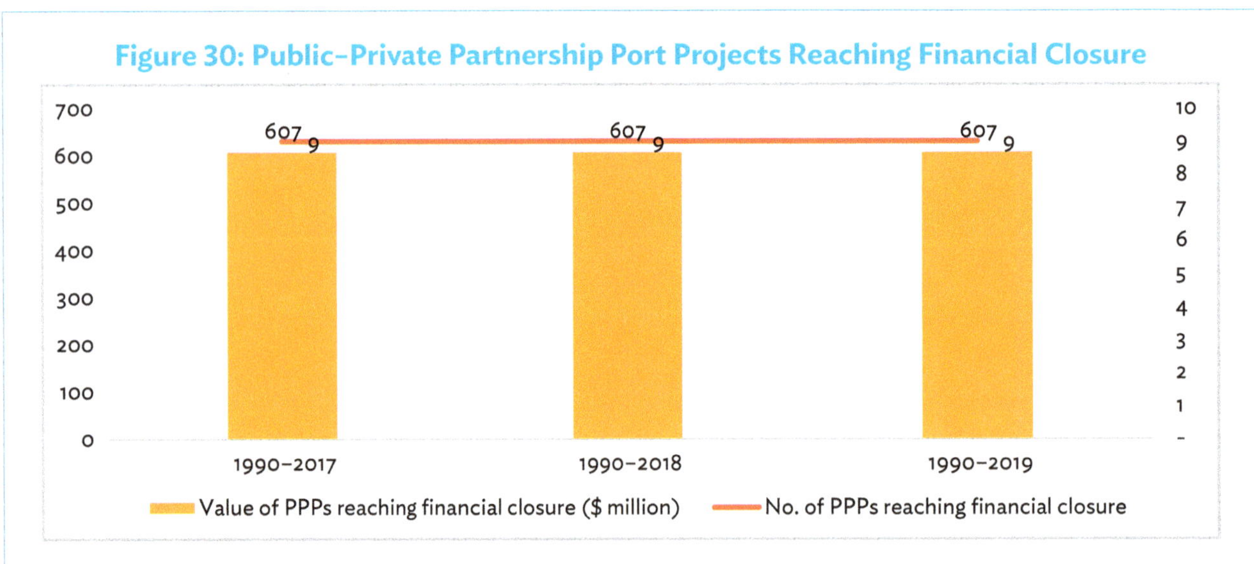


Note: Only active projects are considered in the above graph.

Source: ADB, World Bank. Infrastructure Finance, PPPs and Guarantees. Country Snapshots. Philippines. https://ppi.worldbank.org/en/snapshots/country/philippines (accessed 28 August 2020).

Figure 31 shows the number of PPP projects which have received foreign sponsor participation in the Philippines' port sector.

**Figure 31: Public–Private Partnership Port Projects with Foreign Sponsor Participation**

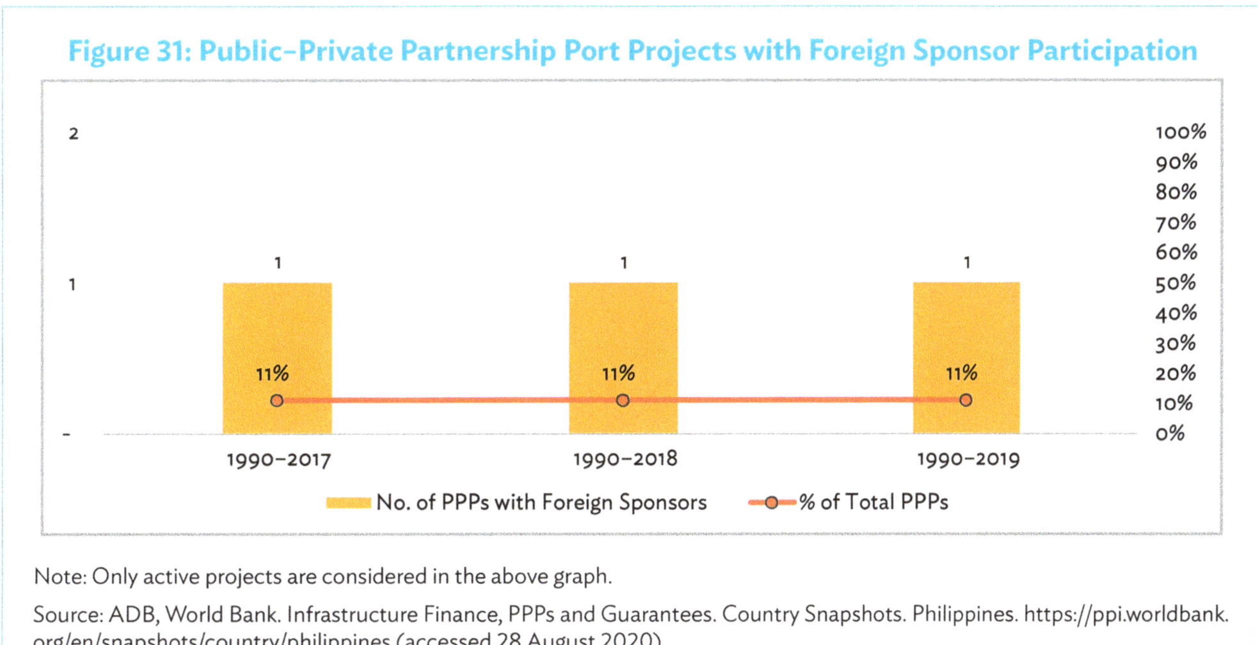


Note: Only active projects are considered in the above graph.

Source: ADB, World Bank. Infrastructure Finance, PPPs and Guarantees. Country Snapshots. Philippines. https://ppi.worldbank.org/en/snapshots/country/philippines (accessed 28 August 2020).

Figure 32 presents the number of PPP projects which have received government support including viability gap funding (VGF) mechanism, government guarantees, and availability/performance payment in the Philippines' port sector.

**Figure 32: Government Support to Public–Private Partnership Port Projects**

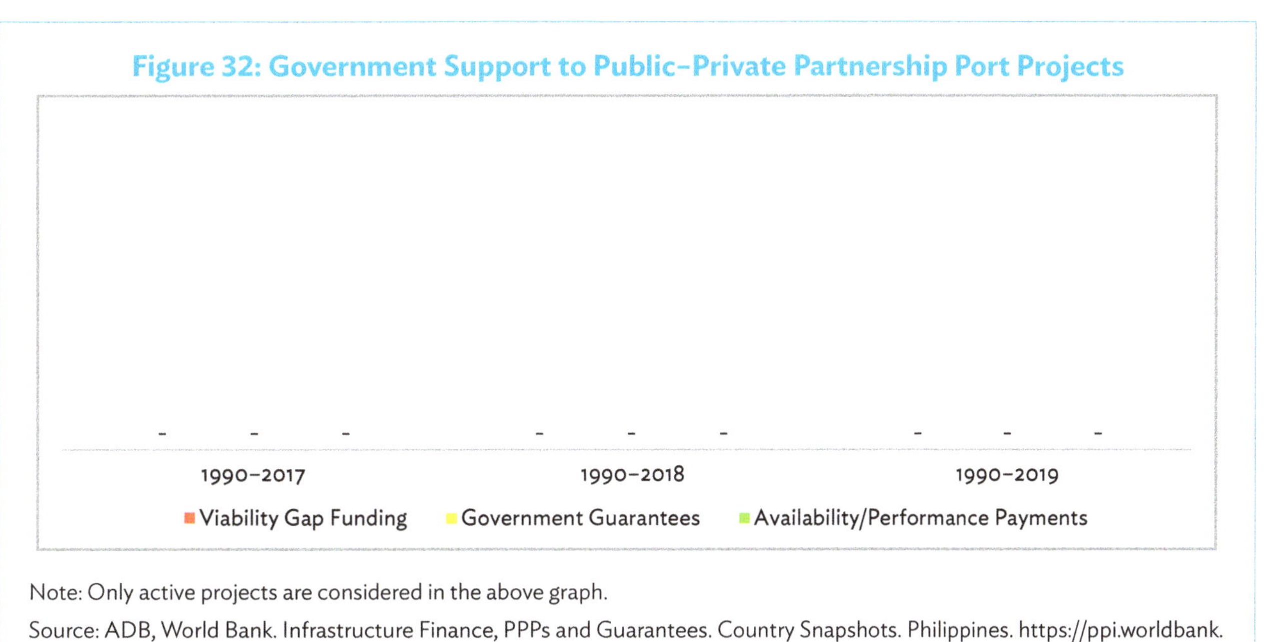


Note: Only active projects are considered in the above graph.

Source: ADB, World Bank. Infrastructure Finance, PPPs and Guarantees. Country Snapshots. Philippines. https://ppi.worldbank.org/en/snapshots/country/philippines (accessed 28 August 2020).

Figure 33 provides the number of PPP projects which have received payment in the form of user charges and government pay (off-take) in the Philippines' port sector.

**Figure 33: Payment Mechanism for Public–Private Partnership Port Projects**

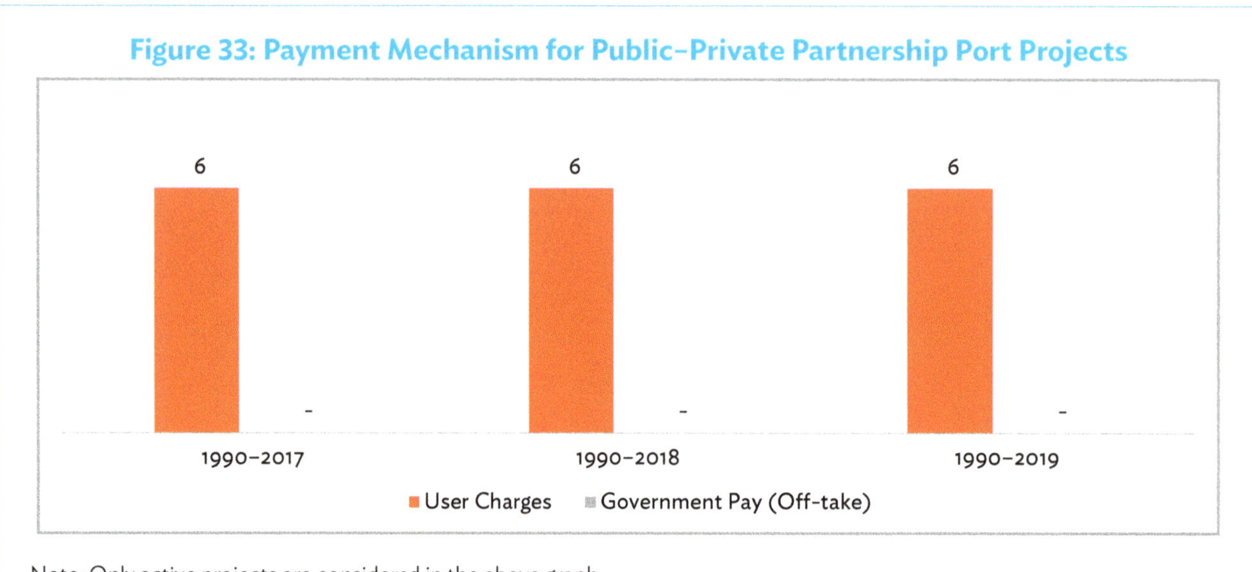


Note: Only active projects are considered in the above graph.

Source: ADB, World Bank. Infrastructure Finance, PPPs and Guarantees. Country Snapshots. Philippines. https://ppi.worldbank.org/en/snapshots/country/philippines (accessed 28 August 2020).

Many projects also receive revenue from land development and advertising rights. Certain projects also pay a revenue share or land lease to the concession authority.

## 4.1 Tariffs in the Port Sector

Tariffs for the port sector are set and regulated by the Philippine Ports Authority. Terminal handling charges (THC) are set by the terminal operators for container movement services at a terminal. For container terminals, THCs cover the movement of a container between the ship's hold and the exit–entry gate via the container terminal yard. Actual THCs may vary from port to port of each country, as the cost of handling depends on the contractual agreement between terminal operators and the relevant shipping line (Table 20) (footnote 1).

**Table 20: Terminal Handling Charges for the Port Sector in the Philippines**

| Designation | Company | Year | Terminal Handling Charge ($) | |
|---|---|---|---|---|
| | | | 20-foot equivalent unit | 40-foot equivalent unit |
| Shipping line | K LINE | 2017 | 133 | 166 |
| Shipping line | OOLA | 2016 | 125 | 155 |
| Terminal operator | MICT | 2015 | 98 | 137 |
| Terminal operator | Philippine Ports Authority | 2013 | 75 | 175 |

K LINE = Kawasaki Kisen Kaisha Ltd, MICT = Manila International Container Terminal.

Source: ADB. 2019. *Public–Private Partnership Monitor.* Second Edition. Manila. https://www.adb.org/sites/default/files/publication/509426/ppp-monitor-second-edition.pdf.

## 4.2 Typical Risk Allocation for Public–Private Partnership Port Projects

| Risk Category | Private | Public | Shared |
|---|---|---|---|
| Demand risk | ✓ | | |
| Competition risk (exclusivity) | ✓ | | |
| Tariff risk | ✓ | | |
| Environmental and social risk | | | ✓ |
| Permits | | | ✓ |
| Geotechnical risk | ✓ | | |

## 4.3 Financing Details of Public–Private Partnerships in the Port Sector

| Parameter | 1990–2017 | 1990–2018 | 1990–2019 |
|---|---|---|---|
| PPP projects with foreign lending participation | 2 | 2 | 2 |
| PPP projects that received export credit agency/international financing institution support | 0 | 0 | 0 |
| Typical debt:equity ratio | 0 | 0 | 0 |
| Time for financial closure | UA | | |
| Typical concession period | 25 years | | |
| Typical Financial Internal Rate of Return | UA | | |

✓ = Yes, × = No, NA = Not Applicable, UA = Unavailable

Source: ADB, World Bank. Infrastructure Finance, PPPs and Guarantees. Country Snapshots. Philippines. https://ppi.worldbank.org/en/snapshots/country/philippines (accessed 28 August 2020).

# 5. Challenges in the Port Sector

- Restriction on foreign investments (capped at 40% for greenfield projects) limits the competition in the sector, as the controlling stake in the project company belongs to local companies. The government is taking steps to ease the restriction on foreign investment to attract international investors.
- The combined regulatory and development function of the Philippine Ports Authority creates conflict of interest.
- There are cases where tenders have been canceled, and this has led to uncertainty among bidders.

# AIRPORTS

| Parameter | Value | Unit |
|---|---|---|
| No. of airports | 247.00 | No. |
| Total passenger capacity | 43.08 | million passengers |
| Quality of air transport infrastructure | 4.10 | 1 (low) – 7 (high) |
| Total number of projects with cumulative lending, grant, and technical assistance commitments in the transport sector | 79 | Number |
| Total amount of cumulative lending, grant, and technical assistance commitments in the transport sector | 2,052 | $ million |

✓ = Yes, × = No, NA = Not Applicable, UA = Unavailable

Sources: City Population. Airports. https://www.citypopulation.de/en/world/bymap/airports.html; World Bank. Air Transport, Passengers Carried. https://data.worldbank.org/indicator/is.air.psgr?locations=bd-kh-ge-kz-mm-pk-pg-lk-uz-vn-cn-in-id-ph-th; The Global Economy. Compare Countries. https://www.theglobaleconomy.com/compare-countries/; ADB. Cumulative Lending, Grant, and Technical Assistance Commitments. https://data.adb.org/dataset/cumulative-lending-grant-and-technical-assistance-commitments.

## 1. Contracting Agencies in the Airport Sector

Most airports in the Philippines are owned by either the DOTr through executive agencies, such as the Manila International Airport Authority, or the Civil Aviation Authority of the Philippines. However, DOTr is identified as the implementing agency for most airport projects in NEDA's *Revised List of Infrastructure Flagship Projects* (published on 17 February 2020).[42]

## 2. Airport Sector Laws and Regulations

There are several regulations that have an impact on PPP projects:

- The Association of Southeast Asian Nations (ASEAN) Single Aviation Market was established in January 2015. This policy aims to liberalize the air transport market in the ASEAN countries to improve the region's connectivity and competitiveness and reduce airfares. The single market enables ASEAN-based carriers to carry passengers and cargo from and to any third country to an ASEAN member state. This requires each state to fully open up their international airports to other ASEAN members and eliminate restrictions on the frequency and maximum capacity of flights. The Philippines has withheld Manila airport, the country's largest, from the ASEAN provisions due to the slot-constrained nature of the airport (footnote 1).
- The Manila and Cebu airports are subject to slot coordination to manage any spare capacity efficiently. Slots are either allocated by an independent slot coordination body based on a number of allocation rules or, in the case of Cebu, by the Mactan–Cebu International Airport Authority. Slots are usually allocated for each summer and winter season (footnote 1).
- To ensure safe and secure air transport operations, the International Civil Aviation Organization has published a number of regulations that airport operators have to adopt. These regulations set out the physical requirements for any type of civil airport to receive an operating license from the National Civil Aviation Authority, as well as various security measures to safeguard the aviation industry against acts of unlawful interference (footnote 1).
- The local and national police provide policing services to airports. Regulations on security, customs, quarantine, and immigration specify the functions to be undertaken by the state or public authorities (footnote 1).
- It is necessary to monitor development-related regulations for areas around airports to ensure that obstacle limitation surfaces are maintained for the safety of flight operations (Table 21).

---

42 The Civil Aviation Authority of the Philippines (CAAP) was the concession authority for Caticlan Airport Development Project. The DOTr and the Mactan–Cebu International Airport Authority (MCIAA) offered the concession for the Mactan–Cebu International Airport Passenger Terminal Building.

### Table 21: Functions of Airport Sector Regulatory Agencies in the Philippines

| Agency | Function |
|---|---|
| Department of Transport | • Provides oversight and strategic direction for air transport and for the airports within its control; and serves as avenue for central government funding for its airports |
| Civil Aviation Authority of the Philippines | • Acts as one of the governing bodies of the aviation industry (by virtue of Republic Act 9497, 2008, An Act Creating the Civil Aviation Authority of the Philippines, Authorizing the Appropriation of Funds thereof, and for Other Purposes, also known as the CAAP Law)<br>• Regulates compliance to certain International Civil Aviation Organization provisions<br>• Provides air navigation services; owns and operates some airports; and owns, operates, and maintains air navigation equipment |
| Civil Aeronautics Board | • Negotiates air traffic rights and supports slot allocation processes |
| Office of Transportation Security | • Provides human resources for security screening and regulates aviation security |

CAAP = Civil Aviation Authority of the Philippines.

Sources: ADB. 2019. *Public–Private Partnership Monitor.* Second Edition. Manila. https://www.adb.org/sites/default/files/publication/509426/ppp-monitor-second-edition.pdf; Government of the Philippines. Official Gazette. Republic Act No. 9497. https://www.officialgazette.gov.ph/2008/03/04/republic-act-no-9497/

## 2.1 Foreign Investment Restrictions in the Airport Sector

The maximum equity investment allowed for foreign investors in greenfield projects is 40% (footnote 33).

| Parameter | 2017 | 2018 | 2019 |
|---|---|---|---|
| Maximum allowed foreign ownership of equity in greenfield projects | 40% | 40% | 40% |

## 2.2 Standard Contracts in the Airport Sector

| Type of Contract | Availability |
|---|---|
| PPP/concession agreement | × |
| Performance-based operation and maintenance contract | × |
| Engineering procurement and construction contract | × |

✓ = Yes, × = No, NA = Not Applicable, UA = Unavailable

# 3. Airport Sector Master Plan

The airports sector does not have a sector specific master plan. Table 22 outlines the priority projects identified in the airports sector for the PPP mode of implementation based on NEDA's *Revised List of Infrastructure Flagship Projects* (published on 17 February 2020).

### Table 22: Public–Private Partnership Priority Airport Projects

| No. | Project Name | Implementing Agency | Estimated Project Cost ($ million) | (₱ billion) | Status |
|---|---|---|---|---|---|
| 1. | Clark International Airport Expansion Project Phase 1[a] | DOTr/ BCDA | 296 | 14.97 | Ongoing implementation |
| 2. | New Manila International Airport | DOTr | 14,521 | 735.63 | Awarded |
| 3. | Ninoy Aquino International Airport | DOTr | 2,016 | 102.12 | To commence construction in 6 to 8 months |
| 4. | Bacolod–Silay International Airport | DOTr | 400 | 20.26 | Advanced stages of government approval |
| 5. | Iloilo International Airport | DOTr | 91 | 4.59 | Advanced stages of government approval |
| 6. | New Bohol (Panglao) International Airport | DOTr | 75 | 3.79 | To commence construction in 6 to 8 months |
| 7. | Kalibo International Airport | DOTr | 76 | 3.84 | Under preparation |
| 8. | Laguindingan Airport | DOTr | 903 | 45.75 | Under preparation |
| 9. | Davao International Airport | DOTr | 967 | 48.97 | Under preparation |

₱1 = $0.01974

BCDA = Bases Conversion and Development Authority, DOTr = Department of Transportation

[a] The Bases Conversion and Development Authority (BCDA) engages in public–private partnerships to push forward vital public infrastructure such as tollways, airports, seaports, and major real estate developments.

Source: NEDA. 2020. *Revised List of Infrastructure Flagship Projects*. Manila. https://www.neda.gov.ph/infrastructure-flagship-projects/.

## 3.1 Projects under Preparation and Procurement in the Airport Sector

Figure 34 presents the number of PPP projects which are under preparation and procurement in the Philippines' airport sector.

### Figure 34: Public–Private Partnership Airport Projects under Preparation and Procurement

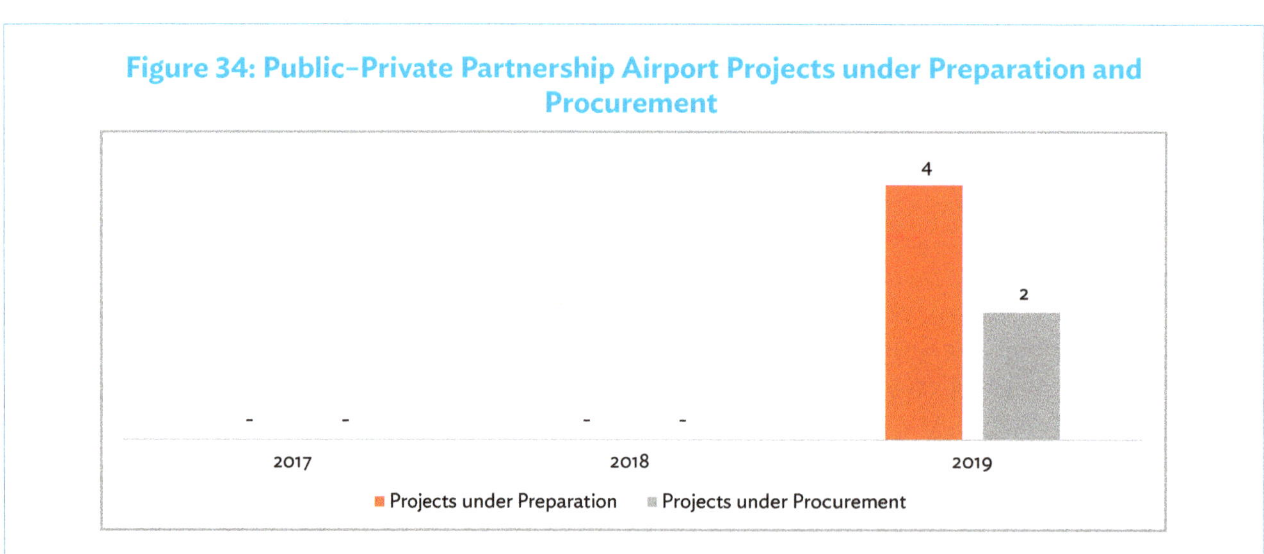


Source: Public–Private Partnership Center. List of Projects. https://ppp.gov.ph/list-of-projects/ (accessed 28 August 2020); Public–Private Partnership Center. 2019. *Investment Opportunities*. Manila. https://ppp.gov.ph/investors-corner/investment-opportunities-2/.

The Public–Private Partnership Center tracks the progress of a pipeline of PPP projects in the Philippines, which is updated regularly and published on the PPP Center website (Table 23).

## Table 23: List of Public–Private Partnership Airport Projects under Preparation

| No. | Project | Implementing Agency | Estimated Total Investment ($ million) | Estimated Total Investment (₱ billion) |
|---|---|---|---|---|
| 1. | 50-year Integrated Development Plan for Mactan Cebu International Airport (MCIA) Project | Department of Transportation | 3,169 | 160.56 |
| 2. | Davao International Airport Development, Operation, and Management | Department of Transportation | 963 | 48.8 |
| 3. | O&M and Facility Upgrade of Kalibo International Airport | Department of Transportation | 76 | 3.84 |
| 4. | Upgrade, Expansion, Operations and Maintenance of Laguindingan Airport | Department of Transportation | 843 | 42.7 |

₱1 = $0.01974

Source: Public–Private Partnership Center. List of Projects. https://ppp.gov.ph/list-of-projects/ (accessed 28 August 2020); Public–Private Partnership Center. 2019. *Investment Opportunities*. Manila. https://ppp.gov.ph/investors-corner/investment-opportunities-2/.

The Public–Private Partnership Center tracks the progress of a pipeline of PPP projects in the Philippines, which is updated regularly and published on the PPP Center website (Table 24).

## Table 24: List of Public–Private Partnership Airport Projects under Procurement

| No. | Project | Implementing Agency | Estimated Total Investment ($ million) | Estimated Total Investment (₱ billion) |
|---|---|---|---|---|
| 1. | Sangley Point International Airport Phase 1 | Department of Transportation | 505 | 25.450 |
| 2. | New Bohol (Panglao) Airport Privatization | Department of Transportation | 4,000 | 201.480 |

Source: Public–Private Partnership Center. List of Projects. https://ppp.gov.ph/list-of-projects/ (accessed 28 August 2020); Public–Private Partnership Center. 2019. *Investment Opportunities*. Manila. https://ppp.gov.ph/investors-corner/investment-opportunities-2/.

## 4. Features of Past Public–Private Partnership Project in the Airport Sector

Figure 35 shows the number of PPP projects procured through various modes including direct appointment, unsolicited bids, and competitive bids in the Philippines' airport sector.

Figure 35: Modes of Procurement for Public–Private Partnership Airport Projects

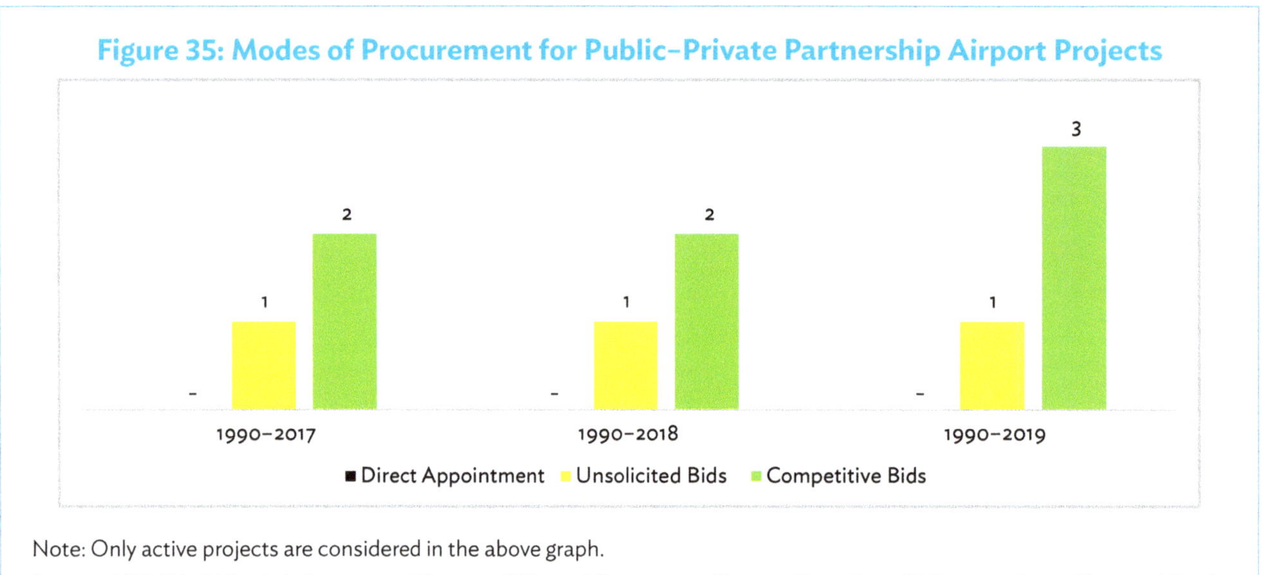


Note: Only active projects are considered in the above graph.

Source: ADB, World Bank. Infrastructure Finance, PPPs and Guarantees. Country Snapshots. Philippines. https://ppi.worldbank.org/en/snapshots/country/philippines (accessed 28 August 2020).

Figure 36 presents the number of PPP projects which have reached financial closure and the total value of those projects in the Philippines' airport sector.

Figure 36: Public–Private Partnership Airport Projects Reaching Financial Closure

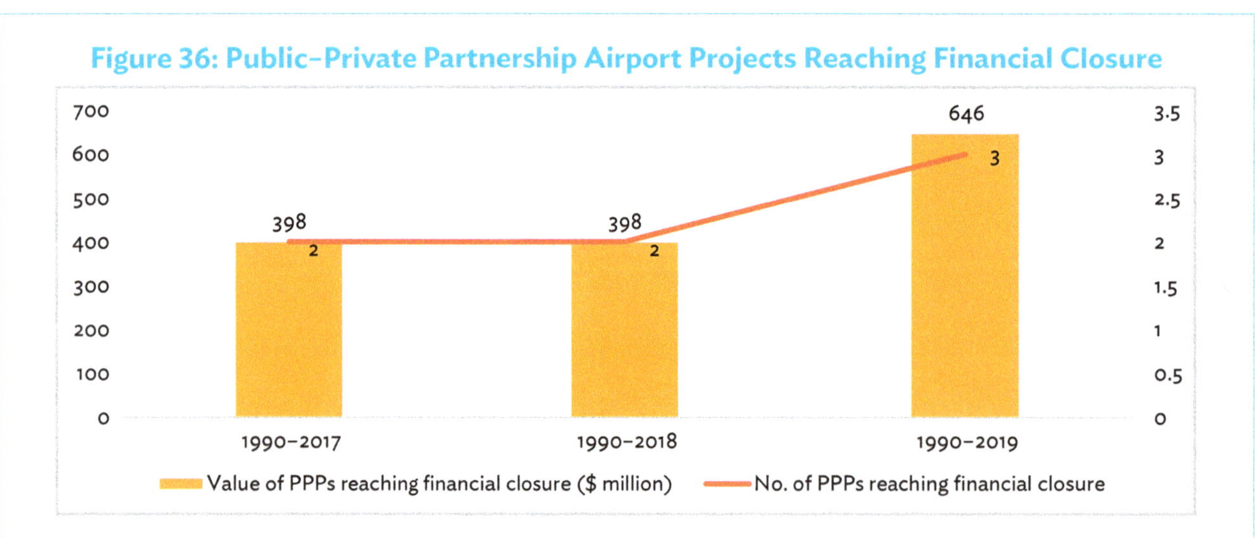


Note: Only active projects are considered in the above graph.

Source: ADB, World Bank. Infrastructure Finance, PPPs and Guarantees. Country Snapshots. Philippines. https://ppi.worldbank.org/en/snapshots/country/philippines (accessed 28 August 2020).

Figure 37 shows the number of PPP projects which have received foreign sponsor participation in the Philippines' airport sector.

**Figure 37: Public–Private Partnership Airport Projects with Foreign Sponsor Participation**

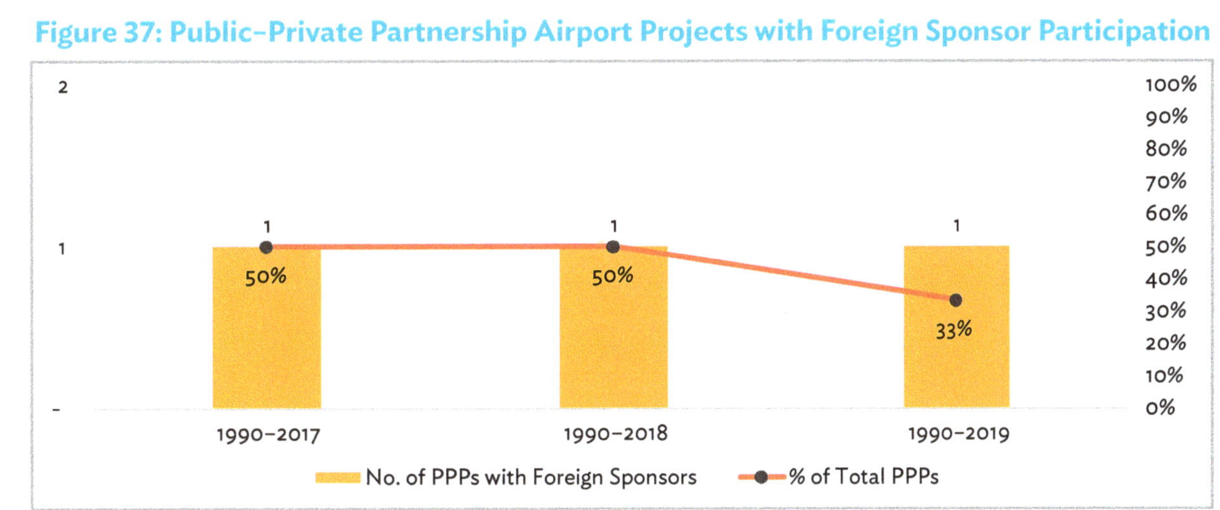


Note: Only active projects are considered in the above graph.

Source: ADB, World Bank. Infrastructure Finance, PPPs and Guarantees. Country Snapshots. Philippines. https://ppi.worldbank.org/en/snapshots/country/philippines (accessed 28 August 2020).

Figure 38 shows the number of PPP projects which have received government support including viability gap funding (VGF) mechanism, government guarantees, and availability/performance payment in the Philippines' airport sector.

**Figure 38: Government Support to Public–Private Partnership Airport Projects**

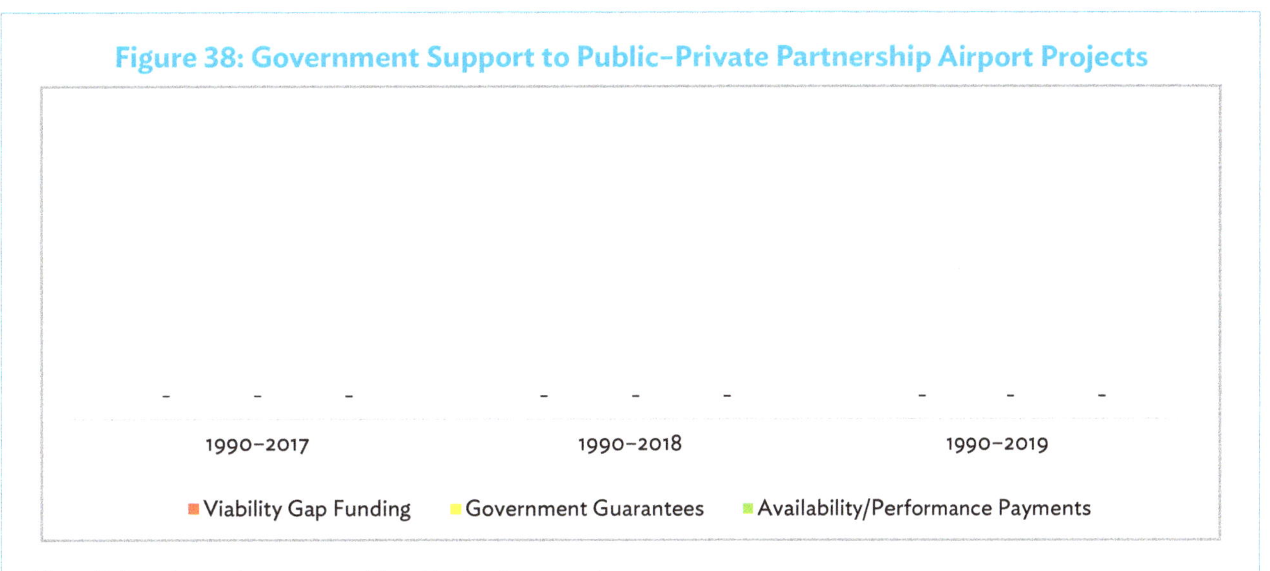


Note: Only active projects are considered in the above graph.

Source: ADB, World Bank. Infrastructure Finance, PPPs and Guarantees. Country Snapshots. Philippines. https://ppi.worldbank.org/en/snapshots/country/philippines (accessed 28 August 2020).

Figure 39 presents the number of PPP projects which have received payment in the form of user charges and government pay (off-take) in the Philippines' airport sector.

**Figure 39: Payment Mechanisms for Public–Private Partnership Airport Projects**

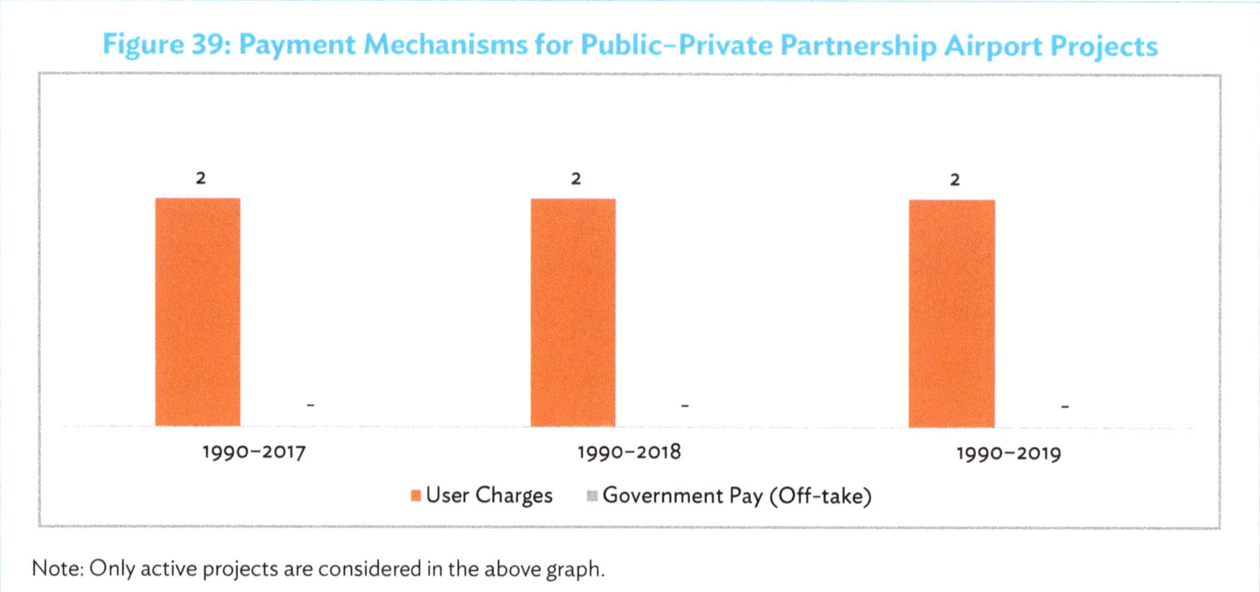


Note: Only active projects are considered in the above graph.

Source: ADB, World Bank. Infrastructure Finance, PPPs and Guarantees. Country Snapshots. Philippines. https://ppi.worldbank.org/en/snapshots/country/philippines (accessed 28 August 2020).

Many projects also receive revenues/fees for various aeronautical services they provide such as for landing, aircraft parking, boarding bridge, and terminal service. Projects also receive ancillary and commercial revenues.

It is noteworthy that the duty-free retail is a state-owned enterprise with monopoly provision rights. The income from duty-free activities is generally outside the provisions of PPP agreements (footnote 1).

## 4.1 Tariffs in the Airport Sector

The approach with passenger service charge and ancillary charges tariff setting has been to provide a form of regulation with the government maintaining control via the Mactan–Cebu International Airport Authority. Passenger service charge escalation is also set out with a concession agreement (footnote 1).

## 4.2 Typical Risk Allocation for Public–Private Partnership Airport Projects

| Risk Category | Private | Public | Shared |
|---|---|---|---|
| Demand | ✓ | | |
| Revenue collection | | | ✓ |
| Tariff | ✓ | | |
| Government payment | | ✓ | |
| Environment and social | ✓ | | |
| Land acquisition | ✓ | | |

*continued on next page*

*continued from previous page*

| Risk Category | Private | Public | Shared |
|---|---|---|---|
| Interface | | | ✓ |
| Handover | ✓ | | |
| Political | ✓ | | |
| Foreign exchange (FOREX) | ✓ | | |

## 4.3 Financing Details of Public–Private Partnerships in the Airport Sector

| Parameter | 1990–2017 | 1990–2018 | 1990–2019 |
|---|---|---|---|
| PPP projects with foreign lending participation | 0 | 0 | 0 |
| PPP projects that received export credit agency/international financing institution support | 1 | 1 | 2 |
| Typical debt:equity ratio | 80:20 | | |
| Time for financial closure | UA | | |
| Typical concession period | UA | | |
| Typical Financial Internal Rate of Return | UA | | |

✓ = Yes, × = No, NA = Not Applicable, UA = Unavailable

Source: ADB, World Bank. Infrastructure Finance, PPPs and Guarantees. Country Snapshots. Philippines. https://ppi.worldbank.org/en/snapshots/country/philippines (accessed 28 August 2020).

The Mactan–Cebu International Airport received debt financing from the Asian Development Bank, while the Clark International Airport (operations and maintenance concession) received debt financing from the International Finance Corporation.

# 5. Challenges in the Airport Sector

- Restriction on foreign investments (capped at 40% for greenfield projects) limits the competition in the sector, as the controlling stake in the project company belongs to local companies. The government is taking steps to ease the restriction on foreign investment to attract international investors.
- There have been cancellations of PPP tenders (five in 2017) in the past. The *Revised List of Priority Projects* indicates that most PPP airport projects were sought to be procured through unsolicited proposals. Furthermore, these projects have not been prepared or structured by the public sector which may result in commercially unviable development propositions (footnote 1).

# ENERGY

| Parameter | Value | Unit |
|---|---|---|
| Electric power consumption | 699 | kilowatt-hour per capita |
| Share of clean energy | 27.45 | % of total energy use |
| Access to electricity | 95 | % of population |
| Getting electricity (score out of 100) | 87.40 | Number |

*continued on next page*

*continued from previous page*

| Parameter | Value | Unit |
|---|---|---|
| Energy imports | 45.77 | % of total energy use |
| Investment in energy with private participation | 2,478 | current $ million |
| Total number of projects with cumulative lending, grant, and technical assistance commitments in the energy sector | 76 | Number |
| Total amount of cumulative lending, grant, and technical assistance commitments in the energy sector | 3,414 | $ million |

✓ = Yes, × = No, NA = Not Applicable, UA = Unavailable

Sources: The Economist Intelligence Unit. Philippines. https://infrascope.eiu.com/; The Global Economy. Share of Clean Energy—Country Rankings. https://www.theglobaleconomy.com/rankings/share_of_clean_energy/; World Bank. Access to Electricity. https://data.worldbank.org/indicator/eg.elc.accs.zs?end=2018&locations=mm-kh-uz-cn-bd-ge-in-id-kz-pk-ph-lk-th-vn&start=2018&view=bar; Doing Business. Getting Electricity. https://www.doingbusiness.org/en/data/doing-business-score?topic=getting-electricity; The Global Economy. Energy Imports. https://www.theglobaleconomy.com/rankings/energy_imports/; ADB. Cumulative Lending, Grant, and Technical Assistance Commitments. https://data.adb.org/dataset/cumulative-lending-grant-and-technical-assistance-commitments

## 1. Contracting Agencies in the Energy Sector

The Energy Regulatory Commission (ERC) is an independent body responsible for regulating the power industry. It is also responsible for approving bilateral power supply agreements and Ancillary Service Procurement Agreements, and for setting the distribution wheeling rates of distribution utilities and electric cooperatives.[43]

## 2. Energy Sector Laws and Regulations

The Department of Energy and various agencies and companies are in charge of the transmission and distribution network. The National Grid Corporation of the Philippines is a privately owned corporation that has been in charge of operating, maintaining, and developing the country's state-owned power grid since 2007. There is a mix of long-term bilateral contracts (80%) and wholesale electricity spot market contracts (20%). Contracts vary from 5 to 25 years in length. Meralco is the largest off-taker, covering 25% of population. Power distribution outside the Metro Manila area is handled by private distribution utilities and electric cooperative (footnote 43).

The EPIRA, passed in 2001, is the main foundation of regulation in the energy sector. The legislation sought to liberalize and unbundle the power sector and promote competition, which resulted in a significant transformation of the power sector (footnote 43).

Privatization played an essential role in the EPIRA-driven reform process which established that power generation should no longer be considered a public utility operation. The Power Sector Assets and Liabilities Management Corporation (PSALM), which reports to the DOE, is charged with selling both the government-owned power sector assets and the rights to control capacity contracted to the government by the private sector under long-term power purchase agreements (PPAs).[44] By the end of 2013, the power sector in the Philippines had become one of the most extensively privatized power sectors in the Asia and Pacific region (footnote 43).

43 ADB. 2018. *Philippines—Energy Sector Assessment, Strategy, and Road Map*. Manila. https://www.adb.org/sites/default/files/publication/463306/philippines-energy-assessment-strategy-road-map.pdf.

44 PSALM. https://www.psalm.gov.ph/.

The Renewable Energy Act 2008 (Republic Act 9513) lays down various policies for the development of renewable sources of energy. The act calls for a renewable portfolio standard, which requires power suppliers to extract a percentage of energy from renewable sources. A feed-in tariff provision allows renewable energy generators to secure a guaranteed market and a guaranteed price for their power, in addition to tax credits for developers and value added tax and duty-free importation of renewable technologies.[45]

The EPIRA also required the distribution utilities to procure power in the "least-cost manner" for sale to their franchised captive customers, and mandated the establishment of a sophisticated Wholesale Electricity Spot Market (WESM). The WESM, established in 2006, is operated by the Philippine Electricity Market Corporation (footnote 43).

Since the passage of the EPIRA, the power sector restructuring in the Philippines has achieved the following:

- establishment of the WESM in Luzon and Visayas;
- establishment of the ERC as an autonomous sector regulator;
- absorption of debt: following the mandate of the EPIRA, the government absorbed ₱200 billion of the debt liabilities of the National Power Corporation (NPC);
- structural unbundling of electricity provision into generation, transmission, and distribution plus retail supply;
- privatization to the point where the private sector now provides most of the generation, all transmission, and most of the distribution or retail supply;
- introduction of performance-based regulation for electricity transmission and distribution businesses;
- removal of most subsidies and cross-subsidies;
- reduction of transmission and distribution losses; and
- improvements in electrification coverage (footnote 43).

The Energy Virtual One-Stop Shop (EVOSS) Act 2019 (Republic Act 11234) was implemented to establish EVOSS under the supervision of DOE. The prospective developers can use the EVOSS online paperless platform to apply, monitor, and receive all the needed permits and applications; submit all the documentary requirements; and pay for charges and fees. The EVOSS platform serves as a decision-making portal for approval of new projects in the energy sector. The portal also accepts the submissions of all the required data and information and undertakes synchronous processing of the data/information. EVOSS has the following characteristics, among others:

- recognizes the legal effect, validity, and enforceability of electronic documents submitted for applications of power generation, transmission, and distribution projects;
- serves as an online platform for payment fees and taxes imposed for the applications of power generation, transmission, and distribution projects;
- offers a secure system for collection of application forms, submission of applications, payment of fees, and monitoring the status of applications, among others; and
- offers a unified system for all government agencies involved in the permission of energy projects. The platform uses standard templates and is governed by a mandated processing time.

45 Clean Energy Solutions. Home. http://cleanenergysolutions.org/.

The law applies to new power projects in generation, transmission, or distribution projects. The system is used by major entities involved in the permitting process of energy projects including all national government departments/agencies, government-owned and controlled corporations, and local government units.

### Table 25: Energy Sector Regulatory Authorities in the Philippines

| Agency | Function |
|---|---|
| Department of Energy | Formulates and implements all government policies and programs for energy exploration, development, distribution, and conservation to ensure sustainable, secure, reliable, and accessible energy. It is the government's supervisory arm for all energy sector-related initiatives. |
| Energy Regulatory Commission | An independent commission comprised of five members, nominated by the President of the Philippines, to regulate all sectors of the electricity market and protect consumer interests. It promulgates the policies created by the Department of Energy and the guidelines formulated by the Joint Congressional Power Commission; issues licenses to electricity suppliers; and ensures compliance with the power sector laws. It is also responsible for setting the transmission, distribution, and retail fees charged to end users. |
| National Power Corporation (NPC) | Prior to the deregulation of the power industry by the Electric Power Industry Reform Act in 2001, the NPC was the largest electric power company in the Philippines. Most of the NPC's generation assets have been privatized. |
| National Transmission Corporation (TransCo) | A state-owned enterprise which has taken over the transmission function and related assets of the NPC. TransCo is now responsible for linking the power plants, owned by both the NPC and independent power producers, to the distribution utilities and electricity cooperatives which, in turn, provide electricity to end users. |
| Power Sector Asset and Liabilities Management | Created to privatize and liquidate the NPC's assets and independent power producers' contracts and liabilities. It also assumes the ownership of TransCo along with all its debt obligations and oversees the transfer of control of its transmission assets through a 25-year concession agreement to private parties. The Power Sector Asset and Liabilities Management has a 25-year corporate life (by 2026), at the end of which, its assets and liabilities would be transferred to the Government of the Philippines. |
| Energy Investment Coordinating Council | Established by Executive Order 30 on 28 June 2017 (Creating the Energy Investment Coordinating Council in order to Streamline the Regulatory Procedures Affecting Energy Projects). The Energy Investment Coordinating Council is mandated to coordinate and facilitate energy investments in the energy sector. |
| Philippine Competition Commission | Mandated to promote free and fair competition across all sectors, including energy. The Philippine Competition Commission penalizes monopolistic and anticompetitive behavior, and has the authority to approve asset transactions in the power sector. |
| Philippine Electricity Market Corporation (PEMC) | A non-profit entity that reports administratively to the DOE and has the mandate to manage the WESM. The PEMC produces the hourly generation schedules (based on generator market offers), which the system operator then uses to instruct the dispatch of the generation plants. |

DOE = Department of Energy, NPC = National Power Corporation, TransCo = National Transmission Corporation, WESM = Wholesale Electricity Spot Market.

Source: ADB. 2019. *Public–Private Partnership Monitor.* Second Edition. Manila. https://www.adb.org/sites/default/files/publication/509426/ppp-monitor-second-edition.pdf.

## 2.1 Foreign Investment Restrictions in the Energy Sector

| Business Activity | 2017 | 2018 | 2019 |
|---|---|---|---|
| Power generation (traditional sources) | 100% | 100% | 100% |
| Power generation (renewable energy, except geothermal which can be up to 100% based on regulations) | 40% | 40% | 40% |
| Power transmission | 40% | 40% | 40% |
| Power distribution | 40% | 40% | 40% |
| Oil and gas | 40% | 40% | 40% |

## 2.2 Standard Contracts in the Energy Sector

| Type of Contract | Availability |
|---|---|
| PPP/concession agreement | × |
| Power purchase agreement | × |
| Capacity take-or-pay contract | × |
| Fuel supply agreement | × |
| Transmission and use of system agreement | × |
| Engineering procurement and construction contract | × |

✓ = Yes, × = No, NA = Not Applicable, UA = Unavailable

# 3. Energy Sector Master Plan

The Department of Energy has developed the Philippine Energy Plan (PEP) 2017–2040 in line with the *"Ambisyon Natin"* 2040 (Our Ambition). The plan sets the following targets, among others:

- 100% electrification by 2022;
- additional capacity of 43.765 gigawatts (GW), from the 2016 base capacity of 21.424 GW;
- additional 20 GW of renewable power capacity (from 6.96 GW capacity in 2016);[46]
- increase reserves and production of local oil, gas, and coal;
- delivery of quality, reliable, affordable, and secure power supply;
- expanded access to electricity;
- transparent and fair power sector playing field;
- establishment of a world class and investment driven natural gas industry in the Philippines; and
- stable energy supply through a technologically responsive energy sector.

46 Government of the Philippines, Department of Energy. 2017. *Power Development Plan and Status of Renewable and Fossil-Based Power Sources.* Manila. http://erdt.coe.upd.edu.ph/images/congress/6thERDTCongress/01_Nuclear%20Energy%20Forum_Aug%2018%20no%20script.pdf.

## 3.1 Projects under Preparation and Procurement in the Energy Sector

Figure 40 presents the number of PPP projects which are under preparation and procurement in the Philippines' energy sector.

**Figure 40: Public–Private Partnership Energy Projects under Preparation and Procurement**

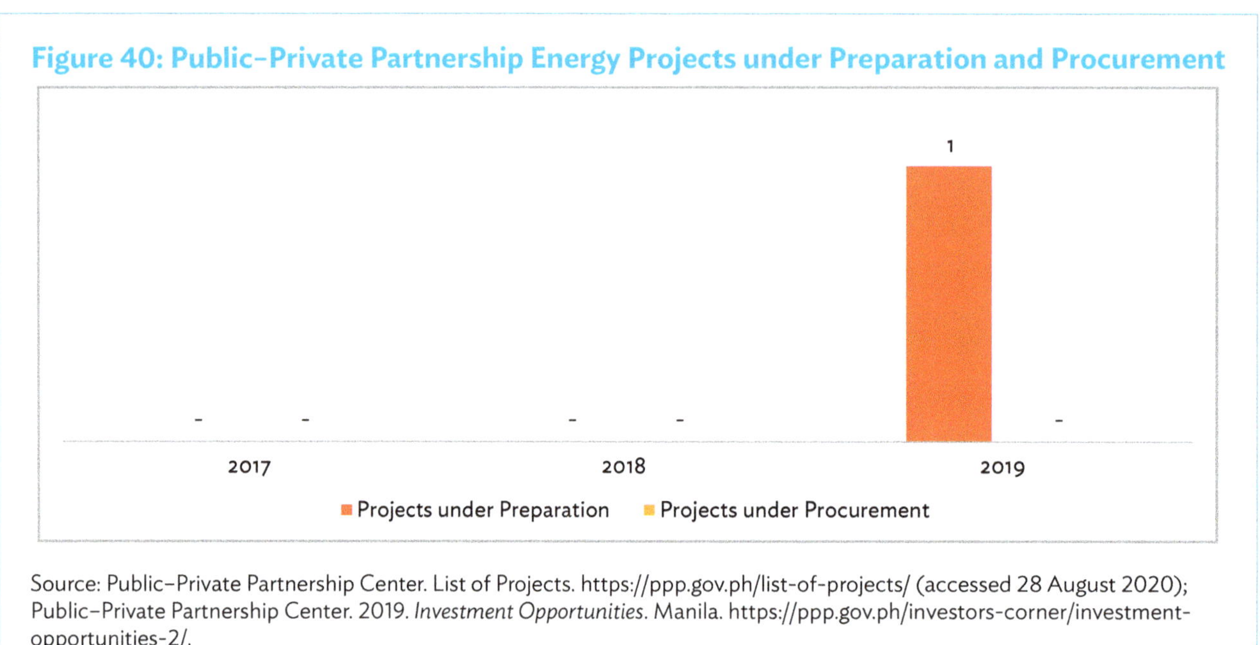


Source: Public–Private Partnership Center. List of Projects. https://ppp.gov.ph/list-of-projects/ (accessed 28 August 2020); Public–Private Partnership Center. 2019. *Investment Opportunities*. Manila. https://ppp.gov.ph/investors-corner/investment-opportunities-2/.

The Public–Private Partnership Center tracks the progress of a pipeline of PPP projects in the Philippines, which is updated regularly and published on the PPP Center website (Table 26).

**Table 26: List of Public–Private Partnership Energy Projects**

| No. | Project | Implementing Agency | Estimated Total Investment |
|---|---|---|---|
| 1. | Angat Hydroelectric Power Plant (AHEPP) Project Rehabilitation, Operation and Maintenance of Auxiliary #4 and #5 | Department of Energy | To be decided |

Source: Public–Private Partnership Center. List of Projects. https://ppp.gov.ph/list-of-projects/ (accessed 28 August 2020); Public–Private Partnership Center. 2019. *Investment Opportunities*. Manila. https://ppp.gov.ph/investors-corner/investment-opportunities-2/.

# 4. Features of Past Public–Private Partnership Projects

Figure 41 shows the number of PPP projects procured through various modes including direct appointment, unsolicited bids, and competitive bids in the Philippines' energy sector.

**Figure 41: Modes of Procurement for Public–Private Partnership Energy Projects**

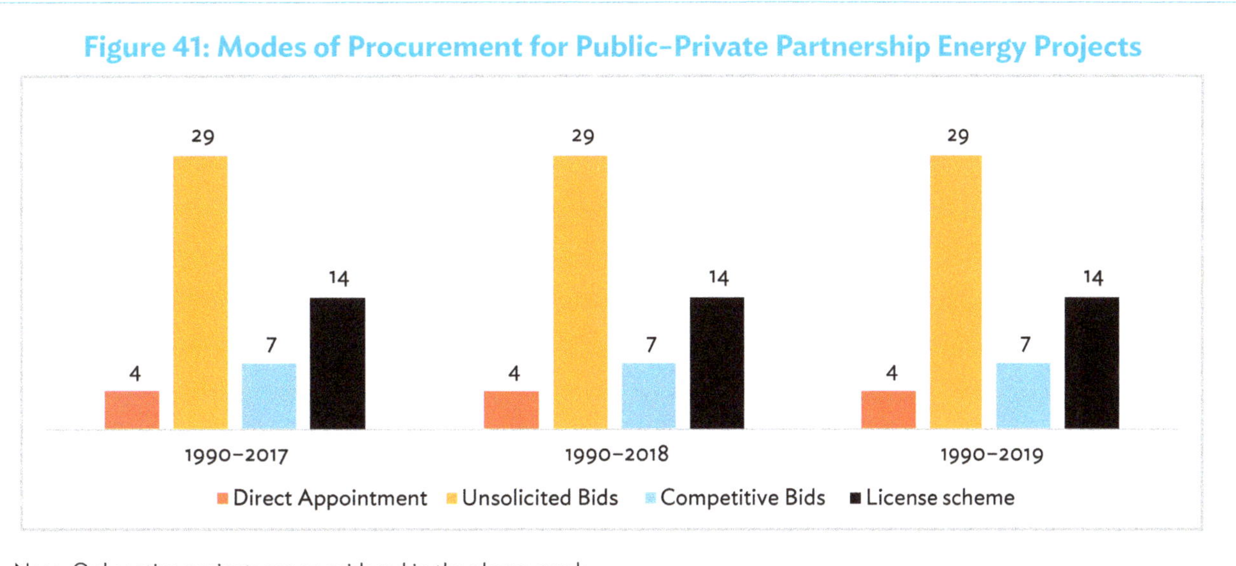


Note: Only active projects are considered in the above graph.

Source: ADB, World Bank. Infrastructure Finance, PPPs and Guarantees. Country Snapshots. Philippines. https://ppi.worldbank.org/en/snapshots/country/philippines (accessed 28 August 2020).

Figure 42 shows the number of PPP projects which have reached financial closure and the total value of those projects in the Philippines' energy sector.

**Figure 42: Independent Power Producer/Public–Private Partnership Energy Projects Reaching Financial Closure**

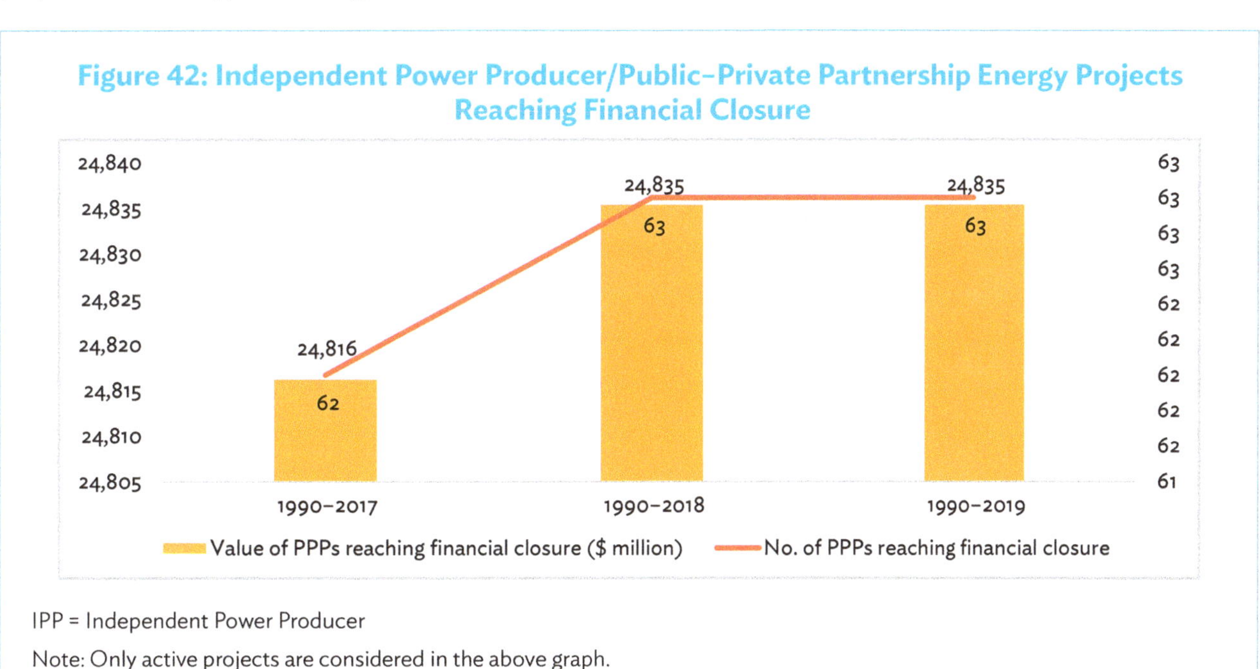


IPP = Independent Power Producer

Note: Only active projects are considered in the above graph.

Source: ADB, World Bank. Infrastructure Finance, PPPs and Guarantees. Country Snapshots. Philippines. https://ppi.worldbank.org/en/snapshots/country/philippines (accessed 28 August 2020).

Figure 43 presents the number of PPP projects which have received foreign sponsor participation in the Philippines' energy sector.

**Figure 43: Independent Power Producer/Public–Private Partnership Energy Projects with Foreign Sponsor Participation**

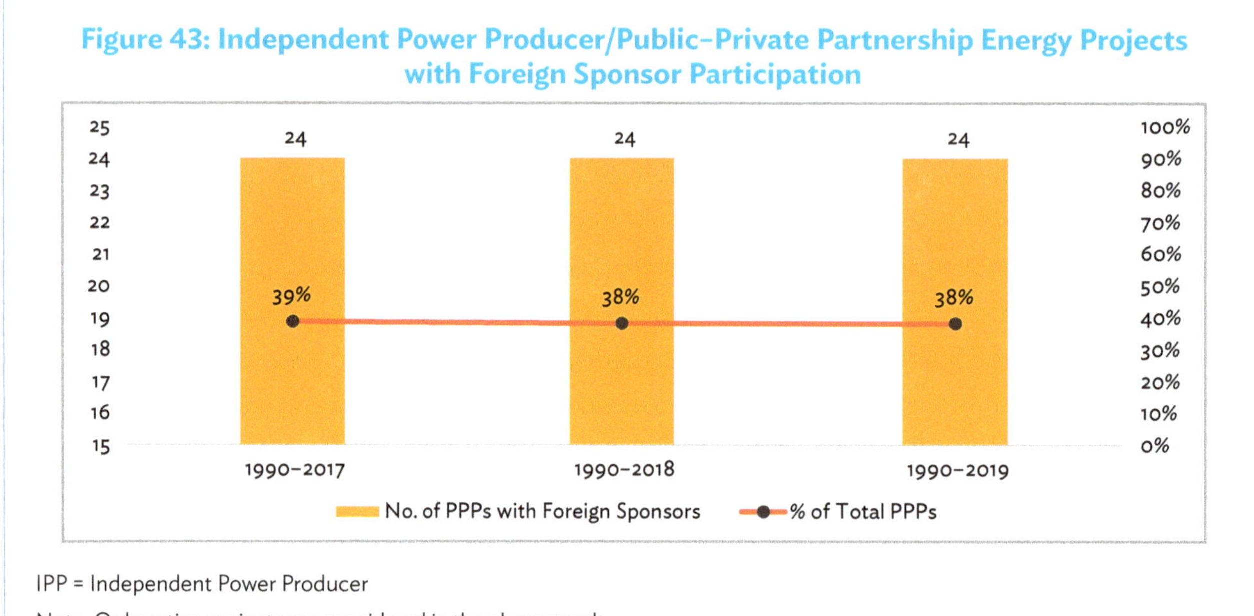


IPP = Independent Power Producer

Note: Only active projects are considered in the above graph.

Source: ADB, World Bank. Infrastructure Finance, PPPs and Guarantees. Country Snapshots. Philippines. https://ppi.worldbank.org/en/snapshots/country/philippines (accessed 28 August 2020).

Figure 44 shows the number of PPP projects which have received government support including viability gap funding (VGF) mechanism, government guarantees, and availability/performance payment in the Philippines' energy sector.

**Figure 44: Government Support to Public–Private Partnership Energy Projects**

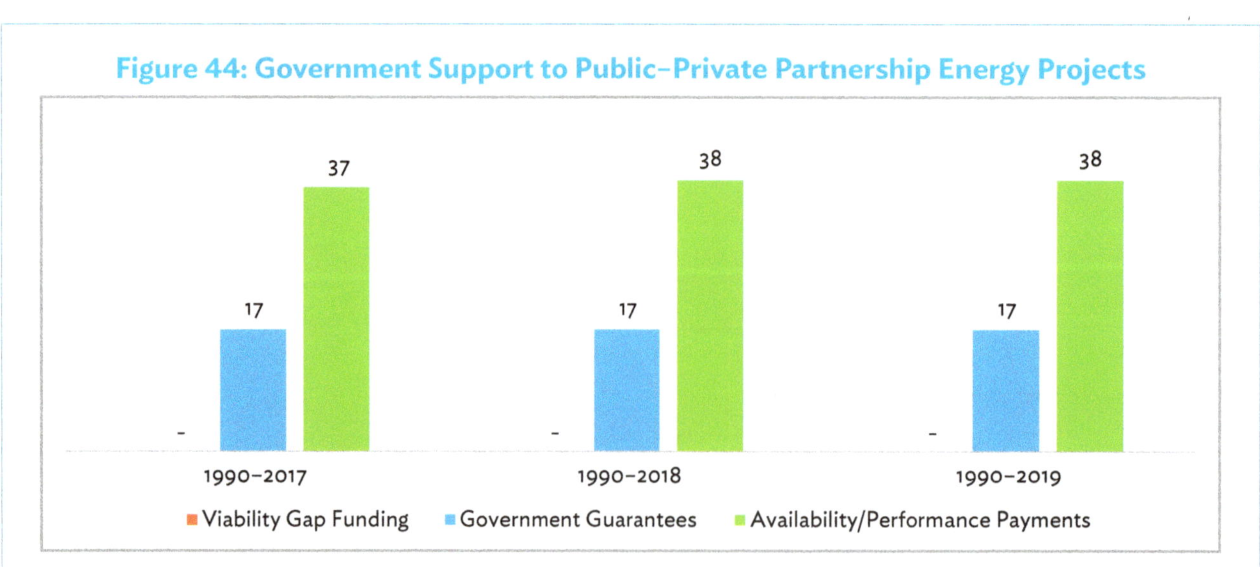


Note: Only active projects are considered in the above graph.

Source: ADB, World Bank. Infrastructure Finance, PPPs and Guarantees. Country Snapshots. Philippines. https://ppi.worldbank.org/en/snapshots/country/philippines (accessed 28 August 2020).

Figure 45 presents the number of PPP projects which have received payment in the form of user charges and government pay (off-take) in the Philippines' energy sector.

**Figure 45: Payment Mechanisms for Public–Private Partnership Energy Projects**

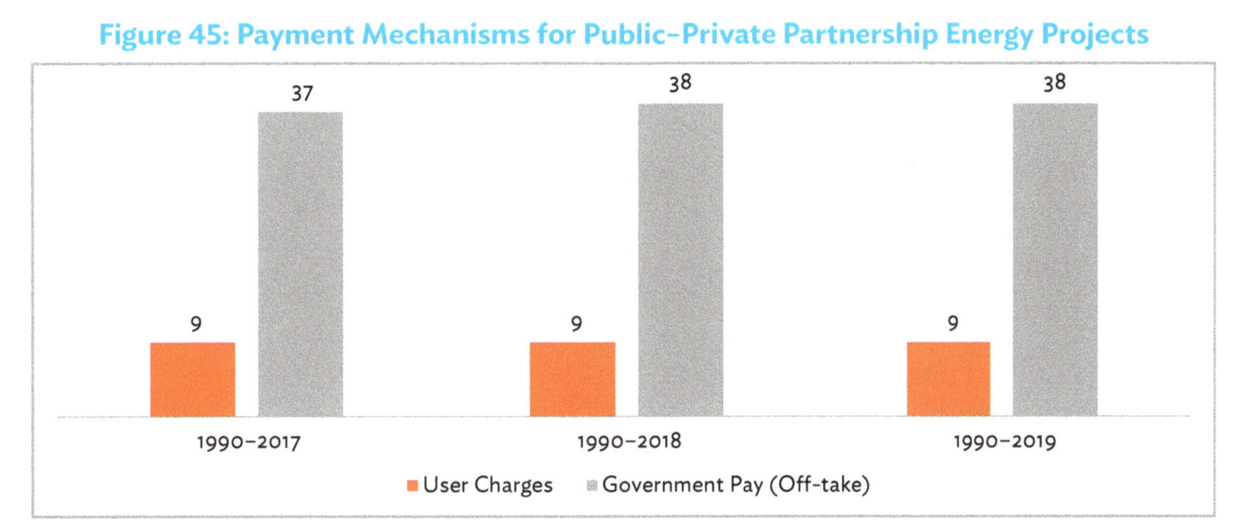


Note: Only active projects are considered in the above graph. User charges include wholesale and sale toward Power Purchase Agreements or transmission fees to private entities.

Source: ADB, World Bank. Infrastructure Finance, PPPs and Guarantees. Country Snapshots. Philippines. https://ppi.worldbank.org/en/snapshots/country/philippines (accessed 28 August 2020).

## 4.1 Tariffs in the Energy Sector

The Feed-In-Tariff (FIT) support applies to renewable energy projects—hydro, wind, solar, ocean, and biomass. To be eligible for a FIT, power utilities must receive a Certificate of Compliance from the ERC.

Under the FIT, generators with eligible renewable energy capacity are paid a FIT rate that is guaranteed for 20 years from the date of effectivity. Funding of the FIT rate for which renewable energy generators are paid comprises two interacting components: (i) a cost recovery rate based on the prevailing WESM price, and (ii) a universal subsidy known as the FIT-All paid by end users and set annually (footnote 43).

The tariff system is financed by a fixed charge on electricity bills referred to as the Feed-In-Tariff Allowance (FIT-ALL). The FIT-ALL Fund, administered by the National Grid Corporation of the Philippines, is then redistributed to eligible renewable energy developers. The FIT decreases over time, according to fixed digression rates, to mirror progressive drops in cost of technologies (Table 27).[47]

[47] IEA. Feed-in Tariff Rules. http://www.iea.org/policies/4805-feed-in-tariff-rules.

## Table 27: Feed-In-Tariffs

| Technology | Feed-In-Tariff (₱/kwh) | Signed Renewable Energy Payment Agreement (REPA) | | Effective Renewable Energy Payment Agreement (REPA) as of 5 September 2018 | |
|---|---|---|---|---|---|
| | | Number | Capacity (mw) | Number | Capacity (mw) |
| Solar | | **24** | **525.95** | **23** | **484.65** |
| | FIT 1: 9.68 | 7 | 108.90 | 6 | 67.60 |
| | FIT 2: 8.69 | 17 | 417.05 | 17 | 417.05 |
| Wind | | **7** | **426.90** | **7** | **426.90** |
| | FIT 1: 8.53 | 3 | 249.90 | 3 | 249.90 |
| | FIT 2: 7.40 | 3 | 144.00 | 3 | 144.00 |
| | Bangui 1 and 2: 5.96 | 1 | 33.00 | 1 | 33.00 |
| Hydro | | **7** | **45.50** | **6** | **43.10** |
| | FIT 1: 5.9 | 5 | 34.60 | 5 | 34.60 |
| | Digression Rate: 5.8705 | 2 | 10.90 | 1 | 8.50 |
| Biomass | | **19** | **138.13** | **16** | **131.63** |
| | FIT 1: 6.63 | 14 | 121.56 | 12 | 117.06 |
| | Digression Rate: 6.5969 | 5 | 16.56 | 4 | 14.56 |
| Total | | **57** | **1,136.48** | **52** | **1,086.28** |

FIT = feed-in-tariff.

Source: Transco. 2018 and 2019. *Feed-In-Tariff Allowance Rate Application*. ERC Case No. 2018-085. RC Expository Presentation. Manila. https://www.transco.ph/downloads/fitall/2019FIT-AllRateExpositoryPresentation-Davao.pdf.

## 4.2 Typical Risk Allocation for Public–Private Partnership Energy Projects

| Risk Category | Private | Public | Shared |
|---|---|---|---|
| Demand risk | | ✓ | |
| Revenue collection risk | | ✓ | |
| Tariff risk | | | ✓ |
| Government payment risk | | | |
| Environmental and social risk | | | ✓ |
| Land acquisition risk | | ✓ | |
| Permits | | | ✓ |
| Handover risk | | | ✓ |
| Political risk | ✓ | | |
| Regulatory risk | ✓ | | |
| Interconnection risk | | | ✓ |
| Brownfield risk: asset condition | ✓ | | |
| Grid performance risk | | ✓ | |
| Hydrology risk | | | ✓ |
| Exploration and drilling risk | | | ✓ |

✓ = Yes, × = No, NA = Not Applicable, UA = Unavailable

### 4.3 Financing Details of Public–Private Partnerships in the Energy Sector

| Parameter | 1990–2017 | 1990–2018 | 1990–2019 |
|---|---|---|---|
| PPP projects with foreign lending participation | 14 | 14 | 14 |
| PPP projects that received export credit agency/international financing institution support | 13 | 13 | 13 |
| Typical debt:equity ratio | UA | UA | UA |
| Time for financial closure | UA | | |
| Typical concession period | 20–25 years | | |
| Typical Financial Internal Rate of Return | UA | | |

✓ = Yes, × = No, NA = Not Applicable, UA = Unavailable

Source: ADB, World Bank. Infrastructure Finance, PPPs and Guarantees. Country Snapshots. Philippines. https://ppi.worldbank.org/en/snapshots/country/philippines (accessed 28 August 2020).

## 5. Challenges in the Energy Sector

- Planning of the power system requires improvement as the country's needs are not always addressed because of constraints in the transmission system and overcapacity in some areas.
- Project developers face challenges in obtaining funding, as lenders generally seek payment guarantees from the government off-takers.
- The variable nature of renewable energy technologies presents additional challenges in managing the stability of the Philippine grid and in securing a reliable supply of energy, particularly when amplified through geographic concentration such as in Negros (footnote 1).
- Effectiveness of the EVOSS system is critical to harmonize the procedures in obtaining permits and licenses.

## WATER AND WASTEWATER

| Parameter | Value | Unit |
|---|---|---|
| Improved water source access | 82.80 | % of population with access |
| Improved sanitation facilities access | 93.70 | % of population with access |
| Investment in water and sanitation with private participation | 488.80 | current $ million |
| Total number of projects with cumulative lending, grant, and technical assistance commitments in water and other urban infrastructure and services | 74 | Number |
| Total amount of cumulative lending, grant, and technical assistance commitments in water and other urban infrastructure and services | 1,258 | $ million |

✓ = Yes, × = No, NA = Not Applicable, UA = Unavailable

Sources: ADB. 2018. *Philippines, 2018–2023 — High and Inclusive Growth*. Philippines. https://www.adb.org/sites/default/files/institutional-document/456476/cps-phi-2018-2023.pdf; The Economist Intelligence Unit. Philippines. https://infrascope.eiu.com/; ADB. Cumulative Lending, Grant, and Technical Assistance Commitments. https://data.adb.org/dataset/cumulative-lending-grant-and-technical-assistance-commitments.

## 1. Contracting Agencies in Water and Wastewater Sector

The institutional arrangement for the water and sanitation (wastewater) sector in the Philippines has been complicated with overlaps between the executive, regulatory, and service provision functions. There is no central organization tasked to oversee the operations of the entire water supply and sanitation system. The entities/institutions providing water supply and sanitation services that may act as contracting agencies for PPP water and sanitation projects include the following:[48]

- **Government-owned and controlled corporations (GOCCs)** are a branch of the national government that conduct both commercial and non-commercial activities. Water supply and sanitation service providers classified as GOCCs include the following (footnote 48):
  - *Water districts* operate and maintain water supply systems in one or more provincial cities or municipalities. Local government units (LGUs) have the option to establish water districts to provide water supply and sanitation (WSS) services in their area. There are about 844 water districts created, of which, about 576 are operational (footnote 48).
  - *Metropolitan Waterworks and Sewerage System (MWSS)* was created to provide WSS services in the National Capital Region or the Metropolitan Manila including parts of the selected municipalities of the provinces of Rizal, Cavite, and Bulacan that have no water districts (footnote 48).
  - *Tourism Infrastructure and Enterprise Zone Authority (TIEZA)* provides WSS in tourist destinations declared as tourist zones, which include Boracay Island, Tagaytay Resort, and Balicasag Island, among others (footnote 48).
- **Local government units (LGUs)** are responsible for the provision of WSS services, as mandated in the Local Government Code. LGUs may provide WSS services themselves or may establish water districts to provide WSS services (footnote 48).

The GOCCs and LGUs usually operate Level III (piped water supply systems), and for Level III WSS PPPs, the contracting agencies are either GOCCs or LGUs (footnote 48).

- **Community-based organizations (CBOs)** are responsible for providing WSS services in small urban and rural areas. CBOs involved in providing WSS services include approximately 200 cooperatives; 3,100 barangay water and sanitation associations (BWSAs); and 500 rural water supply associations (RWSAs) (footnote 48).

CBOs usually operate Level I (non-piped water systems) or Level II (shared connection pipe system) water supply systems with support from national governments or nongovernment organizations (NGOs). For Levels I and II WSS PPPs, the contracting agencies are the CBOs (footnote 48).

## 2. Water and Wastewater Sector Laws and Regulations

Originally, the WSS services in the Philippines were governed through a centralized system, which have been decentralized over the years through various government initiatives:

- The **Republic Act 1383, 1955** formed the National Waterworks and Sewerage Authority (NAWASA). It had jurisdiction, supervision, and control over all territories served by existing government-owned

[48] World Bank. 2016. *Private Sector Provision of Water and Sanitation Services in Rural Areas and Small Towns: The Role of the Public Sector—Country Report: Philippines.* Manila. https://www.wsp.org/sites/wsp/files/publications/WSP%20SPI%20Country%20Report%20-%20Philippines%20final.pdf.

waterworks, and sewerage and drainage systems within the boundaries of cities, municipalities, and municipal districts in the Philippines, at the time.

- The **Republic Act 6234, 1971** (the **MWSS Charter**) superseded the NAWASA. The water sector was decentralized by dissolving the NAWASA and forming the Metropolitan Waterworks and Sewerage System (MWSS). It is responsible for service provision in Metro Manila. Other municipal and provincial water and sewerage systems in about 1,500 cities and towns became the responsibilities of the local governments(footnote 48).
- The **Presidential Decree 198, 1973** or the **Provincial Water Utilities Act** further strengthens the decentralized system by introducing a new management model for urban water supply and by encouraging LGUs to form water utilities called "water districts." A water district operates with a certain degree of autonomy from LGUs. The same Presidential Decree also established the Local Water Utilities Administration (LWUA), which is a GOCC with a specialized lending function to promote and oversee the development of water supply systems in provincial cities and municipalities outside of Metropolitan Manila (footnote 48).
- The **Presidential Decree 1067, 1976**, or more known as the Water Code of the Philippines, governs the water resource allocation, priority, and use as well as the water supply, distribution, and pricing (footnote 48).
- The **Local Government Code of 1991** reinforces that the LGUs are responsible for the delivery of basic services including water supply and sanitation (footnote 48).

Figure 46 depicts the legal and regulatory framework governing WSS services in the Philippines. The key policy provisions for water supply and sanitation that have an impact on private sector participation include the following:

**Figure 46: Legal and Regulatory Framework for Water Supply and Sanitation Services**

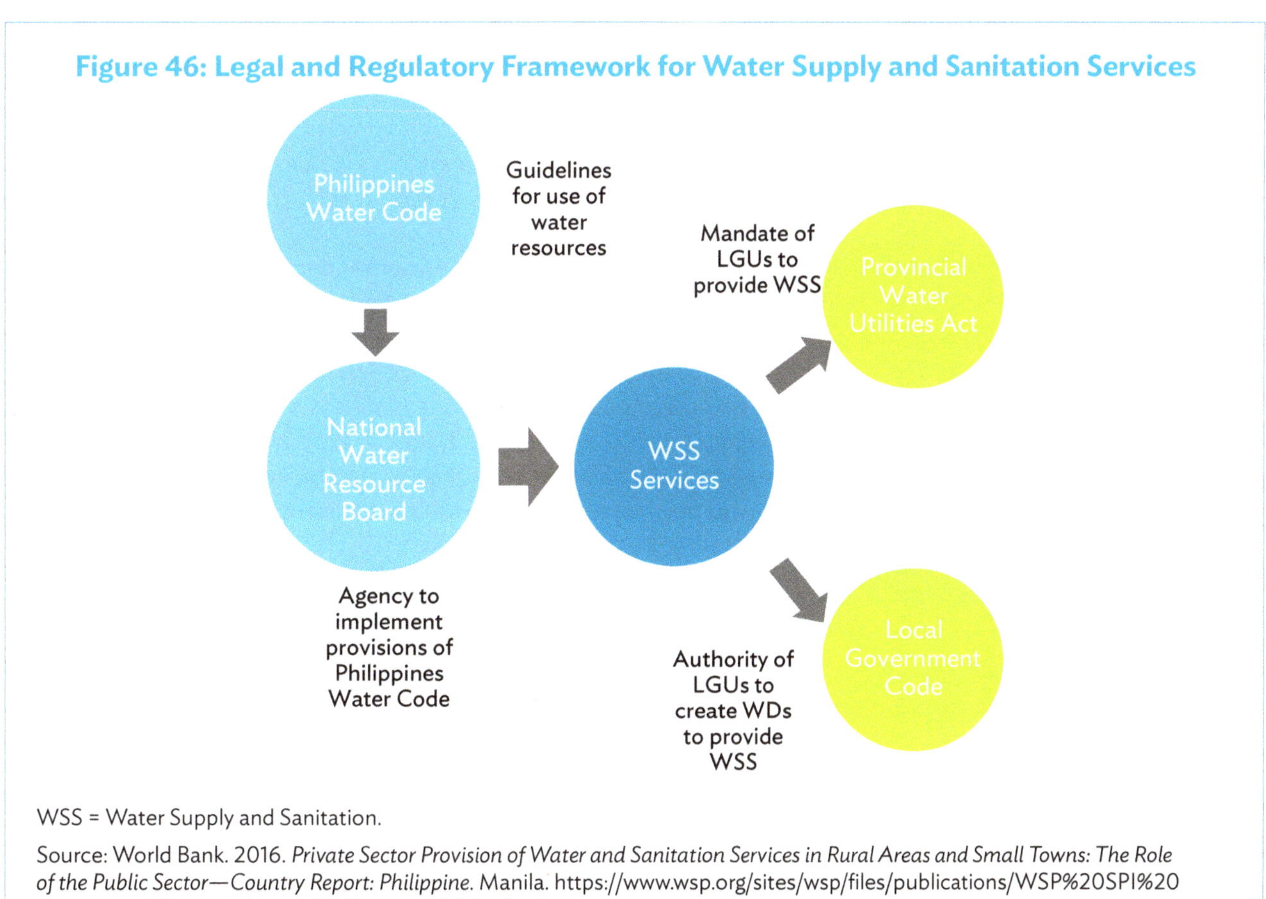


WSS = Water Supply and Sanitation.

Source: World Bank. 2016. *Private Sector Provision of Water and Sanitation Services in Rural Areas and Small Towns: The Role of the Public Sector—Country Report: Philippine.* Manila. https://www.wsp.org/sites/wsp/files/publications/WSP%20SPI%20Country%20Report%20-%20Philippines%20final.pdf.

**Water Code of the Philippines (Presidential Decree 1067, 1976).** Even though the private sector can obtain water abstraction rights, there are restrictions as to who can apply for a permit. As per the Philippines' Water Code (Presidential Decree 1067), only the following groups may apply for a water permit from the National Water Resources Board (NWRB) (footnote 1):

- Citizens of the Philippines
- Duly registered cooperatives, associations, or corporations organized under the laws of the Philippines, at least 60% of the capital of which is owned by citizens of the Philippines
- GOCCs and other government entities and/or instrumentalities

The regulations for raw water extraction are also detailed in the Philippines' Water Code. Treated effluent must comply with quality standards prescribed by the Department of Environment and Natural Resources (DENR) before release.

**National Water Resource Board (Executive Order 124-A-1974).** The NWRB is tasked to advise the National Economic and Development Authority (NEDA) on matters relating to water resources development projects and programs, and recommend general policies and guidelines as well as short- and long-term plans and programs for water resources development (footnote 48).

**Local Government Code of the Philippines (Republic Act 7160, 1991).** LGUs are responsible to provide basic services to the community and are authorized to charge fees for such services. LGUs are also authorized to delegate the responsibility of infrastructure development and public service provision related to WSS services to other institutions or agencies, including the private sector entities. LGUs may enter into contracts with other legal entities, including joint ventures and other forms of cooperative arrangements with people and other nongovernment entities to provide basic services and other developments that will benefit the communities. The Local Government Code authorizes all LGUs to participate in a PPP program for the development of various infrastructure projects in their jurisdictions, including water supply and sanitation facilities and service provision (footnote 48).

**Provincial Water Utilities Act (Presidential Decree 198, 1973).** LGUs are allowed to establish local water districts, which serve as local water utilities. The water districts have the right of acquiring, installing, improving, maintaining, and operating water supply and distribution systems for domestic, industrial, municipal, and agricultural uses for residents and lands within the boundaries of such districts. They also have the right of providing, maintaining, and operating wastewater collection and treatment and disposal facilities, and conducting other functions and operations incidental to water resource development, utilization, and disposal within such districts. To perform their functions, the water districts have the authority to enter into contracts and/or partnerships with any person or legal entities including the private sector entities (footnote 48).

| Parameter | 2016 | 2017 | 2018 |
|---|---|---|---|
| Can the private sector be given water abstraction rights? | ✓ | ✓ | ✓ |
| Are there regulations in place on raw water extraction? | ✓ | ✓ | ✓ |
| Are there regulations in place on the release of treated effluents? | ✓ | ✓ | ✓ |

✓ = Yes, × = No, NA = Not Applicable, UA = Unavailable

Source: World Bank. 2016. *Private Sector Provision of Water and Sanitation Services in Rural Areas and Small Towns: The Role of the Public Sector—Country Report: Philippines*. Manila. https://www.wsp.org/sites/wsp/files/publications/WSP%20SPI%20Country%20Report%20-%20Philippines%20final.pdf

The executive functions, such as policy formulation and general support to the sector in terms of financial and technical support, capacity building, and monitoring, are performed by the Department of the Interior and Local Government (DILG), the Department of Public Works and Highway (DPWH), the Department of Environment and Natural Resources (DENR), and the Department of Health (DOH).

The regulatory functions, such as issuing licenses or permits to abstract water or to operate a water supply and sanitation system, and review and approvals of tariffs, are performed by the Local Water Utilities Administration (LWUA), the National Water Resources Board (NWRB), and the Metropolitan Waterworks and Sewerage Systems (MWSS). The Local Government Code allows self-regulation for the LGUs (footnote 48).

### Table 28: Institutions Performing Executive and Regulatory Functions in the Water and Wastewater Sector

| Agency | Mandate | Functions |
|---|---|---|
| **Institutions performing executive functions** | | |
| **Department of the Interior and Local Government (DILG)** | Strengthen local governments capability in effective delivery of basic services to the community | Within the organizational structure of the DILG is the Water Supply and Sanitation Program Management Office (WSSPMO), under the Office of Project Development Services (OPDS). Its main responsibility is to support the provision of water supply and sanitation services by the local government units (LGUs). The DILG defines and enforces quality and performance standards for the LGU-operated water system. However, the LGUs retain the responsibilities for planning, financing, and regulating the water supply. |
| **Department of Public Works and Highway (DPWH)** | Undertake the planning of infrastructure, including water resources projects and other public works, and the design, construction, and maintenance of national roads and bridges, and major flood control systems. | The DPWH is the umbrella department for the Local Water Utilities Administration (LWUA). The department acts as the lead agency for an inter-agency committee to develop a water resources sector master plan that will effectively address issues and challenges in the water sector in the country. The DPWH also provides support for the improvement of LGU-operated water supply and sanitation system by developing additional water sources to increase the supply capacity in the rural areas, in particular the Level II system (shared connection pipe system). |
| **Department of Environment and Natural Resources (DENR)** | Govern and supervise the exploration, development, utilization, and conservation of the country's natural resources. | The DENR's primary role in the water supply and sanitation sector is to monitor effluent from the wastewater/septage treatment plants prior to its disposal to natural waterways, like rivers, lake, and artificial impounding water. The DENR also sets the monitoring parameters and effluent standards that water supply and sanitation service providers must comply with. |
| **Department of Health (DOH)** | Ensure access to public health services through the provision of quality health care, and the regulation of all health services and products. | In general, the DOH provides leadership and capacity building in health services and administers specific services. The DOH develops national plans, technical standards, and guidelines on health. It also regulates all health services and products and provides special tertiary health care services and technical assistance to health providers and stakeholders. For the water supply and sanitation sector, the DOH provides facilities to monitor and regulate the water quality being distributed to all water consumers by the water and sanitation service provider, and enforces the Philippine National Standards for Drinking Water (PNSDW). |

*continued on next page*

*continued from previous page*

| Agency | Mandate | Functions |
|---|---|---|
| **Institutions performing regulatory functions** | | |
| **National Water Resources Board (NWRB)** | Ensure the optimum exploitation, utilization, development, conservation, and protection of the country's water resource, consistent with the principles of Integrated Water Resource Management. | The NWRB is the main regulatory agency for the water sector. Its regulatory functions include the issuance of water permits for the appropriation and use of water, and the adjudication of disputes regarding the use of water.<br>In terms of economic regulation, the NWRB is tasked to regulate (review and approve) water supply tariffs charged by private operators and private service providers. The NWRB's authority to approve and review the water districts' tariffs was transferred to LWUA.<br>NWRB is also responsible for the issuance of Certificate of Public Convenience (CPC) and Certificate of Public Convenience and Necessity (CPCN)—the permits to provide public services to any private water operators. |
| **Local Water Utilities Administration (LWUA)** | Promote and oversee the development of water supply systems in provincial cities and municipalities outside of Metropolitan Manila, and review tariff proposals from water districts | The LWUA is a government-owned and controlled corporation (GOCC) with a specialized lending function to the water districts. It allocates and re-lends the funds to water districts at competitive terms. Some funds are extended as grants. Under recent enhancements to its charter, the LWUA has been tasked to assist water districts graduate into creditworthy status and access non-traditional sources of funds.<br>The LWUA regulates water districts in terms of tariff setting (including publishing a guideline on how to calculate tariffs, and reviewing and approving tariffs); establish and monitor key performance indicators and business efficiency measures, such as service coverage and collection efficiency; and regulates the prevailing pressure in the distribution system, the Non-Revenue Water (NRW).<br>It also provides institutional development assistance in the form of advisory and managerial services, and transfers policy-making, managerial, and technical competence to water districts. |
| **Metropolitan Waterworks and Sewerage Systems (MWSS)** | Ensure an uninterrupted and adequate supply and distribution of potable water for domestic and other purposes and the proper operation and maintenance of sewerage systems in Metro Manila and parts of the provinces of Cavite, Rizal, and Bulacan. | The MWSS has transferred the operation and management of the entire water supply and sewerage system for 25 years to its two water concessionaires in the east and west zones of Metropolitan Manila.<br>The MWSS Regulatory Office (MWSS-RO) is a separate unit within MWSS tasked with regulating the two concessionaires through contracts.<br>The regulatory functions performed by the MWSS-RO includes tariff reviews and approvals, and performance monitoring in accordance to the contract terms. |

DENR = Department of Environment and Natural Resources, DILG = Department of the Interior and Local Government, DOH = Department of Health, DPWH = Department of Public, LGU = local government unit, LWUA = Local Water Utilities Administration, Works and Highways, MWSS = Metropolitan Waterworks and Sewerage System, MWSS-RO = MWSS Regulatory Office, NWRB = National Water, Resources Board.

Source: World Bank. 2016. *Private Sector Provision of Water and Sanitation Services in Rural Areas and Small Towns: The Role of the Public Sector—Country Report: Philippines*. Manila. https://www.wsp.org/sites/wsp/files/publications/WSP%20SPI%20Country%20Report%20-%20Philippines%20final.pdf

## 2.1 Foreign Investment Restrictions in the Water and Wastewater Sector

The maximum equity investment allowed for foreign investors in greenfield projects is 40% (footnote 33).

| Parameter | 2017 | 2018 | 2019 |
|---|---|---|---|
| Maximum allowed foreign ownership of equity in greenfield projects | | | |
| Bulk water supply and treatment | 40% | 40% | 40% |
| Water distribution | 40% | 40% | 40% |
| Wastewater treatment | 40% | 40% | 40% |
| Wastewater collection | 40% | 40% | 40% |

## 2.2 Standard Contracts in the Water and Wastewater Sector

| Type of Contract | |
|---|---|
| PPP/concession agreement | × |
| Bulk water supply agreement | × |
| Performance-based operation and maintenance contract | × |
| Engineering procurement and construction contract | × |

✓ = Yes, × = No, NA = Not Applicable, UA = Unavailable

Source: ADB. 2019. *Public–Private Partnership Monitor.* Second Edition. Manila. https://www.adb.org/sites/default/files/publication/509426/ppp-monitor-second-edition.pdf.

# 3. Water and Wastewater Sector Master Plan

The Philippine Water Supply Sector Roadmap (PWSSR) is the key policy and planning document for the water supply sector in the Philippines. The Philippine Sustainable Sanitation Roadmap and Plan (PSSR and PSSP) is for the sanitation sector (footnote 48).

The PWSSR has the overall objective of providing "access to safe, adequate and sustainable water for all" with the vision:

> *"By 2025, universal access coverage and sustainable utility operations have been attained, that existing formal/legal utilities continue to expand coverage at par with population growth, and that all water service providers shall have been regulated."*

The PSSR has the overall objective of having "a clean and healthy Philippines through safe, adequate and sustainable sanitation for all" with the vision:

> *"By 2028, universal access to safe and adequate sanitary facilities, behavior change and proper hygiene practices will have become accepted norms within families and communities, and mechanisms for sustainable sanitation (i.e., link with health, agriculture, and environment) will have been institutionalized."*

The other critical policy and planning document for the WSS sector in the Philippines is the National Sewerage and Septage Management Program (NSSMP). The objective of the NSSMP is for all LGUs to have septage management programs serving their urban barangays. For sewerage, the NSSMP is targeting 17 highly urbanized cities outside Metro Manila, serving 50% of urban barangays (footnote 48).

To achieve these objectives and vision, various entities responsible for the WSS service delivery in the Philippines are implementing various WSS infrastructure development projects. Table 29 shows the WSS projects proposed to be implemented through the PPP route based on NEDA's *Revised List of Infrastructure Flagship Projects* (published on 17 February 2020).

**Table 29: Public–Private Partnership Water Supply and Sanitation Projects**

| No. | Project Name | Implementing Agency | Investment | | Status |
|---|---|---|---|---|---|
| | | | ($ million) | (₱ million) | |
| 1 | Kanan Dam Project | MWSS | 1,105 | 56,000 | Under preparation, advanced feasibility studies |
| 2 | Wawa Bulk Water Supply Project | MWSS | 395 | 20,000 | Under pre-construction |

₱1 = $0.01974

MWSS = Metropolitan Waterworks and Sewerage System.

Source: Public–Private Partnership Center. List of Projects. https://ppp.gov.ph/list-of-projects/ (accessed 28 August 2020); Public–Private Partnership Center. 2019. *Investment Opportunities*. Manila. https://ppp.gov.ph/investors-corner/investment-opportunities-2/.

## 3.1 Projects under Preparation and Procurement in the Water and Wastewater Sector

Figure 47 presents the number of PPP projects which are under preparation and procurement in the Philippines' water and wastewater sector.

**Figure 47: Public–Private Partnership Water and Wastewater Projects under Preparation and Procurement**

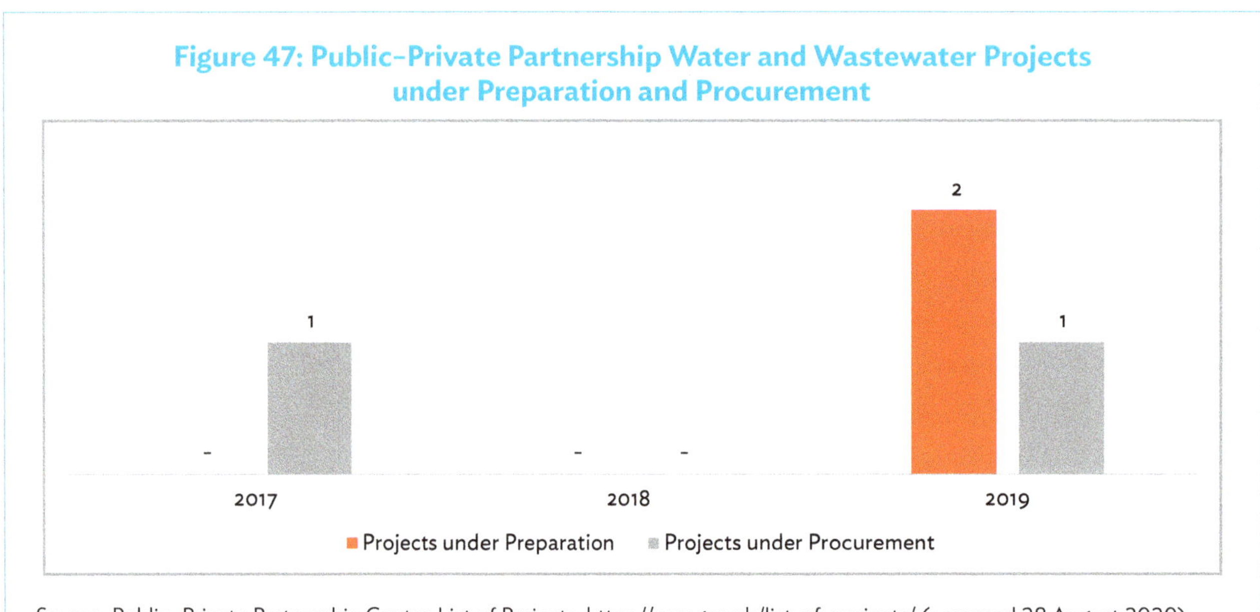


Source: Public–Private Partnership Center. List of Projects. https://ppp.gov.ph/list-of-projects/ (accessed 28 August 2020); Public–Private Partnership Center. 2019. *Investment Opportunities*. Manila. https://ppp.gov.ph/investors-corner/investment-opportunities-2/.

### Table 30: Public–Private Partnership Water Supply and Sanitation Projects under Preparation

| No. | Project Name | Implementing Agency | Investment ($ million) | Investment (₱ million) | Status |
|---|---|---|---|---|---|
| 1 | Bislig City Bulk Water Supply and Septage Project | Bislig City Water District | TBD | TBD | Development – Undergoing project conceptualization |
| 2 | Ormoc City Water Supply System Project | City Government of Ormoc | TBD | TBD | Development – undergoing studies |

TBD = To be decided.

Source: Public–Private Partnership Center. List of Projects. https://ppp.gov.ph/list-of-projects/ (accessed 28 August 2020); Public–Private Partnership Center. 2019. *Investment Opportunities*. Manila. https://ppp.gov.ph/investors-corner/investment-opportunities-2/.

### Table 31: Public–Private Partnership Water Supply and Sanitation Projects under Procurement

| No. | Project Name | Implementing Agency | Estimated Project Cost ($ million) | Estimated Project Cost (₱ million) |
|---|---|---|---|---|
| 1 | Baggao Water Supply Project | Municipal Government of Baggao | 1.67 | 84 |

₱1 = $0.01974

Source: Public–Private Partnership Center. List of Projects. https://ppp.gov.ph/list-of-projects/ (accessed 28 August 2020); Public–Private Partnership Center. 2019. *Investment Opportunities*. Manila. https://ppp.gov.ph/investors-corner/investment-opportunities-2/.

## 4. Features of Past Public–Private Partnership Projects in the Water and Wastewater Sector

Figure 48 shows the number of PPP projects procured through various modes including direct appointment, unsolicited bids, and competitive bids in the Philippines' water and wastewater sector.

### Figure 48: Modes of Procurement for Public–Private Partnership Water and Wastewater Projects

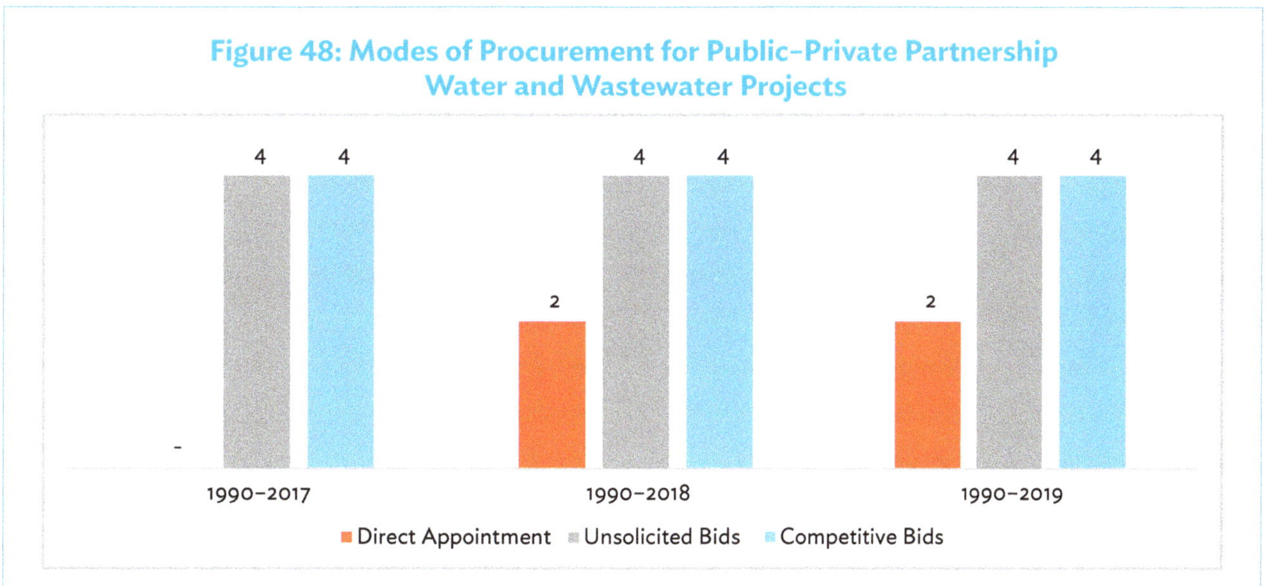


Note: Only active projects are considered in the above graph.

Source: ADB, World Bank. Infrastructure Finance, PPPs and Guarantees. Country Snapshots. Philippines. https://ppi.worldbank.org/en/snapshots/country/philippines (accessed 28 August 2020).

Figure 49 presents the number of PPP projects which have reached financial closure and the total value of those projects in the Philippines' water and wastewater sector.

**Figure 49: Public–Private Partnership Water and Wastewater Projects Reaching Financial Closure**

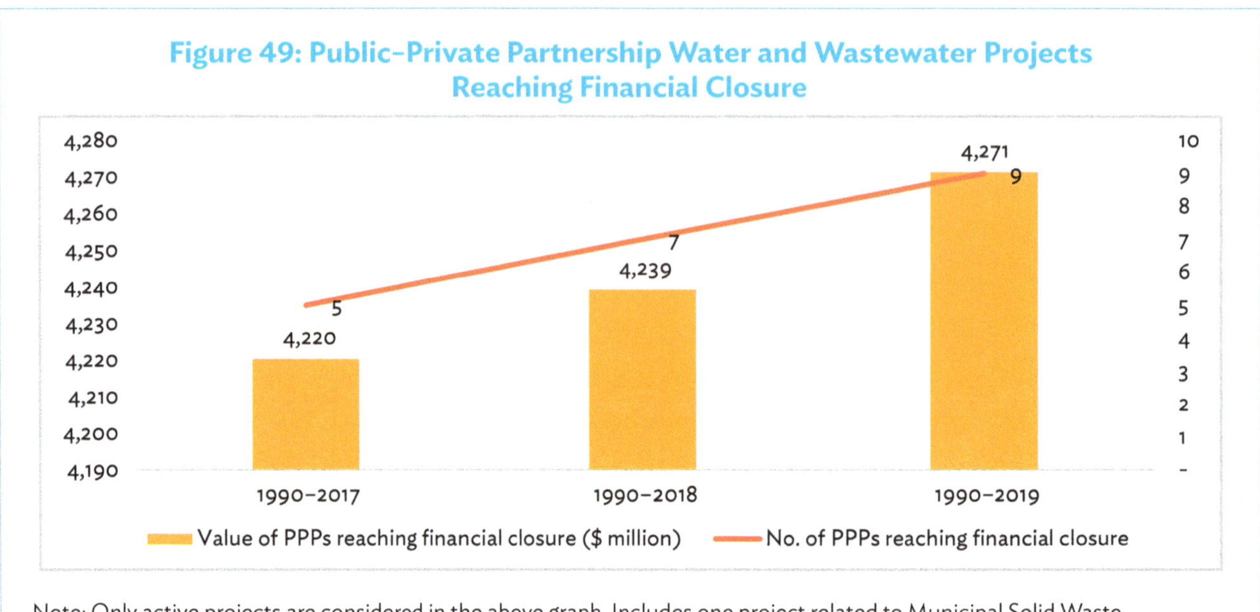


Note: Only active projects are considered in the above graph. Includes one project related to Municipal Solid Waste

Source: ADB, World Bank. Infrastructure Finance, PPPs and Guarantees. Country Snapshots. Philippines. https://ppi.worldbank.org/en/snapshots/country/philippines (accessed 28 August 2020).

Figure 50 shows the number of PPP projects which have received foreign sponsor participation in the Philippines' water and wastewater sector.

**Figure 50: Public–Private Partnership Water and Wastewater Projects with Foreign Sponsor Participation**

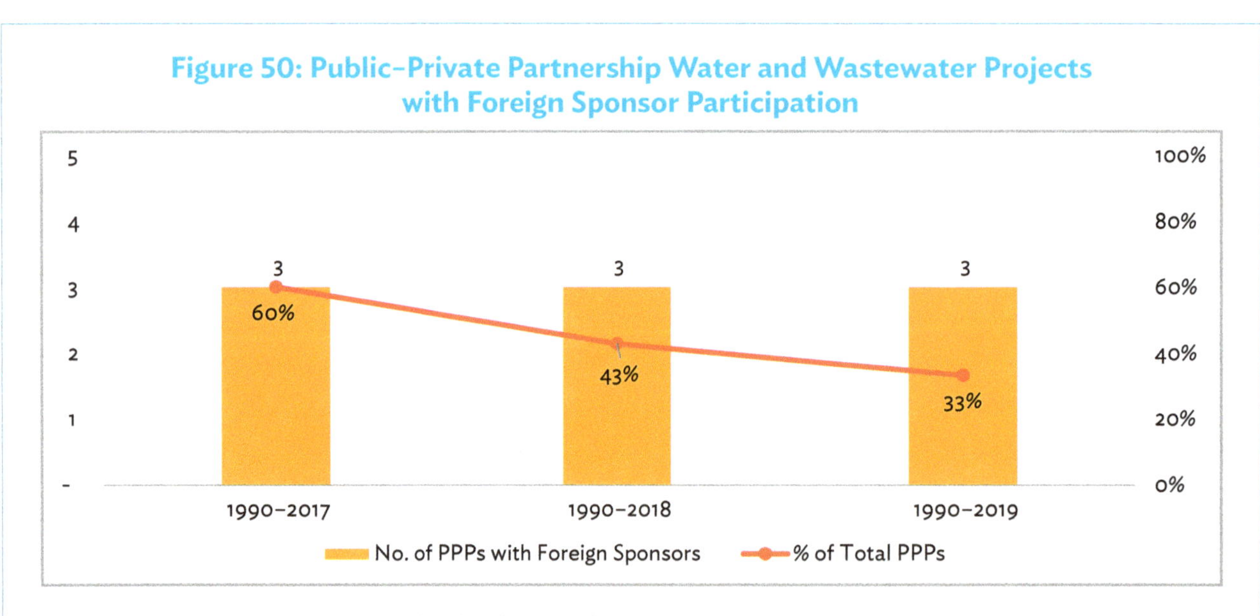


Note: Only active projects are considered in the above graph.

Source: ADB, World Bank. Infrastructure Finance, PPPs and Guarantees. Country Snapshots. Philippines. https://ppi.worldbank.org/en/snapshots/country/philippines (accessed 28 August 2020).

Figure 51 presents the number of PPP projects which have received government support including viability gap funding (VGF) mechanism, government guarantees, and availability/performance payment in the Philippines' water and wastewater sector.

### Figure 51: Government Support for Public–Private Partnership Water and Wastewater Projects

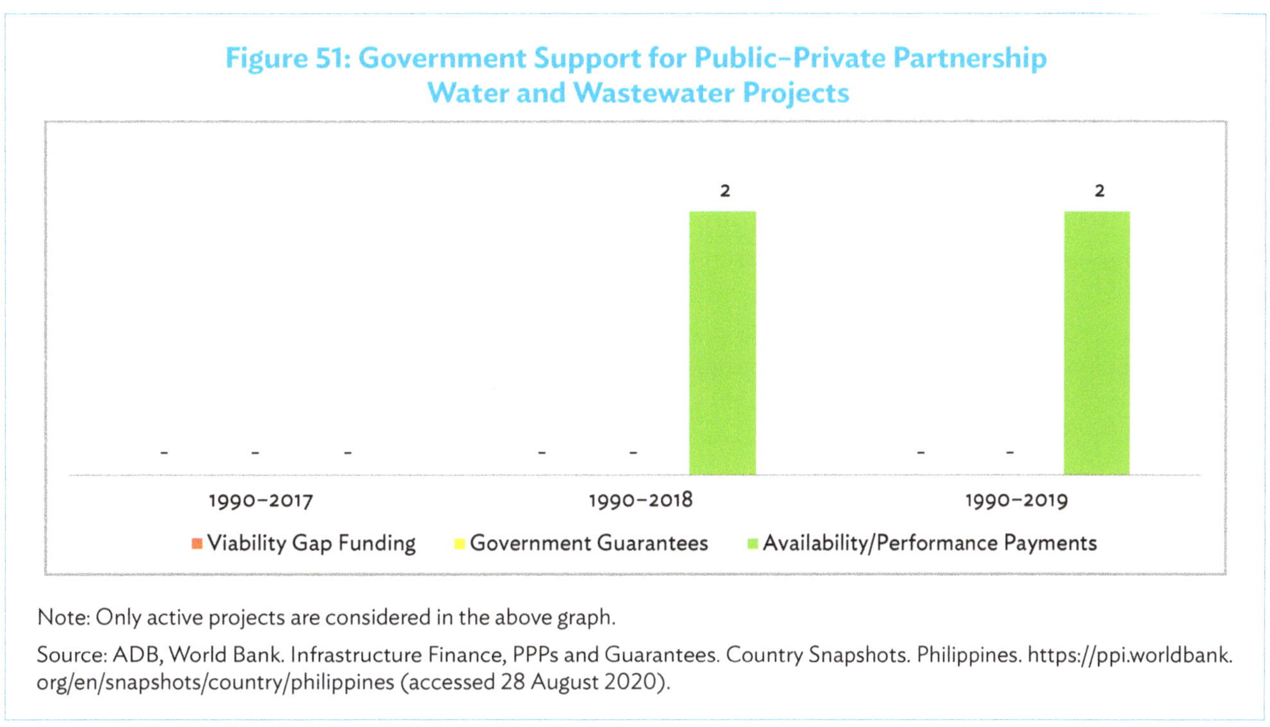


Note: Only active projects are considered in the above graph.

Source: ADB, World Bank. Infrastructure Finance, PPPs and Guarantees. Country Snapshots. Philippines. https://ppi.worldbank.org/en/snapshots/country/philippines (accessed 28 August 2020).

Figure 52 presents the number of PPP projects which have received payment in the form of user charges and government pay (off-take) in the Philippines' water and wastewater sector.

### Figure 52: Payment Mechanisms for Public–Private Partnership Water and Wastewater Projects

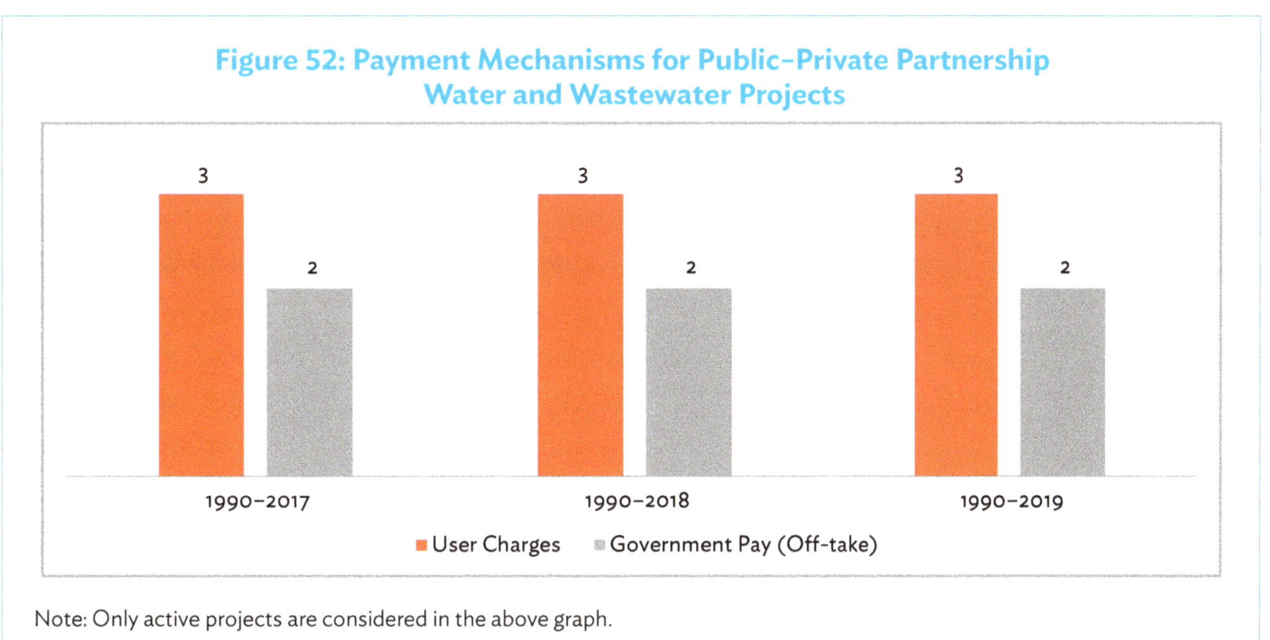


Note: Only active projects are considered in the above graph.

Source: ADB, World Bank. Infrastructure Finance, PPPs and Guarantees. Country Snapshots. Philippines. https://ppi.worldbank.org/en/snapshots/country/philippines (accessed 28 August 2020).

## 4.1 Tariffs in the Water and Wastewater Sector

The tariff structure of the water system varies widely across the country. The tariff structure is similar in water districts and Metro Manila, with an average tariff for the first 10 cubic meters and increasing tariffs for additional consumption (Table 32 and Table 33). For LGU-operated systems, the tariff levels and structures vary widely because most connections are not metered, and LGUs offer different levels of service. The NWRB has issued a document providing basic guidelines on tariff setting to improve cost recovery and regulation (footnote 1).

The tariff levels must be approved by the relevant regulatory authorities based on a range of factors. The Metropolitan Waterworks and Sewerage System is responsible for regulating tariffs in Metro Manila, the Local Water Utilities Administration in water districts, and the NWRB for private operators and other service providers (footnote 1).

For the concession agreements with the Manila Water Company, there are three tariff adjustment mechanisms: (i) inflation adjustment—annual adjustment based on inflation, (ii) extraordinary price adjustment—compensation for extraordinary events (i.e., change in law, government regulation), and (iii) rate rebasing—every 5 years based on historic and future cash flows (footnote 1).

### Table 32: Average Water Tariff in Water Districts in the Philippines, 2015

| Water Consumption (volume in m³) | $/m³ | ₱/m³ |
|---|---|---|
| 0 – 10 | 3.86) | 195.64 |
| 11 – 20 | 0.43 | 21.90 |
| 21 – 30 | 0.47 | 23.89 |
| 31 – 40 | 0.53 | 26.88 |
| 41 – 50 | 0.59 | 29.87 |
| 51 and above | 0.60 | 30.37 |

₱1 = $0.01974, m³ = cubic meter

Note: No further updates to these values have been made available.

Source: IBNET. 2020. IBNET Database. https://database.ib-net.org/DefaultNew.aspx. (accessed 28 August 2020).

### Table 33: Current Domestic Water Tariff in Metro Manila, 2016

| Water Consumption (volume in m³) | Manila Water | | Maynilad | |
|---|---|---|---|---|
| | $/m³ | ₱/m³ | $/m³ | ₱/m³ |
| 0 – 10 | $ 1.92 per connection | ₱ 97.07 per connection | $ 2.85 per connection | ₱ 144.36 per connection |
| 10 – 20 | 0.24 | 11.95 | 0.34 | 17.42 |
| 20 – 40 | 0.44 | 22.4 | 0.66 | 33.35 |
| 40 – 60 | 0.58 | 29.37 | 0.86 | 43.81 |
| 60 – 80 | 0.68 | 34.35 | 1.01 | 51.27 |
| 80 – 100 | 0.75 | 37.83 | 1.06 | 53.76 |

₱1 = $0.01974, m³ = cubic meter

Source: Manila Water Company, Maynilad Water Services. https://www.mayniladwater.com.ph/maynilad-to-adjust-water-tariff-by-april/.

## 4.2 Typical Risk Allocation for Public–Private Partnership Projects in Water and Wastewater Sector

### Typical Risk Allocation Arrangements in Public–Private Partnership Water Concession Contracts

| Risk Type | Private | Public | Shared | Comments |
|---|---|---|---|---|
| Demand | ✓ | | | |
| Revenue collection | ✓ | | | |
| Tariff | ✓ | | | |
| Government payment | ✓ | | | |
| Environment and social | | | ✓ | |
| Land acquisition | ✓ | ✓ | | Public, if solicited.<br>Private, if unsolicited. |
| Interface | | | ✓ | |
| Handover | | | ✓ | |
| Political | | | ✓ | |
| Foreign exchange (FOREX) | | | ✓ | |

Source: Government of the Philippines, Investment Coordination Committee. 2014. Generic Preferred Risk Allocation Matrix (GPRAM). Manila. https://ppp.gov.ph/wp-content/uploads/2015/04/Generic-Preferred-Risk-Allocation-Matrix.pdf; Government of the Philippines, National Economy and Development Authority. 2009. Structuring Public–Private Partnerships (PPPs). Manila. http://www.neda.gov.ph/wp-content/uploads/2014/01/Structuring-Public-Private-Partnerships-PPPs-Handbook.pdf.

### Typical Risk Allocation Arrangements in Public–Private Partnership Bulk Water Supply Contracts

| Risk Type | Private | Public | Shared | Comments |
|---|---|---|---|---|
| Demand | | ✓ | | |
| Revenue collection | | ✓ | | |
| Tariff | | ✓ | | BOT project agreements have generally been drafted with provision for index-linked tariff. |
| Government payment | ✓ | | | |
| Environment and social | | | ✓ | |
| Land acquisition | ✓ | ✓ | | Public, if solicited.<br>Private, if unsolicited. |
| Interface | | | ✓ | |
| Handover | | | ✓ | |
| Political | | | ✓ | |
| Foreign exchange (FOREX) | ✓ | | ✓ | As per the Generic Preferred Risk Allocation Matrix—private sector would bear the risk.<br>As per the National Economic and Development Authority's structured PPP, the risk is shared (the public entity to assume a portion of the risk by allowing the total or partial indexing of bulk water rate to exchange rate, and the private entity to assume the remaining risk). |

### 4.3 Financing Details of Public–Private Partnerships in Water and Wastewater Sector

| Parameter | 1990–2017 | 1990–2018 | 1990–2019 |
|---|---|---|---|
| PPP projects with foreign lending participation | UA | UA | UA |
| PPP projects that received export credit agency/international financing institution support | 2 | 2 | 2 |
| Typical debt:equity ratio | 70:30 | 70:30 | 70:30 |
| Time for financial closure | 6 – 12 months | | |
| Typical concession period | 25 – 30 years | | |
| Typical Financial Internal Rate of Return | UA | | |

✓ = Yes, × = No, NA = Not Applicable, UA = Unavailable

Source: ADB, World Bank. Infrastructure Finance, PPPs and Guarantees. Country Snapshots. Philippines. https://ppi.worldbank.org/en/snapshots/country/philippines (accessed 28 August 2020).

## 5. Challenges in Water and Wastewater Sector

- The cap of 40% on foreign investment and ownership hinders competition and has been a challenge to the development of PPPs in this sector.
- The LGUs are constrained with limited technical resources and budgets for project preparation. Also, guidelines for LGUs to form joint ventures with the private sectors for PPP projects are not in place.
- In LGU projects, tariffs levels are too low for cost recovery.
- The institutional framework is fragmented and there are multiple regulatory agencies for this sector.
- Expenses for environmental and social studies for water project investment are not recoverable through the rate rebasing mechanism under the concession agreements, which also hinders water investment (footnote 1).

## SOCIAL INFRASTRUCTURE

| Parameter | Value | Unit |
|---|---|---|
| Government expenditure on education | 2.80 | % of GDP |
| Education spending as % of government spending | 13.21 | % |
| Primary school gross enrollment | 113.00 | % |
| Adult literacy rate | 96.30 | % |
| Total number of projects with cumulative lending, grant, and technical assistance commitments in the education sector | 42.00 | Number |
| Total amount of cumulative lending, grant, and technical assistance commitments in the education sector | 1,748.93 | $ million |
| Total health expenditure | 4.70 | % of GDP |
| Health spending per capita | 132.90 | $ |
| Maternal mortality ratio (modelled estimates per 100,000 live births) | 114.00 | (per 100,000 live births) |
| Infant mortality rate | 21.00 | (below 1 year/per 1,000 live births) |

*continued on next page*

*continued from previous page*

| Parameter | Value | Unit |
|---|---|---|
| Life expectancy at birth | 68.30 | (years) |
| Child malnutrition | 21.50 | (% below 5 years old) |
| Total number of projects with cumulative lending, grant, and technical assistance commitments in the health sector | 26 | Number |
| Total amount of cumulative lending, grant, and technical assistance commitments in the health sector | 374 | $ million |
| Existing no. of affordable housing units | UA | Number |
| Affordable housing gap | UA | |

✓ = Yes, × = No, NA = Not Applicable, UA = Unavailable

GDP = gross domestic product.

Sources: The Economist Intelligence Unit. Philippines. https://infrascope.eiu.com/; The Global Economy. Education Spending, Percent of Government Spending—Country Rankings. https://www.theglobaleconomy.com/rankings/Education_spending_percent_of_government_spending/; ADB. 2018. *Philippines, 2018–2023—High and Inclusive Growth*. Philippines. https://www.adb.org/sites/default/files/institutional-document/456476/cps-phi-2018-2023.pdf; The Global Economy. Health Spending per Capita—Country Rankings. https://www.theglobaleconomy.com/rankings/Health_spending_per_capita/; ADB. Cumulative Lending, Grant, and Technical Assistance Commitments. https://data.adb.org/dataset/cumulative-lending-grant-and-technical-assistance-commitments.

## 1. Contracting Agencies in the Social Infrastructure Sector

Social infrastructure typically includes projects concerning healthcare infrastructure and services, education infrastructure and services, social housing, prisons and correction centers, government buildings, and sports and leisure facilities. Various departments, bureaus, offices, commissions, authorities, or agencies of the national government (including GOCCs); government financial institutions; state universities and colleges; and LGUs are authorized to enter into PPP contracts. The following departments are currently engaged in implementing one or more projects in the social infrastructure PPP pipeline (footnote 1):

- Department of Health (healthcare)
- Department of Education (education)
- University of the Philippines (education, healthcare, and hospital facilities)
- Cagayan State University (education)
- Bicol University (education)
- Bureau of Corrections (justice)
- Department of Justice (justice)
- Department of Tourism (recreation and culture)
- Tourism Infrastructure and Enterprise Zone Authority (recreation and culture)
- Marikina City Government (parking and commercial building)
- City Government of Panabo, Davao del Norte (government building – town center)
- Provincial Government of Iloilo (commercial building – meat processing facility)
- Provincial Government of Iloilo (commercial building – public market)

# 2. Social Infrastructure Sector Laws and Regulations

## 2.1 Healthcare Sector Regulations

The delivery of healthcare services is governed by the recently enacted Universal Health Care (UHC) Law (i.e., Republic Act 11223). The UHC Law ensures that all Filipino citizens have access to a comprehensive set of health services without financial hardship, by automatically enrolling all Filipinos in PhilHealth's National Health Insurance Program (NHIP). The UHC Law aims to help achieve three critical healthcare sector objectives of the government: (i) achieving universal and sustainable PhilHealth membership; (ii) upgrading and modernizing government health facilities through the Health Facilities Enhancement Program; and (iii) fortifying efforts to achieve the Millennium Development Goal (MDG) targets.[49]

PPPs in the delivery of healthcare services in the Philippines is governed by the Philippine Build–Operate–and–Transfer (BOT) Law (Republic Act 7718). Private healthcare provides a large share of the healthcare services in the Philippines.

Various institutions responsible for different functions in the Philippines healthcare sector are as follows (footnote 49):

- The **Department of Health (DOH)** is the national technical authority on health, and provides national policy direction and strategic plans, regulatory services, standards and guidelines for health, and highly specialized and specific tertiary-level hospital services. It provides leadership, technical assistance, capacity building, and linkages and coordination with other national government agencies, LGUs, and private entities in implementing health policies. The DOH is in charge of licensing hospitals, laboratories, and other health facilities through the Health Facilities and Service Regulatory Bureau (HFSRB) and health products through the Food and Drug Administration (FDA).
- The **LGUs** (i.e., provincial, city, and municipal governments) are responsible for managing and implementing local health programs and services.
- Mindanao, a distinct subnational entity called the Autonomous Region in Muslim Mindanao (ARMM), has its own **regional Department of Health**, which directly administers the provincial, city and municipal health offices, and the provincial and district hospitals within ARMM.
- The **Insurance Commission under the Department of Finance** regulates and supervises the operations of private insurance companies, including health insurance and pre-need companies as well as mutual benefit associations. Health Maintenance Organizations (HMOs) are also regulated by the Insurance Commission.
- The **Department of National Defense** operates and supervises the military hospitals.

49 SEARO. 2017. Executive Summary. Philippines. http://www.searo.who.int/entity/asia_pacific_observatory/publications/hits/executive_summary_philippines_hit_ii.pdf?ua=1.

## 2.2 Education Sector Regulations

PPPs in the delivery of education services in the Philippines is governed by the Philippine Build–Operate–and–Transfer (BOT) Law (Republic Act 7718), and the Expanded Government Assistance to Students and Teachers in Private Education Act (Republic Act 8545). The Education Service Contracting (ESC) Program, a hallmark PPP Program of the Government of Philippines that provides school access for public students via private school places, has been extended under Republic Act 8545 to recognize the complementary roles of public and private schools. The ESC Program aims to improve access to quality basic education at the secondary level through government extension of financial assistance to "poor but deserving" elementary school graduates.

Education in the Philippines is administered and regulated by three different government agencies, each exercising largely exclusive jurisdiction over various aspects of the education system:

- **The Department of Education** oversees all aspects of elementary, secondary, and informal education. The DOE is also responsible for the supervision of all elementary and secondary schools, both public and private. The central office of the Department of Education sets the overall policies for the basic education sector, while the field offices of the Department of Education implement policies at the local level. The Autonomous Region in Muslim Mindanao (ARMM) has an independent department of education, but for the most part follows national guidelines and uses the national school curriculum. The Department of Education is supported by various other agencies in supervising programs. For example, the Bureau of Alternative Learning System (BALS) oversees education programs designed for "out-of-school children, youth and adults who need basic and functional literacy skills, knowledge and values."[50]
- Technical and Vocational Education and Training (TVET) in the Philippines is supervised by the **Technical Education and Skills Development Authority (TESDA)**. TESDA oversees TVET providers, both public and private, and acts as a regulatory body, setting training standards, curricula, and testing requirements for vocational programs (footnote 50).
- Tertiary education in the Philippines is governed by the **Commission on Higher Education (CHED)**. CHED is directly attached to the Office of the President. It develops and implements higher education policies and provides quality assurance through oversight of post-secondary programs and institutions, both public and private. CHED sets the minimum standards for academic programs and for the establishment of new Higher Education Institutions (HEIs). It also suggests funding levels for public HEIs and determines how HEIs can use these funds (footnote 50).

## 2.3 Social Housing Regulations

The social housing agenda of the Government of the Philippines is embodied in a National Shelter Program (NSP) envisioned as a "total systems approach to housing finance, production and regulation" delivered by an interacting network of implementing housing agencies. The core programs and implementing mechanisms were later enacted into law through Executive Order 90 issued in December 1986. Executive Order 90 created the Housing and Urban Development Coordinating Council (HUDCC), charged with coordinating the activities of government housing agencies to ensure the accomplishment of the NSP goals. The following key agencies have been identified to accomplish the NSP goals and fund it:[51]

50 WENR. https://wenr.wes.org/.

51 World Bank Group. 2016. *Closing the Gap in Affordable Housing in the Philippines.* http://documents1.worldbank.org/curated/en/547171468059364837/pdf/AUS13470-REVISED-PUBLIC-WBNationalHousingSummitFinalReport.pdf.

- The **National Housing Authority (NHA)**, established by consolidating People's Homesite and Housing Corporation and seven other corporations and authorities, is the sole government agency engaged in direct shelter production, and focuses on housing assistance to the lowest 30% of urban income earners.
- The **Housing and Land Use Regulatory Board (HLURB)** was the sole regulatory body for housing and land development, charged with "encouraging greater private sector participation in low-cost housing through liberalization of development standards, simplification of regulations and decentralization of approvals for permits and licenses."
- The **National Home Mortgage Finance Corporation (NHMFC)** is responsible for operating a viable home mortgage market utilizing long-term funds principally provided by the support agencies. The Social Housing Finance Corporation (SHFC), a wholly owned subsidiary of NHMFC, develops and administers social housing finance programs for formal and informal low-income households.
- The **Home Development Mutual Fund (HDMF)**, also known as Pag-IBIG Fund, utilizes funds that are not required for provident benefits for housing loans to members; the **Social Security System (SSS)** is the primary provider of funds for long-term mortgages for low and middle-income private sector employees; and the **Government Service Insurance System (GSIS)** is the primary provider of funds for long-term mortgages for low- and middle-income government employees.
- The recently established **Philippine Guarantee Corporation**, a state-owned entity, provides guarantees to loans given for social housing. It offers guarantees which were earlier offered by Home Guaranty Corporation.

To streamline the housing and land use planning by the government, a new law (Republic Act 11201) has been enacted to create the **Department of Human Settlements and Urban Development (DHUD)**. The DHUD is a combination of the Housing and Urban Development Coordinating Council and the Housing and Land Use Regulatory Board. It serves as the primary national government entity responsible for the management of housing, human settlement, and urban development. It is specifically responsible for (i) developing national housing and urban development policy; (ii) keeping records of idle lands, comprehensive land use plans of local governments, housing stocks, and lists of housing beneficiaries; and (iii) owning and administering government-owned lands, and developing and implementing a plan for the establishment of government centers in the country.[52]

## 2.4 Foreign Investment Restrictions in the Social Infrastructure Sector

| Parameter | 2017 | 2018 | 2019 |
|---|---|---|---|
| **Maximum allowed foreign ownership of equity in greenfield projects** | | | |
| • Healthcare infrastructure | 40% | 40% | 40% |
| • Healthcare services | 40% | 40% | 40% |
| • Education infrastructure | 40% | 40% | 40% |
| • Education services | 0% | 0% | 0% |

52 Rappler. Nation. https://www.rappler.com/nation/223856-new-law-creates-department-housing-urban-development.

## 2.5 Standard Contracts in the Social Infrastructure Sector

| Parameter | 2017 | 2018 | 2019 |
|---|---|---|---|
| **What standardized contracts are available and used in the market?** | | | |
| • PPP/concession agreement | × | × | × |
| • Performance-based operation and maintenance contract | × | × | × |
| • Engineering procurement and construction contract | × | × | × |

✓ = Yes, × = No, NA = Not Applicable, UA = Unavailable

# 3. Social Infrastructure Sector Master Plan

Agencies and LGUs implementing the projects are tasked to prepare the infrastructure delivery programs and identify priority projects, which should be consistent with the Philippine Development Plan and the Provincial Development and Physical Framework Plan (footnote 1).

The Public Investment Program and the Comprehensive and Integrated Infrastructure Program are considered to constitute the list of national priority projects. Local priority projects include the provincial and/or local development investment programs. There is an expressed intention to periodically update the Public Investment Program, Comprehensive and Integrated Infrastructure Program, and Provincial Development Investment Program and/or Local Development Investment Program (footnote 1).

The PPP Center maintains a pipeline of PPP projects in the Philippines, which is updated regularly and published on the PPP Center website (Table 34).

**Table 34: List of Pipeline Public–Private Partnership Social Infrastructure Projects**

| No. | Project Name | Implementing Agency | Investment ($ million) | Investment (₱ million) | Status |
|---|---|---|---|---|---|
| 1. | Philippine General Hospital (PGH) Diliman Project | University of the Philippines | TBD | TBD | Development – Undergoing studies |
| 2. | Development of the former Manila Seedling Site owned by the National Housing Authority | National Housing Authority | TBD | TBD | Approval – Under evaluation by relevant approving body |
| 3. | Baguio General Hospital and Medical Center Renal Center Building Project | Baguio General Hospital and Medical Center and Department of Health | TBD | TBD | Development – Project conceptualization |
| 4. | Cagayan Valley Medical Center - Hemodialysis Unit | Cagayan Valley Medical Center and Department of Health | TBD | TBD | Development – Project conceptualization |
| 5. | UP PGH Manila Cancer Center | Philippine General Hospital | TBD | TBD | Development – Undergoing studies |

*continued on next page*

*continued from previous page*

| No. | Project Name | Implementing Agency | Investment ($ million) | (₱ million) | Status |
|---|---|---|---|---|---|
| 6. | UP Los Baños Agro-Industrial Information and Technology Parks | UP Los Baños | TBD | TBD | Development – Undergoing studies |
| 7 | Rizal Park Western Section Development Project | Tourism Infrastructure and Enterprise Zone Authority (TIEZA) | TBD | TBD | Development – Project conceptualization |
| 8. | Cagayan State University - Piat Mixed-Use Tourism Project | Cagayan State University | TBD | TBD | Development – Project conceptualization |
| 9. | Cagayan de Oro Convention Center Project | TIEZA | TBD | TBD | Development – Project conceptualization |
| 10. | Redevelopment of Panabo Town (Unsolicited) | Local Government of Panabo City (Davao Del Notre) | TBD | TBD | Development – Project conceptualization |
| 11. | Footbridge Development Project (Quezon City) | Quezon City Government | TBD | TBD | Approval – Under evaluation by relevant approving body |
| 12. | Iloilo City Central and Terminal Public Markets | City Government of Iloilo | TBD | TBD | Development – Undergoing studies |
| 13. | Iloilo City "Triple A" Slaughterhouse Project | City Government of Iloilo | TBD | TBD | Development – Undergoing studies |
| 14. | Cauayan Mega Market (Unsolicited) | Local Government of Cauayan City | 5.96 | 300 | Pre-construction |
| 15. | National Government Administrative Center Phase I and Mixed Use Industrial Development Phase I | Bases Conversion and Development Authority | 357.36 | 18,000 | Under implementation |

₱1 = $0.01974

PGH = Philippine General Hospital, TIEZA = Tourism Infrastructure and Enterprise Zone Authority, TBD = To be decided.

Source: Public–Private Partnership Center. List of Projects. https://ppp.gov.ph/list-of-projects/ (accessed 28 August 2020); Public–Private Partnership Center. 2019. *Investment Opportunities*. Manila. https://ppp.gov.ph/investors-corner/investment-opportunities-2/; NEDA. 2020. *Revised List of Infrastructure Flagship Projects*. Philippines. http://www.neda.gov.ph/wp-content/uploads/2020/03/Revised-List-of-Infrastructure-Flagship-Projects-as-of-2.17.2020.pdf.

## 3.1 Projects under Preparation and Procurement in the Social Infrastructure Sector

Figure 53 shows the number of PPP projects which are under preparation and procurement in the Philippines' social infrastructure sector.

## Figure 53: Public–Private Partnership Social Infrastructure Projects under Preparation and Procurement

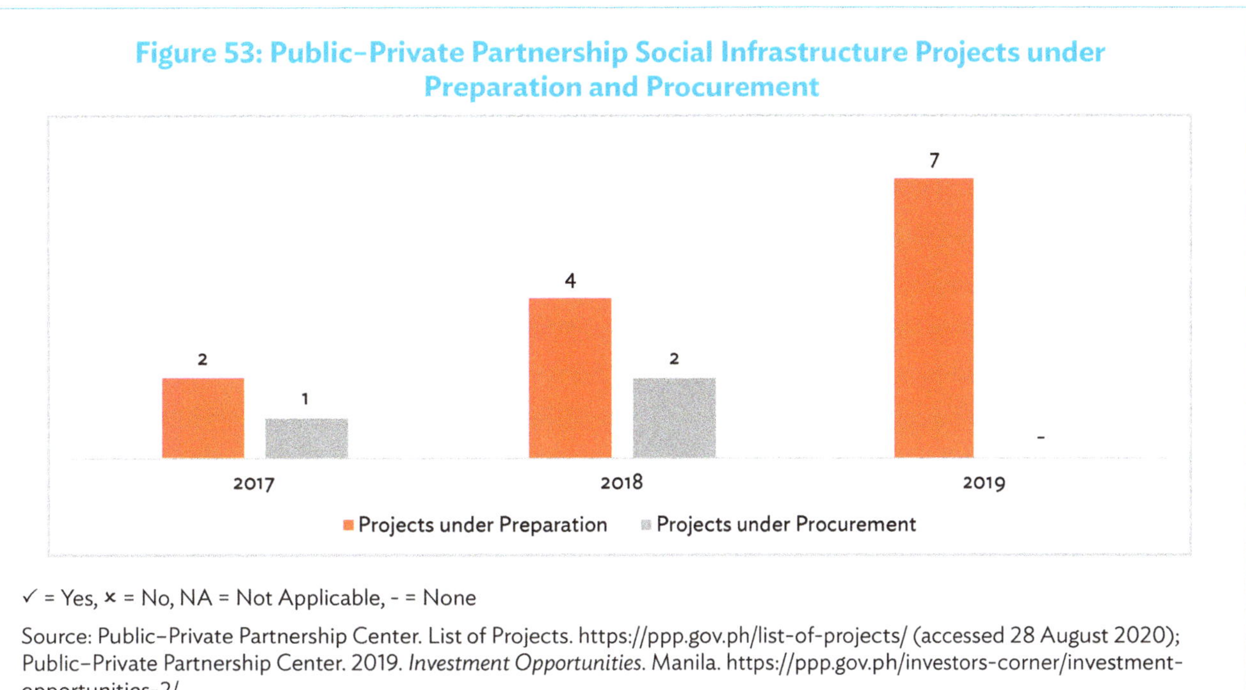


✓ = Yes, × = No, NA = Not Applicable, - = None

Source: Public–Private Partnership Center. List of Projects. https://ppp.gov.ph/list-of-projects/ (accessed 28 August 2020); Public–Private Partnership Center. 2019. *Investment Opportunities*. Manila. https://ppp.gov.ph/investors-corner/investment-opportunities-2/.

The Public–Private Partnership Center tracks the progress of a pipeline of PPP projects in the Philippines, which is updated regularly and published on the PPP Center website (Table 35).

## Table 35: List of Public–Private Partnership Social Infrastructure Projects under Preparation

| No. | Project Name | Implementing Agency | Investment ($ million) | Investment (₱ million) | Status |
|---|---|---|---|---|---|
| 1. | Philippine General Hospital (PGH) Diliman Project | University of the Philippines | TBD | TBD | Development – Undergoing studies |
| 2. | Development of the former Manila Seedling Site owned by the National Housing Authority (NHA) | National Housing Authority | TBD | TBD | Approval – Under evaluation by relevant approving body |
| 3. | UP PGH Manila Cancer Center | Philippine General Hospital | TBD | TBD | Development – Undergoing studies |
| 4. | UP Los Baños Agro-Industrial Information and Technology Parks | UP Los Baños | TBD | TBD | Development – Undergoing studies |
| 5. | Footbridge Development Project (Quezon City) | Quezon City Government | TBD | TBD | Approval – Under Evaluation by relevant approving body |
| 6. | Iloilo City Central and Terminal Public Markets | City Government of Iloilo | TBD | TBD | Development – Undergoing studies |
| 7. | Iloilo City "Triple A" Slaughterhouse Project | City Government of Iloilo | TBD | TBD | Development – Undergoing studies |

✓ = Yes, × = No, NA = Not Applicable, - = None;

PGH = Philippine General Hospital, TBD = To be decided.

Source: Public–Private Partnership Center. List of Projects. https://ppp.gov.ph/list-of-projects/ (accessed 28 August 2020); Public–Private Partnership Center. 2019. *Investment Opportunities*. Manila. https://ppp.gov.ph/investors-corner/investment-opportunities-2/.

# 4. Features of Past Public–Private Partnership Projects in the Social Infrastructure Sector

Figure 54 presents the number of PPP projects procured through various modes including direct appointment, unsolicited bids, and competitive bids in the Philippines' social infrastructure sector.

**Figure 54: Modes of Procurement for Public–Private Partnership Social Infrastructure Projects**

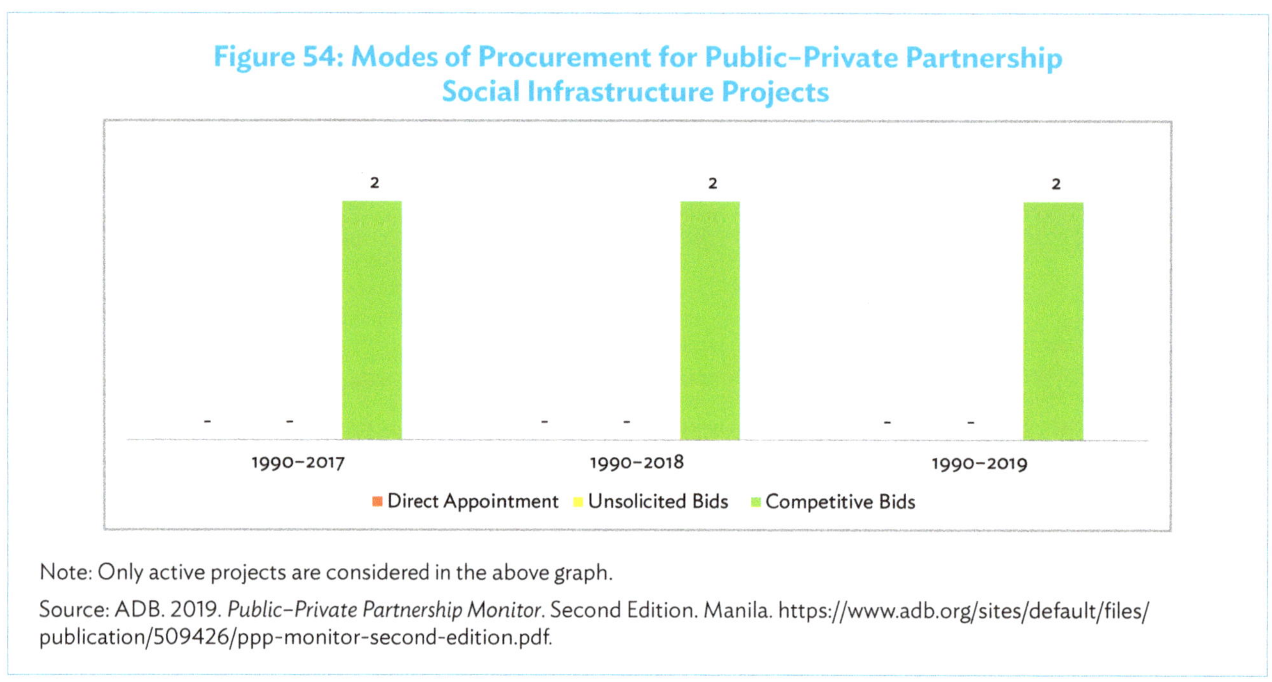


Note: Only active projects are considered in the above graph.

Source: ADB. 2019. *Public–Private Partnership Monitor*. Second Edition. Manila. https://www.adb.org/sites/default/files/publication/509426/ppp-monitor-second-edition.pdf.

Figure 55 provides the number of PPP projects which have reached financial closure and the total value of those projects in the Philippines' social infrastructure sector.

**Figure 55: Public–Private Partnership Social Infrastructure Projects Reaching Financial Closure**

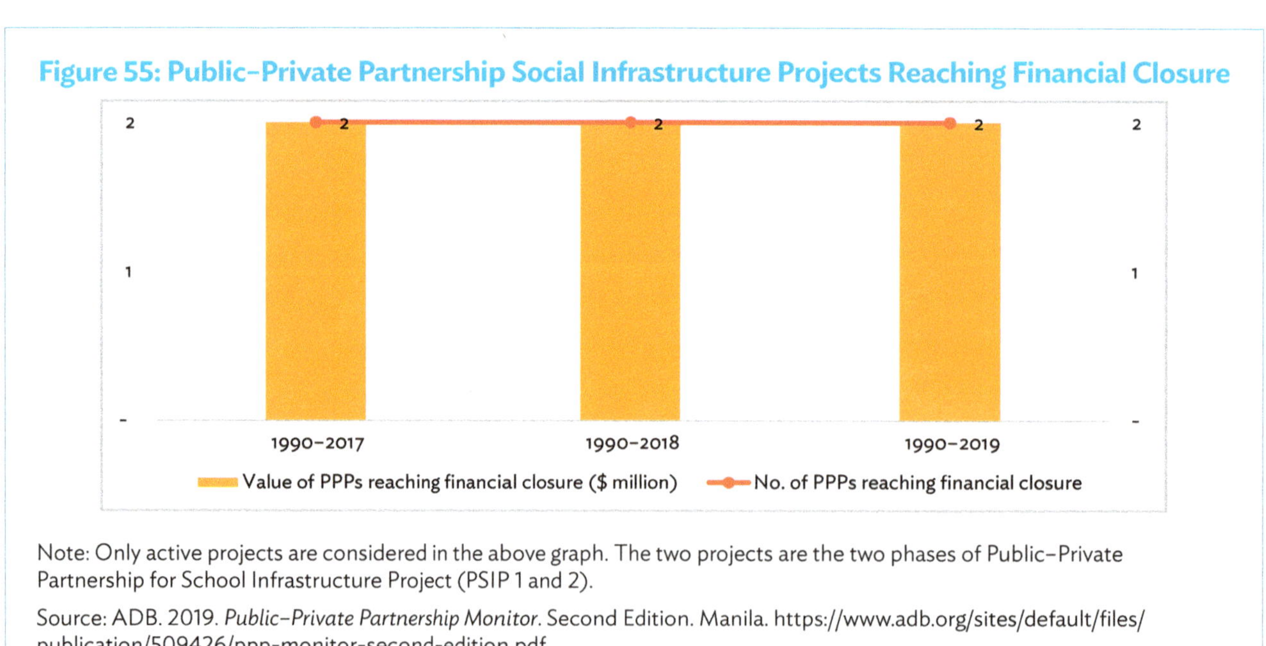


Note: Only active projects are considered in the above graph. The two projects are the two phases of Public–Private Partnership for School Infrastructure Project (PSIP 1 and 2).

Source: ADB. 2019. *Public–Private Partnership Monitor*. Second Edition. Manila. https://www.adb.org/sites/default/files/publication/509426/ppp-monitor-second-edition.pdf.

Figure 56 shows the number of PPP projects which have received foreign sponsor participation in the Philippines' social infrastructure sector.

## Figure 56: Public–Private Partnership Social Infrastructure Projects with Foreign Sponsor Participation

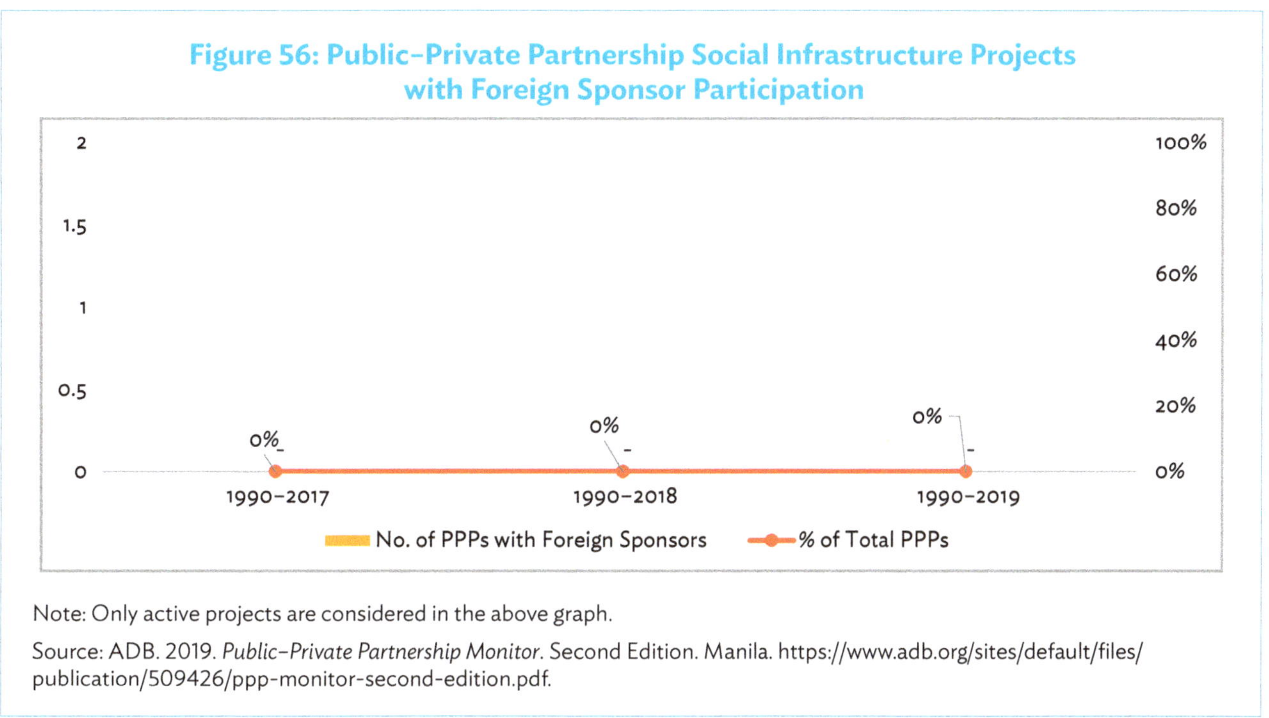


Note: Only active projects are considered in the above graph.

Source: ADB. 2019. *Public–Private Partnership Monitor.* Second Edition. Manila. https://www.adb.org/sites/default/files/publication/509426/ppp-monitor-second-edition.pdf.

Figure 57 presents the number of PPP projects which have received government support including Viability Gap Funding (VGF) mechanism, government guarantees, and availability/performance payment in the Philippines' social infrastructure sector.

## Figure 57: Government Support to Public–Private Partnership Social Infrastructure Projects

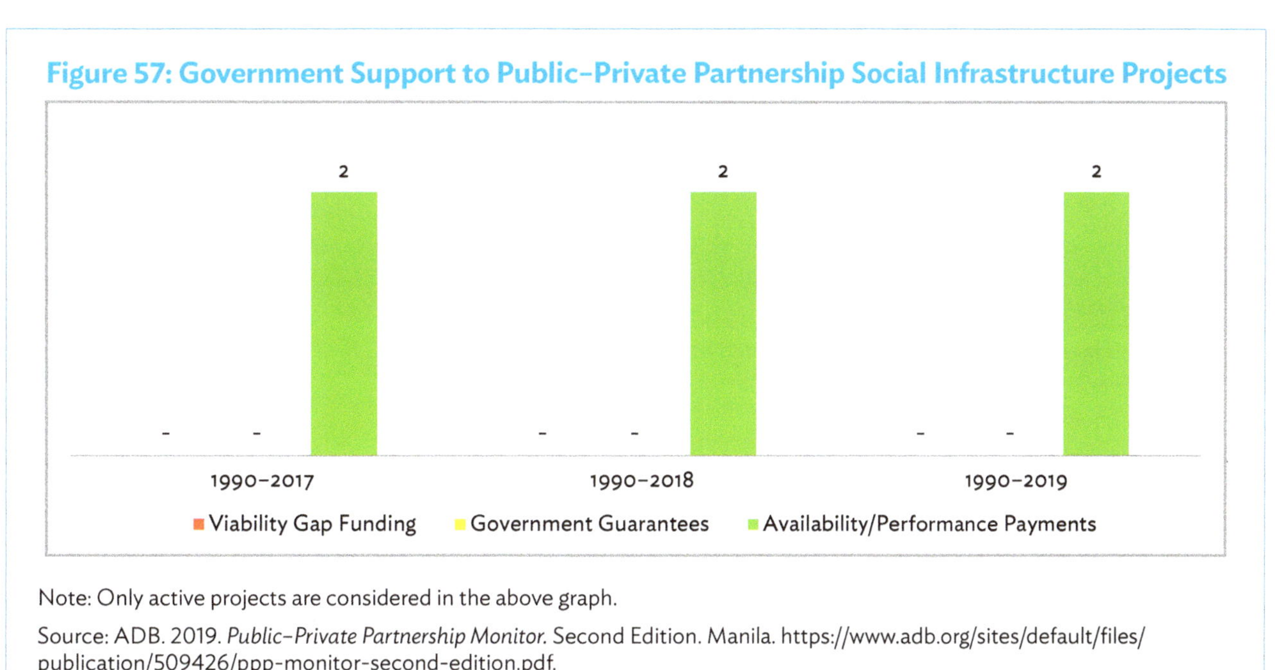


Note: Only active projects are considered in the above graph.

Source: ADB. 2019. *Public–Private Partnership Monitor.* Second Edition. Manila. https://www.adb.org/sites/default/files/publication/509426/ppp-monitor-second-edition.pdf.

Figure 58 shows the number of PPP projects which have received payment in the form of user charges and government pay (off-take) in the Philippines' social infrastructure sector.

**Figure 58: Payment Mechanisms for Public–Private Partnership Social Infrastructure Projects**

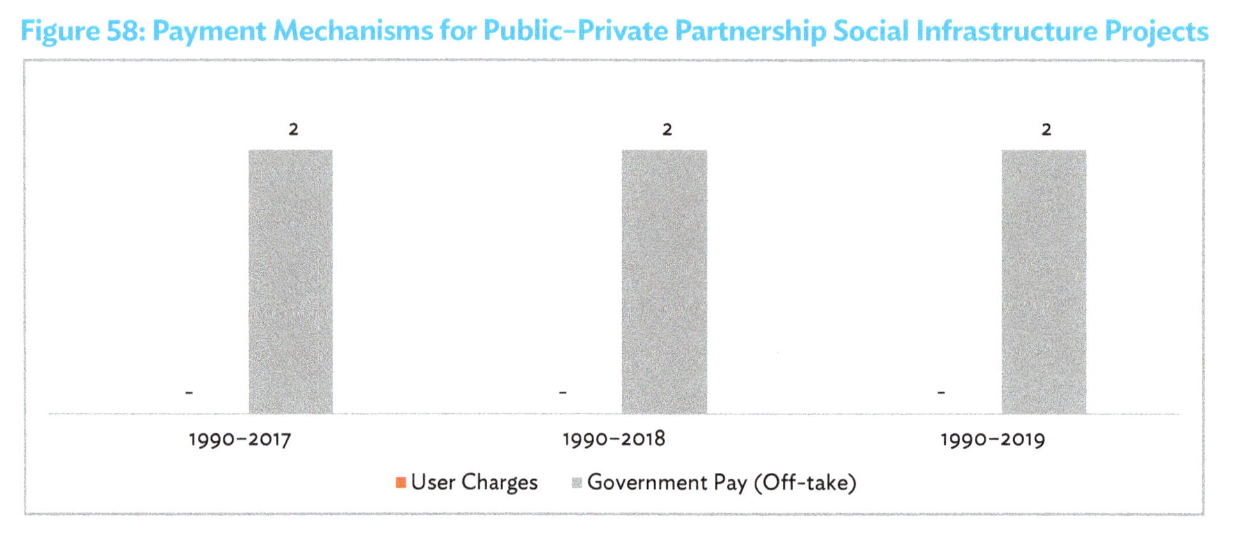


Note: Only active projects are considered in the above graph.

Source: ADB. 2019. *Public–Private Partnership Monitor.* Second Edition. Manila. https://www.adb.org/sites/default/files/publication/509426/ppp-monitor-second-edition.pdf.

## 4.1 Tariffs in the Social Infrastructure Sector

No information on the tariffs for social infrastructure projects is available.

## 4.2 Typical Risk Allocation for Public–Private Partnership Projects in the Social Infrastructure Sector

No information on the risk allocation for social infrastructure projects is available.

## 4.3 Financing Details of Public–Private Partnerships in the Social Infrastructure Sector

| Parameter | 1990–2017 | 1990–2018 | 2019 |
|---|---|---|---|
| PPP projects with foreign lending participation | UA | UA | UA |
| PPP projects that received export credit agency/international financing institution support | UA | UA | UA |
| Typical debt:equity ratio | 80:20 | 80:20 | 80:20 |
| Time for financial closure | Not later than 90 days from commercial close | | |
| Typical concession period | UA | | |
| Financial Internal Rate of Return | UA | | |

✓ = Yes, ✗ = No, NA = Not Applicable, UA = Unavailable

Source: ADB, World Bank. Infrastructure Finance, PPPs and Guarantees. Country Snapshots. Philippines. https://ppi.worldbank.org/en/snapshots/country/philippines (accessed 28 August 2020).

## 5. Challenges in the Social Infrastructure Sector

- Restriction on foreign investments (capped at 40% for greenfield projects) limits the competition in the sector, as the controlling stake in the project company belongs to local companies. The government is taking steps to ease the restriction on foreign investment to attract international investors.
- The market for social infrastructure PPPs is relatively untested because of only a few projects that have entered the award/construction stage.

# OTHER SECTORS

Table 36 presents the potential PPP projects for sectors not covered in the preceding sections. The Public–Private Partnership Center tracks the progress of a pipeline of PPP projects in the Philippines, which is updated regularly and published on the PPP Center website.

### Table 36: List of Public–Private Partnership Projects for Other Sectors, as of March 2020

| No. | Project Name | Implementing Agency | Investment | | Status |
|---|---|---|---|---|---|
| | | | ($ million) | (₱ million) | |
| 1. | Integrated Waste Management Project (Marikina City) | Marikina City Government | 25.8 | 1,300 | Under evaluation – Proposal received by the implementing agency |
| 2. | Cebu City Solid Waste Management Project | City Government of Cebu | TBD | TBD | UA |
| 3. | Iloilo City Integrated Solid Waste Facility Management Project | Provincial Government of Iloilo | TBD | TBD | Development – Undergoing studies |

₱1 = $0.01974, TBD = To be decided, UA = Unavailable

Source: Public–Private Partnership Center. 2019. *Investment Opportunities*. Manila. https://ppp.gov.ph/investors-corner/investment-opportunities-2/.

# IV. Local Government Public–Private Partnership Landscape

Table 37: Local Government Public–Private Partnership Landscape Key Indicators

| Parameter | Value | Unit |
|---|---|---|
| **Number of Subnational Governments (SNGs)** | | |
| - *Municipal level* | 42,028 | Number |
| - *Intermediate level* | 1,594 | Number |
| - *Regional or state level* | 81 | Number |
| Total number of SNGs | 43,703 | Number |
| **SNG Expenditure Profile** | | |
| Total SNG expenditure as % of GDP | 12.30 | % |
| - *SNG current expenditure as % of GDP* | 11.30 | % |
| - *SNG staff expenditure as % of GDP* | UA | % |
| - *SNG investment as % of GDP* | UA | % |
| Total SNG expenditure as % of the total general government (% of total public expenditure) | 16.20 | % |
| - *SNG current expenditure as a % of total current expenditure of the general government* | UA | % |
| - *SNG staff expenditure as a % of total staff expenditure of the general government* | UA | % |
| - *SNG investment as a % of total investment of the general government* | UA | % |
| Current expenditure of SNG as a % of total SNG expenditure | 92.10 | % |
| Staff expenditure of SNG as a % of total SNG expenditure | UA | % |
| Investments of SNG as a % of total SNG expenditure | UA | % |
| **SNG Expenditure by Function** | | |
| - *General public services* | 47.30 | % |
| - *Defence* | UA | % |
| - *Security and public order* | UA | % |
| - *Economic affairs* | 10.70 | % |
| - *Environmental protection* | UA | % |
| - *Housing and community amenities* | UA | % |
| - *Health* | UA | % |
| - *Recreation, culture, and religion* | UA | % |
| - *Education* | UA | % |
| - *Social protection* | 10.70 | % |

*continued on next page*

*continued from previous page*

| Parameter | Value | Unit |
|---|---|---|
| **SNG Revenue Profile** | | |
| Total SNG revenue as a % of GDP | 14.80 | % |
| – *SNG tax revenue as a % of GDP* | 3.60 | % |
| – *SNG grants and subsidies as a % of GDP* | 9.60 | % |
| – *SNG other revenues as a % of GDP* | 1.50 | % |
| Total SNG revenue as % of total general government revenue | 22.7 | % |
| – *SNG tax revenue as a % of total general government tax revenue* | 6.30 | % |
| – *SNG grants and subsidies as a % of total general government grants and subsidies* | – | % |
| – *SNG other revenues as a % of total other revenues* | – | % |
| SNG tax revenue as a % of total SNG revenue | 24.70 | % |
| SNG grants and subsidies as a % of total SNG revenue | 65.30 | % |
| SNG other revenues as a % of total SNG revenue | 10.00 | % |
| **SNG Debt Profile** | | |
| Outstanding SNG debt as % of GDP | UA | % |
| Outstanding SNG debt as % of total outstanding debt of general government | UA | % |
| **Parameters for transfers to the Subnational Governments from the National Government** | | |
| Score on transfers to Subnational Governments | A | |
| – *Score on system for allocating transfers* | A | |
| – *Score on timeliness of information on transfers* | A | |
| – *Score on extent of collection and reporting of consolidated fiscal data for general government* | NA | |
| Value of central government transfers to subnational governments | UA | % of the GDP |
| Value of actual budgetary allocation to subnational governments from national government | UA | % of total expenditure |
| Value of deviation of actual against the budgeted transfers to subnational governments | UA | % of budgeted transfers |

✓ = Yes, × = No, NA = Not Applicable, UA = Unavailable

GDP = Gross Domestic Product, SNG = subnational governments.

Source: UCLG. 2016. *Subnational Governments around the World—Structure and Finance.* https://www.uclg.org/sites/default/files/global_observatory_of_local_finance-part_iii.pdf; PEFA. 2016. *Republic of the Philippines PFM Strategy Implementation Support.* Manila. https://www.pefa.org/sites/pefa/files/assessments/reports/PH-Jun16-PFMPR-Public-with-PEFA-Check-Meth16.pdf.

## Local Governance System in the Philippines

The Philippines has a decentralized system of government, with three tiers of local governance: (i) 81 provinces; (ii) 1,489 municipalities and 105 cities; and (iii) 42,028 barangays. The province is the highest tier of local governance and is made up of a cluster of municipalities and/or cities. Some cities, which are highly urbanized, are considered independent from the province. Municipalities and cities are made of barangay, or villages, which is the lowest tier of decentralization. In addition to these jurisdictions, the Philippines also comprises the Autonomous Region in Muslim Mindanao (ARMM).[53]

The legal and regulatory provisions for the local governments operating framework are set in the Local Government Code of 1991. The local government autonomy is combined with a supervision of higher level of government, especially regarding the budget approval process and local government legal accountability (footnote 53).

## Infrastructure Development Plan of Local Governments

In the Philippines, development planning and investment programming follows a dynamic and iterative process whereby the national, regional, and local levels of governance adhere to support and reaffirm each other's priority development thrusts and objectives.[54]

The national government provides guidance and directions for the preparation of sector and lower level plans in terms of policies and macroeconomic targets taking into account the prevailing development issues and concerns affecting national, regional, and local conditions at the planning stage. From these national planning guidelines, regional and local level development plans and investment programs are then prepared with consideration of the local development needs and service delivery gaps. These documents serve as bases for the preparation of sector plans and investment programs which become the components of the national medium-term development plan and investment program (footnote 54).

The local government development plans contain programs, projects, and activities (PPAs) responding to the development needs and gaps of the local governments. The local government investment plans outline a set of prioritized PPAs, their specific timeframes of implementation, and their budget requirements. The local governments also propose suitable fund sourcing alternatives and resource mobilization strategies to ensure that these identified and prioritized PPAs are implemented (footnote 54).

The Provincial Development Council undertakes the formulation of medium-term, long-term, and annual socioeconomic development plans for the province. It also prepares the public investment programs, undertakes project appraisal, and prioritizes development projects. Tasks such as coordination, monitoring, and evaluation of the implementation of development projects are also undertaken by the Provincial Development Council.

At the city/municipal level, the City/Municipal Development Council is tasked with the formulation of long-term, medium-term, and annual socioeconomic development plans and public investment programs; appraisal and prioritization of development projects; and coordination, monitoring, and evaluation of the implementation of development projects.

The provincial, city, and municipal government development and investment plans present opportunities to engage the private sector, identify projects for private investment, and offer incentives for the private sector (footnote 54).

53 OECD. Regional Policy. Philippines. https://www.oecd.org/regional/regional-policy/profile-Philippines.pdf.
54 PPP Center. 2012. *A PPP Manual for LGUs*. Philippines. https://ppp.gov.ph/wp-content/uploads/2012/07/PPP-Manual-for-LGUs-Volume-1.pdf.

# Public–Private Partnership Enabling Framework for Local Government Projects

## 1. Public–Private Partnership Legal Framework for Local Government Projects

The Local Government Code (LGC) of 1991 (Republic Act 7160) has institutionalized decentralization from the national government to LGUs. It provides the legal basis for the participation of the private sector in local governance, particularly in the delivery of basic services. The LGC allows LGUs to enter into joint ventures and other forms of cooperative arrangements with the private sector to deliver basic services such as health care, social welfare, agricultural extension, and other revenue-generating infrastructure facilities eligible under the LGC (described subsequently under section 1.4.4). Cooperation with the private sector could be for financing, construction, maintenance, operation, and management of infrastructure projects.

The LGC further provides that projects may be financed, constructed, operated, and maintained by the private sector, and these projects should be included in the LGU's local development plans and public investment programs and be disclosed to the public and to the duly registered contractors. The projects also need to be confirmed by the local development councils based on the plans and specifications submitted. The contracts for approved projects should be awarded to the lowest complying bidder in a public bidding (footnote 31).

To finance public and infrastructure facilities and other capital investment projects that may not be financially viable or self-liquidating, LGUs are authorized by the LGC to contract loans, credits, or other forms of indebtedness with government or domestic private banks. The LGUs are also authorized by the LGC to accept financial grants or donations in kind from local and foreign assistance agencies, without prior approval of the national government or any higher LGU (footnote 31).

## 2. Public–Private Partnership Policy Framework for Local Government Projects

The Department of Finance (DOF) and NEDA have formulated a robust policy framework to rationalize the use of available financial resources and help achieve the vision and goals of the LGC with respect to the roles and responsibilities of LGUs in helping achieve national objectives.

### *LGU Financing Policy Framework*

In 1996, the DOF, in consultation with key stakeholders, formulated the LGU Financing Policy Framework to wean off LGUs from the national government and promote their effective partnership with the private sector. The ultimate objective of the framework is to step up the more creditworthy LGUs to private sources of capital, at least for their revenue-generating or self-liquidating projects. Under the LGU Financing Policy Framework, the First Tier LGUs are allowed to directly contract loans not only with government financial institutions (GFIs) and the DOF Municipal Development Fund Office (MDFO), but also with multilateral financial institutions created by treaties to which the Philippines is a signatory.[55] The project to be financed should be certified by the LGU's Planning and Development Office to be included in the Annual Investment Plan of the LGU (footnote 31).

55 First Tier LGUs refer to provinces, cities, or municipalities whose 3-year average proportion of regular locally sourced income to total regular income is at least 60% as per certification of the Bureau of Local Government Finance (BLGF) of the DOF.

### *National Government–Local Government Units Cost-Sharing Policy Framework*

In 1996, the NEDA Board approved a policy framework for financial assistance from the national government for LGU projects with social and/or environmental objectives. This framework provides for national government support to projects with social and/or environmental objectives in the form of matching grants that are for specific purposes, performance-based, limited in amount and duration, and based on the following: (i) cost recovery through user charges shall be maximized and PSP shall be elicited whenever possible, (ii) recurrent operation and maintenance expenditures shall not be included, and (iii) the amount of national government exposure in any devolved project/program is set at about 50% and allowed to vary depending on the type of project and the LGU income class (footnote 31).

The framework also specifies the percentage of the project cost that could be given by the national government as capital grants and the types of projects and income classes of LGUs that would be eligible for the grants.

### *Performance-Based Incentive Policy for Local Government Units*

The MDFO Policy Governing Board approved the Performance-Based Incentive Policy (PBIP) in 2008. This policy was subsequently re-affirmed by the Development Budget Coordination Committee of the NEDA Board in 2009. The PBIP aims to rationalize intergovernmental fiscal transfers from the national government to LGUs to improve overall LGU governance and delivery of basic services (footnote 31).

The maximum subsidy for a municipality is ₱1 million ($19,740 as of April 2020); for a city, ₱3 million ($59,220 as of April 2020); and for a province, ₱7 million ($98,700 as of April 2020). LGUs are required to put up at least the same amount as their counterpart fund. The subsidy together with the LGU counterpart may be used for any of the following purposes: (i) as subsidy for high-impact capital investment projects of the LGU, (ii) as counterpart funds for foreign-assisted projects of the LGU, (iii) as co-financing for joint projects with other LGUs, and (iv) as counterpart for projects of the LGU with the private sector in the context of PPPs in creating more economic activities. Projects eligible for subsidy are those geared toward the achievement of national government priorities, such as the attainment of the Millennium Development Goals, adaptation to climate change, disaster preparedness, local economic development, and solid waste management (DILG 2010) (footnote 31).

## 3. Public–Private Partnership Institutional Framework for Local Government Projects

Along with the various institutions responsible for PPPs at the national level, specific institutions responsible for PPPs at the local government level include: (i) regional development councils, (ii) provincial legislative and development councils, (iii) city/municipal legislative and development councils, and (iv) PPP subcommittees in LGUs.

## 4. Public–Private Partnership Financing Institutions for Local Government Public–Private Partnership Projects

### *Municipal Development Fund Office (MDFO)*

The Municipal Development Fund (MDF) is a special revolving fund for re-lending to local government units (LGUs). The Project Technical Assistance and Contingency Fund (PTACF) provides optional financing with low interest rates (0% to 1.5% interest payable in 3 years) for LGUs (except for highly urbanized cities in Metro Manila) in funding the contingency requirements and technical assistance needed for LGU projects financed by MDFO.[56]

### *Cities Development Initiative for Asia (CDIA)*

The CDIA is an initiative that provides assistance to medium-sized cities to bridge the gap between their development plans and the implementation of their infrastructure investments. It provides consultancy and advisory support for (i) identifying potential private sector involvement at the early stages of a project design and structuring the project for such involvement, (ii) conducting pre-feasibility studies for high priority infrastructure projects, (iii) strengthening local institutional capacity on infrastructure investment planning and programming, and (iv) marketing local investment proposals to potential financiers (footnote 56).

### *Asia Pacific Project Preparation Facility (AP3F)*

The AP3F aims to assist the ADB developing member countries (DMCs) and their public sector agencies in preparing and structuring infrastructure projects with private sector participation, including PPP modalities, and bring them to the global market. The AP3F also provides assistance for capacity building, particularly in reforming and improving policy, legislative, regulatory, and institutional practices in DMCs. It also provides ongoing project performance assistance, including project monitoring and project restructuring (footnote 56).

### *Project Development and Monitoring Facility (PDMF)*

The PDMF is a revolving fund managed by the PPP Center. It is used to engage consultants for Project Preparation and Transaction Support to conduct feasibility studies, structure projects, prepare tender documents, manage the bid process, and provide assistance until financial closure. The fund can also be tapped to involve a probity advisor for the bidding process, and consultants for monitoring of project implementation (footnote 56).

### *Asia Infrastructure Center for Excellence (AICOE)*

The AICOE assists ASEAN countries in (i) building capacity to identify, screen, and prioritize projects for private sector participation, and develop a pipeline of financeable PPP projects; and (ii) funding project structuring support to prepare PPP transactions for financing (footnote 56).

## Sectors for Potential Public–Private Partnership with Local Governments

According to the Constitution and the Local Government Code of 1991, local governments are mainly responsible for basic public services provision. Provinces are mostly responsible for competences that imply inter-municipal services provision, such as tertiary health care services and maintenance of hospital covering several municipalities, social housing, and social welfare services. Municipalities and barangays have been assigned with proximity services, such as primary health care, primary school building and maintenance, waste collection, and cultural centers. Due to their importance, cities are responsible for both inter-municipal and municipal competences (footnote 53).

[56] PPP Center. https://ppp.gov.ph/.

Section 17 of the Local Government Code of 1991 provides a list of eligible sectors under which PPP projects can be implemented by local governments (Table 37). Table 38 shows the various levels of approvals for these projects and Table 39 shows the list of local government projects in the PPP pipeline as per the PPP Center.

### Table 38: Sectors where Local Governments can Implement Public–Private Partnerships

| Infrastructure Sectors | Eligible Projects |
|---|---|
| Agriculture and Fisheries | Agricultural development facilities, such as agricultural produce storage and warehousing facilities; agricultural produce processing and post-harvest facilities; livestock facilities<br>Fisheries and aquatic resources facilities, such as public fish ports, fish ponds, fisheries storage facilities, and fisheries processing facilities |
| Commercial and Industrial Development | Local trading support infrastructure, such as markets and slaughterhouses; business district development facilities, such as business district establishment, expansion, and revitalization/rehabilitation |
| Education | School buildings, dormitories, hostels, hometels, and student centers |
| Environmental and Solid Waste Management | Solid waste collection equipment, sanitary landfills, composting plans and facilities, tidal barriers |
| Government Buildings | Government buildings and operations centers |
| Forestry | Community-based forestry projects |
| Healthcare | Hospitals, clinics, health centers, lying-in centers, emergency medical stations, pharmacies, drug stores, animal bite centers |
| Housing | Housing projects |
| Information and Communication Technology (ICT) Systems and Facilities | IT modernization, cadastral survey for resource accounting and planning, geospatial resource mapping |
| Land Use | Land reclamation and dredging |
| Roads and Bridges | Provincial, city, and municipal roads and bridges |
| Social Welfare | Day care centers, social welfare distribution centers, emergency response units |
| Transportation | Transportation facilities and infrastructure, such as transport management system and transport terminals |
| Water and Sanitation | Local water supply systems, septage management or sewerage systems; drainage facilities |

Source: Government of the Philippines. Local Government Code of 1991. Section 17. https://www.officialgazette.gov.ph/1991/10/10/republic-act-no-7160/#:~:text=SECTION%2017.,functions%20currently%20vested%20upon%20them.

### Table 39: Levels of Approval for Local Government Public–Private Partnership Projects

| Infrastructure Sectors | Eligible Projects |
|---|---|
| President | All Build-Operate-Own projects and other schemes not defined in Section 2 of RA 7718, subject to the recommendation of the NEDA Board's Investment Coordination Committee |
| Investment Coordination Committee (ICC) | Local projects costing above ₱200 million ($3.9 million as of April 2020); and all unsolicited proposals regardless of project cost |
| Regional Development Council (RDC) | Local projects costing above ₱50 million ($1 million as of April 2020) up to ₱200 million ($3.9 million as of April 2020) |
| City Development Council (CDC) | Local projects costing up to ₱50 million |

*continued on next page*

*continued from previous page*

| Infrastructure Sectors | Eligible Projects |
|---|---|
| Provincial Development Council (PDC) | Local projects costing above ₱20 million ($0.39 million as of April 2020) up to ₱50 million ($1 million as of April 2020) |
| Municipal Development Council (MDC) | Local projects costing up to ₱20 million ($0.39 million as of April 2020) |

₱1 = $0.01974, NEDA = National Economic and Development Authority, RA = Republic Act.

Sources: Public–Private Partnership Center. 2012. *A PPP Manual for LGUs*. Philippines. https://ppp.gov.ph/wp-content/uploads/2012/03/Volume-2-LGU-PPP-Manual.pdf; Public–Private Partnership Center. 2012. *The Philippine Amended BOT Law*. Philippines. https://ppp.gov.ph/wp-content/uploads/2013/02/BOT-IRR-2012_FINAL.pdf.

## Table 40: List of Local Government Public–Private Partnership Projects in the Public–Private Partnership Pipeline

| Project Name | Implementing Agency | Estimated Project Cost | | Status |
|---|---|---|---|---|
| | | ($ million) | (₱ million) | |
| Integrated Waste Management Project (Marikina City) (Unsolicited) | Marikina City Government | 26 | 1,300 | Under evaluation – Proposal received by implementing agency |
| Ormoc City Water Supply System Project | City Government of Ormoc | TBD | TBD | Development – Undergoing studies |
| Puerto Galera Sewerage and Wastewater Treatment Plant Project | Local Government of Puerto Galera (Mindoro Oriental) | TBD | TBD | NA |
| Cauayan Mega Market (Unsolicited) | Local Government of Cauayan City | 6 | 300 | Pre-construction |
| Iloilo City "Triple A" Slaughterhouse Project | City Government of Iloilo | TBD | TBD | Development – Undergoing studies |
| Iloilo City Central and Terminal Public Markets | City Government of Iloilo | TBD | TBD | Development – Undergoing studies |
| Iloilo City Integrated Solid Waste Facility Management Project | City Government of Iloilo | TBD | TBD | Development – Undergoing studies |
| Bislig City Bulk Water Supply and Septage Project | Bislig City Water District | TBD | TBD | Development – Project conceptualization |
| Cebu City Solid Waste Management Project | City Government of Cebu | TBD | TBD | UA |
| IT Project for LGU City of Naga – Unlad Bayan Local Government Information System (Unsolicited) | Naga City Local Government | TBD | TBD | Technical Board deliberation / endorsement |
| Baggao Water Supply Project | Municipal Government of Baggao | 1.6 | 84 | Procurement |
| Unsolicited Proposal for the Redevelopment of Panabo Town | Local Government of Panabo City (Davao Del Norte) | TBD | TBD | UA |

₱1 = $0.01974, TBD = To be decided, UA = Unavailable.

LGU = local government unit.

Source: Public–Private Partnership Center. List of Projects. https://ppp.gov.ph/list-of-projects/ (accessed 28 August 2020); Public–Private Partnership Center. 2019. *Investment Opportunities*. Manila. https://ppp.gov.ph/investors-corner/investment-opportunities-2/.

## Revenues for Local Governments

The local governments have three sources of revenue: tax revenues; grants and subsidies, including intergovernmental transfers and shared revenues from national tax collection; and other revenues.[57]

- *Tax revenue.* Principal local government tax revenue includes basic real property tax (43% of tax revenues), business tax (51% of tax revenues), and a few other local taxes, such as the special education tax. Provinces and cities have to share some of their revenues with the municipalities and barangays and are restricted on the set of taxes they can collect.
- *Grants and subsidies.* In addition to the local taxes, local governments also receive a share of national tax collection through a formula-based grant, the Internal Revenue Allotment (IRA), which varies according to the type of local government: 23% to provinces, 23% to cities, 34% to municipalities, and 20% to barangays. The IRA is calculated according to population, land area, and equal sharing formula. The intergovernmental transfer system also includes shares from government corporations, such as the Philippine Amusement and Gaming Corporation, Philippine Charity Sweepstakes Office, ECOZONE (economic zones); and shares from the Expanded Value-Added Tax Act (EVAT) and tobacco and excise tax. Shared taxation represents a major part of overall subnational governments' revenues (between 75% and 85%). Subnational governments may also receive inter-local transfers, extraordinary resources, and grants and donations; however, these types of revenues remain a very small part of their total revenues.
- *Other revenues.* These include regulatory fees, receipts from economic enterprises, and diverse fees and charges.

The revenue surplus after meeting the revenue expenditures from the above sources of revenue is typically used for financing capital investment and infrastructure projects, including PPPs.

## Borrowings by Local Governments

Local governments can borrow through government mechanisms to finance local infrastructures based on the approved local development plan and public investment program. The local debt should not exceed 20% of the regular income of the local government unit concerned. The Bureau of Local Government Finance (BLGF) certifies debt service ceiling and net borrowing capacity of local governments.[58]

Borrowings of local governments are limited to the following purposes:

- Construction, installation, improvement, expansion, operation or maintenance of public facilities, infrastructure facilities, and housing projects; acquisition of real property; and implementation of other capital investment projects
- Establishment, development, or expansion of agricultural, industrial, commercial, house financing, and livelihood projects; and other economic enterprises
- Acquisition of property, plant, machinery, equipment, and the necessary accessories
- Financing of self-liquidating, income-producing development or livelihood projects

57 UCLG. https://www.uclg.org/.
58 ADB. 2019. *Credit Financing for Local Development: The Subnational Debt in the Philippines.* Manila. https://www.adb.org/sites/default/files/publication/506931/adbi-wp966.pdf.

### Table 41: Average Lending Rates for Local Governments

| Year | Bank Average Lending Rates | Interest Rate per BLGF Certificate | GFIs | PFIs |
|---|---|---|---|---|
| 2015 | 5.58% | 5.75% | 5.74% | 5.84% |
| 2016 | 5.64% | 5.46% | 5.50% | 5.10% |
| 2017 | 5.63% | 5.00% | 5.10% | 4.60% |
| Average | 5.62% | 5.40% | 5.45% | 5.18% |

BLGF = Bureau of Local Government Finance, GFI = government financial institution, PFI = private financing institution.

Source: ADB. 2019. *Credit Financing for Local Development: The Subnational Debt in the Philippines.* Manila. https://www.adb.org/sites/default/files/publication/506931/adbi-wp966.pdf.

Relevant financing facilities are made available for capital investments and infrastructure projects, including PPPs (Table 42).

### Table 42: Financing Facilities Available for Capital Investments and Infrastructure Projects

| Financing Window | Objectives | Eligible Borrowers | Eligible Proposals/ Subprojects | Interest Rates |
|---|---|---|---|---|
| Municipal Development Fund Project | Provide concessional financing assistance to lower-income-class LGUs with revenue-generating subprojects | All LGUs nationwide | Revenue- and non-revenue-generating projects; Other infrastructure projects | 3.75% to 4.5% |
| Philippine Water Revolving Fund | Leverage Official Development Assistance (ODA) Private Financing Institution (PFI) funding; Develop financing mechanism acceptable to PFIs but at the same time affordable to water utilities; Develop financing mechanism with revolving capacity | Water districts, LGUs' consortium or joint ventures; Privately owned corporations; Private financial institutions | Water extraction, transmission, supply treatment, and distribution; Wastewater collection, treatment, and disposal; Non-Revenue Water (NRW) reduction and efficiency-enhancing measures; Refinancing of water project loans | Variable |
| Program Lending (ProLend) | Assist provincial LGUs in financing development projects with the provision that they will pursue a policy reform agenda | All provinces | Revenue generation; Expenditures planning and management; Service delivery; Congruence with national policy objectives and programs | Fixed based on the 10- year Treasury Bond on the day of the loan approval |

*continued on next page*

*continued from previous page*

| Financing Window | Objectives | Eligible Borrowers | Eligible Proposals/ Subprojects | Interest Rates |
|---|---|---|---|---|
| Project Technical Assistance and Contingency Fund (PTACF) | Assist in accelerating LGU preparation and submission of feasibility studies and detailed engineering design; Create a fund to finance the actual foreign exchange differentials of LGUs incurred in their project implementation; Provide a source of financing for other technical assistance needs of LGUs | All LGUs except highly urbanized cities | Feasibility studies; Detailed Engineering Design (DED); Other technical assistance requirements of LGUs | 0% to 1.5% |
| Refinancing Facility | Lower the loan amortization payment of LGUs; Reduce the LGUs' risk from paying a variable interest rate offered by other banks by switching to a fixed-rate loan; Decrease the financial burden of LGUs | All provinces, cities, municipalities, and highly urbanized cities | Refinancing of existing debts, such as the outstanding loan and other fees and charges the lending institution may impose due to contract pretermination | Fixed based on the prevailing market rate at the time of loan approval |
| Public–Private Partnership Fund | Support the current administration's thrust of moving the PPP to the LGU level | All LGUs, with a condition that the LGU will partner with a private entity | Public economic enterprise/revenue generating subprojects, social and environmental subprojects, solid waste management facilities | 3.75% |

LGU = local government unit.

Sources: ADB. 2019. *Credit Financing for Local Development: The Subnational Debt in the Philippines.* Manila. https://www.adb.org/sites/default/files/publication/506931/adbi-wp966.pdf; Base Data: MDFO. www.mdfo.gov.ph.

## Budgetary Allocation to Local Governments

Budgetary allocation to local governments follows a medium-term expenditure framework based on their budget requests as per their annual investment plans.

## Credit Rating of Local Governments

The Bureau of Local Government Finance (BLGF) is setting up the LGU Creditworthiness Rating Index (CRI) to be issued to all provinces, cities, and municipalities on a regular basis to improve planning and resource mobilization strategies. The CRI will serve as a rating mechanism for the fiscal health and credit viability of LGUs. It seeks to determine the conditions, red flags, and relevant signals in which the risk of default on debt obligations may be considered low or the probability of paying back a loan on time is assuredly high (footnote 58).

In determining the individual CRIs, the BLGF assesses five core areas of LGU performance: (i) revenue generation, (ii) investment and debt capacity, (iii) rigidity of expenditures, (iv) financial management capacity, and (v) borrowing history.

Capping of an LGU's borrowing capacity based on CRI rating is being explored to foster fiscal discipline and minimize haphazard borrowings, and therefore counter any resulting soft budget constraints. LGUs with AAA to A ratings are considered automatically certified with 100% of their borrowing capacity. LGUs with a BBB rating can only avail themselves of 90%, those rated BB 80%, the B-rated LGUs 70%, and LGUs with a score less than 40 and a rating of C would get a 60% cap on the loanable amount that will be certified by the BLGF.

Putting a cap on borrowing could influence lending institutions in negotiating the loan tenure, interest rates, and grace periods. Correspondingly, it would make LGUs look for lending institutions that offer the lowest or most advantageous interest rate. The CRI is envisioned to help LGUs constructively and effectively link their physical and capital investment plans with the appropriate resource mobilization agenda. On the other hand, capping based on CRI would force small- and low-income LGUs to start modestly with their borrowings, and eventually expand when capacity is built over time.

Once established, the CRI would be able to expand further the vision of the LGU Financing Framework to (i) identify the status of LGUs in terms of credit financing, (ii) aid the lending institutions by supplementing their risk assessment tools using government-issued creditworthiness ratings, and (iii) enable LGUs to plan and strategize on resource mobilization using debt performance rating and related metrics (footnote 58).

## Mandaluyong City Public Market Public–Private Partnership Project: A Case Study

### Background

The previous Mandaluyong Public Market was razed by a fire accident in 1990. The vendors who had carried out business in this market were transferred to street sidewalks and parks while the lot where the previous public market was established remained idle.

The occupation of the sidewalks by the vendors inconvenienced the general public who were using the sidewalks for their commute. The City Government decided to develop the public market to provide the vendors a place to carry out their business and free the sidewalks for the commuters.

### Physical Infrastructure

A seven-story commercial center, named The Marketplace, was designed to include a public market, street-front stores, a parking garage, commercial shops, department stores, a bowling alley, and a movie theater.

### Description of the Public–Private Partnership

In 1991, the Mandaluyong City Government (the local government) entered into a PPP contract agreement to develop the marketplace. The project was awarded through a solicited proposal mode. The winning bid for the ₱300 million ($6 million as of April 2020) project came from the Macro Founders and Developers, Inc. (MFD), a business consortium formed for this project.

The private developer constructed the public market on the ground floor of the commercial center and transferred control to the Mandaluyong City government immediately following completion. Half of the stalls in the public market were constructed by the city government and the other half were constructed by the stall owners, per the agreement between the city and the Association of Stall Owners. The government was designated as the operator of the public market and engaged in the collection of stall fees. Maintenance and security for the public market were outsourced to the MFD.[59]

The remainder of The Marketplace, the commercial complex, fell under the BOT scheme. The Mandaluyong City government offered a 40-year concession to the MFD for the operation and maintenance of this portion of the complex. Though the government retained ownership of the land used in the project, it did not require lease payments from the MFD for its use. The government does not have a share in any of the revenue generated by the commercial complex, and that revenue is used by the MFD to recoup the capital and operating costs. At the end of 40 years, the MFD will transfer the operation and maintenance of the commercial complex to the Mandaluyong City government (footnote 59).

Tenantable areas have been leased to banks, pawnshops, service shops, dry goods stores, restaurants, cinemas, amusement facilities, and other third parties. The rental and other revenues are expected to enable the private contractor to recover the cost of its investment and realize a reasonable rate of return (footnote 31).

**Table 43: Risk Matrix for the Build-Operate-Transfer Arrangement**

| Risk Category | Private | Public | Shared |
|---|---|---|---|
| Construction | ✓ | | |
| Demand | ✓ | | |
| Revenue | ✓ | | |
| Competition | ✓ | | |
| Environmental and social | | | ✓ |
| Land acquisition | | ✓ | |

## Project finance

The original project cost estimate was ₱300 million ($6 million as of April 2020), and the project financing is given below.

- 50% of the project cost was financed by debt and the remaining was financed by equity contribution from the MFD and advances from shops and charitable institutions
- The equity contribution from the MFD was 25% of the project cost, and 25% of the project cost came from advances paid by shops and charitable contributions[60]
- 50% of the project cost was financed by debt. The Asian Financing and Investment Corporation, a subsidiary of the Asian Development Bank, provided a 10-year loan at concessional rates for the project.

59 ESC-PAU. 2012. *Case Study (Public Buildings)*. Manila. https://www.esc-pau.fr/ppp/documents/featured_projects/philippines_mandaluyong_city.pdf.

60 ESCAP. 2008. *Case study 6: The Mandaluyong market, Philippines*. Philippines. https://www.unescap.org/ttdw/ppp/ppp_primer/96_the_mandaluyong_market_philippines.html.

The final project cost was ₱450 million ($9 million as of April 2020). As the project had high commercial potential, the MFD took on all the construction risk and absorbed this increase by making incremental equity infusion (footnote 59).

## Project construction

Under the build–transfer arrangement, the new public market was turned over to the city government for its exclusive supervision and control in 1993. The MFD constructed one-half of the stalls inside the market and leased them to market vendors while the remaining stalls were constructed by the stallholders themselves (footnote 31).

## Project revenues

The project is considered a success, generating sufficient revenues for the private developer to achieve a reasonable rate of return.

The Mandaluyong City Government has been earning revenues from the operation of the wet public market as well as from the business taxes, licenses, and fees paid by the lessees of the commercial complex.

## Key learnings

- Well-planned PPP projects can help local governments deliver the necessary infrastructure services to the public.
- Stakeholder engagement and involvement is a major driver for the project success. The project received commitment from the local communities and the Mandaluyong City Government.
- Transparent procurement of this project ensured selection of the most qualified bidder at amicable terms for both the public and private sector.
- Mixed-use land development has helped the Mandaluyong City Government develop this project without any capital outlay. Moreover, the Mandaluyong City Government benefits from incremental revenues from collecting taxes from the businesses in the marketplace.

# Appendixes

## Appendix 1: Methodology

### 1.1 Research Period

The research was carried out in 2020.

### 1.2 List of Indicators

Table A1.1 through Table A1.6 present a list of indicators for each major topic, including the definition and/or explanation of certain indicators where it is deemed necessary.

**Table A1.1: Overview**

| Subcategory | Supporting Indicators | Units | Definition |
|---|---|---|---|
| Overview | None | Description | • Overview of the PPP legal and regulatory framework<br>• Number of PPP projects reaching financial close from 1990 till end of 2019 across sectors<br>• Total investment made in PPPs from 1990 to 2019 across sectors<br>• Features of past PPP projects including the number of PPPs procured through various modes of PPP procurement<br>• Number of PPP projects under preparation and procurement<br>• Number of PPP projects supported by the government<br>• Payment mechanism for PPPs<br>• Foreign sponsor participation in PPPs from 1990 to 2019<br>• Major sponsors active in the country's infrastructure sector<br>• Challenges associated with the PPP landscape in the country |

## Table A1.2: National Public–Private Partnership Landscape

| Subcategory | Supporting Indicators | Units | Definition |
|---|---|---|---|
| National PPP legal and regulatory framework | Does the country have— | Yes/No/Not Applicable/ Unavailable | Details on the legal and regulatory framework applicable to PPPs and its evolution since the introduction of PPPs in the country<br><br>Details on other supporting laws and regulations governing PPPs in the country |
| | • National PPP laws and regulations? | Yes/No/Not Applicable/ Unavailable | |
| | • Public financial management laws and regulations? | Yes/No/Not Applicable/ Unavailable | |
| | • Sector-specific laws and regulations? | Yes/No/Not Applicable/ Unavailable | |
| | • Procurement laws and regulations? | Yes/No/Not Applicable/ Unavailable | |
| | • Environmental laws and regulations? | Yes/No/Not Applicable/ Unavailable | |
| | • Laws and regulations for social compliance? | Yes/No/Not Applicable/ Unavailable | |
| | • Laws and regulations governing land acquisition and ownership? | Yes/No/Not Applicable/ Unavailable | |
| | • Taxation laws and regulations? | Yes/No/Not Applicable/ Unavailable | |
| | • Employment laws and regulations? | Yes/No/Not Applicable/ Unavailable | |
| | • Licensing requirements? | Yes/No/Not Applicable/ Unavailable | |
| | Evolution of the PPP legal and regulatory framework in the country | Description | |
| | What are the other components of the PPP legal and regulatory framework? | Description | |
| PPP types | Number of PPP types defined in the PPP regulations | Number | Details on the PPP types allowed to be used as per PPP legal and regulatory framework. In case the PPP legal and regulatory framework doesn't specify the PPP types, this section provides the details on the specific PPP types which have been adopted for various PPP projects at various stages of the PPP lifecycle. |
| Eligible sectors | • Transportation infrastructure | Yes/No/Not Applicable/ Unavailable | Details on various infrastructure sectors for which projects could be procured through the PPP route as per the PPP legal and regulatory framework |
| | • Road infrastructure | Yes/No/Not Applicable/ Unavailable | |
| | • Water resources and irrigation infrastructure | Yes/No/Not Applicable/ Unavailable | |
| | • Water supply infrastructure | Yes/No/Not Applicable/ Unavailable | |
| | • Infrastructure for centralized water waste management systems | Yes/No/Not Applicable/ Unavailable | |

*continued on next page*

*continued from previous page*

| Subcategory | Supporting Indicators | Units | Definition |
|---|---|---|---|
| | • Infrastructure for local water waste management system | Yes/No/Not Applicable/ Unavailable | |
| | • Infrastructure for waste management system | Yes/No/Not Applicable/ Unavailable | |
| | • Telecommunication and informatics infrastructure | Yes/No/Not Applicable/ Unavailable | |
| | • Energy and electricity infrastructure including renewable energy | Yes/No/Not Applicable/ Unavailable | |
| | • Energy conservation infrastructure | Yes/No/Not Applicable/ Unavailable | |
| | • Urban facilities infrastructure | Yes/No/Not Applicable/ Unavailable | |
| | • Zone infrastructure | Yes/No/Not Applicable/ Unavailable | |
| | • Tourism infrastructure (e.g., tourism information center) | Yes/No/Not Applicable/ Unavailable | |
| | • Education facilities, research and development infrastructure | Yes/No/Not Applicable/ Unavailable | |
| | • Health infrastructure | Yes/No/Not Applicable/ Unavailable | |
| | • Public housing infrastructure | Yes/No/Not Applicable/ Unavailable | |
| Public–private partnership institutional framework | Does the country have a national PPP unit? | Yes/No/Not Applicable/ Unavailable | Details on the PPP institutional framework including availability of a PPP Unit, functions of the PPP Unit, principal public entities associated with PPPs and their respective functions, and details of public entities responsible for PPP project identification, appraisal, approval, oversight, and monitoring |
| | What are the functions of the national PPP unit? | | |
| | • Supporting the design and operationalization of the National PPP Enabling Framework? | Yes/No/Not Applicable/ Unavailable | |
| | • Helping develop a national PPP pipeline? | Yes/No/Not Applicable/ Unavailable | |
| | • Supporting the arrangement of funding for project preparation (budgetary allocations, technical assistance funding from multilateral development agencies, operating a dedicated project preparation/project development fund)? | Yes/No/Not Applicable/ Unavailable | |
| | • Guidance for project preparation to and coordination with the government agencies responsible for sponsoring the projects? | Yes/No/Not Applicable/ Unavailable | |
| | • Making recommendations to the PPP Committee and/or other approving authorities to provide approvals associated with various stages of the PPP process? | Yes/No/Not Applicable/ Unavailable | |

*continued on next page*

*continued from previous page*

| Subcategory | Supporting Indicators | Units | Definition |
|---|---|---|---|
| Entities responsible for PPP project identification, approval, and oversight | Who is responsible for identifying, preparing, and procuring the PPP projects? | Description | |
| | Is there a PPP Committee for providing approvals at various stages of PPP projects? | Yes/No/Not Applicable/ Unavailable | |
| | Who are the approving authorities other than the PPP Committee for the PPP projects? | | |
| | Does the country have an independent think tank for various PPP planning, budgeting, and policy decisions? | Yes/No/Not Applicable/ Unavailable | |
| | Is there a legislature for the PPP program oversight? | Yes/No/Not Applicable/ Unavailable | |
| Entities responsible for PPP project monitoring | Is there an entity for monitoring of PPP projects post commercial close? | Yes/No/Not Applicable/ Unavailable | |
| | Is there an entity for monitoring and management of fiscal risks and liabilities from PPP projects for the Ministry of Finance (MOF)? | Yes/No/Not Applicable/ Unavailable | |
| The public–private partnership process | Does the PPP legal and regulatory framework provide for a PPP implementation process covering the entire PPP lifecycle? | Yes/No/Not Applicable/ Unavailable | Details on various stages of the PPP process including PPP project identification, preparation, structuring, procurement, and management as per the PPP legal and regulatory framework in the country |
| | Does the Feasibility Assessment Stage cover— | Yes/No/Not Applicable/ Unavailable | |
| | • Technical feasibility? | Yes/No/Not Applicable/ Unavailable | |
| | • Socioeconomic feasibility? | Yes/No/Not Applicable/ Unavailable | |
| | • Environmental sustainability? | Yes/No/Not Applicable/ Unavailable | |
| | • Financial feasibility? | Yes/No/Not Applicable/ Unavailable | |
| | • Fiscal affordability assessment? | Yes/No/Not Applicable/ Unavailable | |
| | • Legal assessment? | Yes/No/Not Applicable/ Unavailable | |
| | • Risk assessment and PPP project structuring? | Yes/No/Not Applicable/ Unavailable | |
| | • Value for Money assessment? | Yes/No/Not Applicable/ Unavailable | |
| | • Market sounding with stakeholders? | Yes/No/Not Applicable/ Unavailable | |
| | Is the PPP procurement plan required? | Yes/No/Not Applicable/ Unavailable | |

*continued on next page*

*continued from previous page*

| Subcategory | Supporting Indicators | Units | Definition |
|---|---|---|---|
| | Is there a need to set up a separate PPP procurement committee? | Yes/No/Not Applicable/ Unavailable | |
| | Is competitive bidding the only method for selection of PPP private developer? | Yes/No/Not Applicable/ Unavailable | |
| | Is the prequalification stage necessary? Or does the PPP legal and regulatory framework allow flexibility to skip the prequalification stage? | Yes/No/Not Applicable/ Unavailable | |
| | Does the PPP legal and regulatory process provide the option to the preferred bidder for contract negotiations? | Yes/No/Not Applicable/ Unavailable | |
| | Does the PPP Legal and Regulatory Framework allow unsuccessful bidders to challenge the award/ submit complaints? | Yes/No/Not Applicable/ Unavailable | |
| | What is the maximum time allowed for submitting a complaint/ challenging the award by unsuccessful bidders from the announcement of the preferred bidder? | Yes/No/Not Applicable/ Unavailable | |
| | Does the PPP legal and regulatory framework provide for transparency? | Yes/No/Not Applicable/ Unavailable | |
| | Which of the following are required to be published? | Yes/No/Not Applicable/ Unavailable | |
| | • Findings from the feasibility assessment? | Yes/No/Not Applicable/ Unavailable | |
| | • Procurement notice? | Yes/No/Not Applicable/ Unavailable | |
| | • Outcome of stakeholder consultations from market sounding? | Yes/No/Not Applicable/ Unavailable | |
| | • Clarifications to prequalification queries? | Yes/No/Not Applicable/ Unavailable | |
| | • Prequalification results? | Yes/No/Not Applicable/ Unavailable | |
| | • Clarifications to pre-bid queries? | Yes/No/Not Applicable/ Unavailable | |
| | • Results for the bid stage and selection of preferred bidder? | Yes/No/Not Applicable/ Unavailable | |
| | • Final concession agreement to be entered between the government agency and the preferred bidder? And other PPP project agreements executed between government agency and preferred bidder? | Yes/No/Not Applicable/ Unavailable | |
| | • Confidentiality | Yes/No/Not Applicable/ Unavailable | |

*continued on next page*

*continued from previous page*

| Subcategory | Supporting Indicators | Units | Definition |
|---|---|---|---|
| PPP standard operating procedures, toolkits, templates, and model bid documents | Does the country have PPP Guidelines/PPP Guidance Manual? | Yes/No/Not Applicable/ Unavailable | Details on standard operating procedures and standard templates or model bidding documents available for PPPs, if any.<br><br>Details on the key clauses in a PPP Agreement based on the review of select PPP Agreements already executed, and/or the review of the PPP legal and regulatory framework |
| | Does the PPP Guidelines/PPP Guidance Manual adequately cover the process, entities involved, roles and responsibilities of various entities, approvals required at various stages, and the timelines for the various stages of the PPP project lifecycle? | Yes/No/Not Applicable/ Unavailable | |
| | What are the templates and checklists available in the PPP Guidelines/PPP Guidance Manual? | Yes/No/Not Applicable/ Unavailable | |
| | • Project Needs Assessment and Options Analysis checklist? | Yes/No/Not Applicable/ Unavailable | |
| | • Project Due Diligence checklist? | Yes/No/Not Applicable/ Unavailable | |
| | • Technical Assessment checklist? | Yes/No/Not Applicable/ Unavailable | |
| | • Environmental Assessment checklist? | Yes/No/Not Applicable/ Unavailable | |
| | • PPP Procurement Plan template? | Yes/No/Not Applicable/ Unavailable | |
| | Does the country have standardized/ model bidding documents for PPPs? | Yes/No/Not Applicable/ Unavailable | |
| | • Model Request for Qualification (RFQ) document? | Yes/No/Not Applicable/ Unavailable | |
| | • Model Request for Proposal (RFP) document? | Yes/No/Not Applicable/ Unavailable | |
| | • Model PPP/Concession Agreement? | Yes/No/Not Applicable/ Unavailable | |
| | • State Support Agreement? | Yes/No/Not Applicable/ Unavailable | |
| | • VGF Agreement? | Yes/No/Not Applicable/ Unavailable | |
| | • Guarantee Agreement? | Yes/No/Not Applicable/ Unavailable | |
| | • Power Purchase Agreement? | Yes/No/Not Applicable/ Unavailable | |
| | • Capacity Take-or-Pay Contract? | Yes/No/Not Applicable/ Unavailable | |
| | • Fuel Supply Agreement? | Yes/No/Not Applicable/ Unavailable | |
| | • Transmission and Use of System Agreement? | Yes/No/Not Applicable/ Unavailable | |
| | • Performance-based Operations and Maintenance Contract? | Yes/No/Not Applicable/ Unavailable | |

*continued on next page*

*continued from previous page*

| Subcategory | Supporting Indicators | Units | Definition |
|---|---|---|---|
| | • Engineering, Procurement and Construction Contract? | Yes/No/Not Applicable/ Unavailable | |
| | Does the country have standardized PPP agreement terms? | Yes/No/Not Applicable/ Unavailable | |
| | • PPP Family Indicator? | Yes/No/Not Applicable/ Unavailable | |
| | • PPP Mode Validity Indicator? | Yes/No/Not Applicable/ Unavailable | |
| | • PPP Suitability Filter? | Yes/No/Not Applicable/ Unavailable | |
| | • PPP Screening Tool? | Yes/No/Not Applicable/ Unavailable | |
| | • Financial Viability Indicator Model? | Yes/No/Not Applicable/ Unavailable | |
| | • Economic Viability Indicator Model? | Yes/No/Not Applicable/ Unavailable | |
| | • VFM Indicator Tool? | Yes/No/Not Applicable/ Unavailable | |
| | • Readiness Filter? | Yes/No/Not Applicable/ Unavailable | |
| | Is there a framework for monitoring fiscal risks from PPPs including the following? | Yes/No/Not Applicable/ Unavailable | |
| | • Process for assessing fiscal commitments? | Yes/No/Not Applicable/ Unavailable | |
| | • Process for approving fiscal commitments? | Yes/No/Not Applicable/ Unavailable | |
| | • Process for monitoring fiscal commitments? | Yes/No/Not Applicable/ Unavailable | |
| | • Process for reporting fiscal commitments? | Yes/No/Not Applicable/ Unavailable | |
| | • Process for budgeting fiscal commitments? | Yes/No/Not Applicable/ Unavailable | |
| | Are there fiscal prudence norms/ thresholds to limit fiscal exposure to PPPs? | Yes/No/Not Applicable/ Unavailable | |
| | Is there a process for assessing and budgeting contingent liabilities from PPPs? | Yes/No/Not Applicable/ Unavailable | |
| Lender's security rights | Does the law specifically enable lenders the following rights: | Yes/No/Not Applicable/ Unavailable | The rights of lenders including the charge of project assets |
| | • Security over the project assets | Yes/No/Not Applicable/ Unavailable | |
| | • Security over the land on which they are built (land use right) | Yes/No/Not Applicable/ Unavailable | |
| | • Security over the shares of a PPP project company | Yes/No/Not Applicable/ Unavailable | |

*continued on next page*

*continued from previous page*

| Subcategory | Supporting Indicators | Units | Definition |
|---|---|---|---|
| | • Can there be a direct agreement between the government and lenders? | Yes/No/Not Applicable/ Unavailable | |
| | • Do lenders get priority in the case of insolvency? | Yes/No/Not Applicable/ Unavailable | |
| | • Can lenders be given step-in rights? | Yes/No/Not Applicable/ Unavailable | |
| Termination and compen-sation | Does the law specifically enable compensation payment to the private partner in case of early termination due to: | | Definition on whether the private player is eligible for compensation in case of PPP project termination due to various reasons |
| | • Public sector default or termination for reasons of public interest | Yes/No/Not Applicable/ Unavailable | |
| | • Private sector default | Yes/No/Not Applicable/ Unavailable | |
| | • Force majeure | Yes/No/Not Applicable/ Unavailable | |
| | • Does the law enable the concept of economic/financial equilibrium? | Yes/No/Not Applicable/ Unavailable | |
| | Does the law enable compensation payment to the private partner due to: | Yes/No/Not Applicable/ Unavailable | |
| | • Material adverse government action | Yes/No/Not Applicable/ Unavailable | |
| | • Force majeure | Yes/No/Not Applicable/ Unavailable | |
| | • Change in law | Yes/No/Not Applicable/ Unavailable | |
| Unsolicited PPP proposals | Does the PPP legal and regulatory framework allow submission and acceptance of unsolicited proposals? | Yes/No/Not Applicable/ Unavailable | Details on possibility of submission of unsolicited PPP proposals, and their treatment, including, potential advantages provided to the unsolicited PPP proposal proponent at the PPP procurement stage |
| | What are the advantages provided to the project proponent for an unsolicited bid? | | |
| | • Competitive advantage at bid evaluation? | Yes/No/Not Applicable/ Unavailable | |
| | • Swiss Challenge? | Yes/No/Not Applicable/ Unavailable | |
| | • Compensation of the project development costs? | Yes/No/Not Applicable/ Unavailable | |
| | • Government support for land acquisition and resettlement cost? | Yes/No/Not Applicable/ Unavailable | |
| | Government support in the form of viability gap funding and guarantees? | Yes/No/Not Applicable/ Unavailable | |

*continued on next page*

*continued from previous page*

| Subcategory | Supporting Indicators | Units | Definition |
|---|---|---|---|
| Foreign investor participation restrictions | Is there any restriction for foreign investors on: | | Definition of whether there are any statutory restrictions on foreign equity investments and ownership in PPP projects |
| | • Land use/ownership rights as opposed to similar rights of local investors | Yes/No/Not Applicable/ Unavailable | |
| | • Currency conversion | Yes/No/Not Applicable/ Unavailable | |
| Dispute resolution | Does the country have a dispute resolution tribunal (DRT)? | Yes/No/Not Applicable/ Unavailable | Definition of the dispute resolution process and mechanisms available in the country |
| | Does the country have an institutional arbitration mechanism? | Yes/No/Not Applicable/ Unavailable | |
| | Can a foreign law be chosen to govern PPP contracts? | Yes/No/Not Applicable/ Unavailable | |
| | What dispute resolution mechanisms are available for PPP agreements? | | |
| | • Court litigation | Yes/No/Not Applicable/ Unavailable | |
| | • Local arbitration | Yes/No/Not Applicable/ Unavailable | |
| | • International arbitration | Yes/No/Not Applicable/ Unavailable | |
| | Has the country signed the New York Convention on the Recognition and Enforcement of Foreign Arbitral Awards? | Yes/No/Not Applicable/ Unavailable | |
| Environ-mental and social issues | Is there a local regulation establishing a process for environmental impact assessment? | Yes/No/Not Applicable/ Unavailable | Details on whether the legal and regulatory framework governing PPPs stipulates a mechanism for managing the environmental impact of a PPP project, including the potential environmental issues which could be caused by a PPP project |
| | Is there a legal mechanism for the private partner to limit environmental liability for what is outside of its control or caused by third parties? | Yes/No/Not Applicable/ Unavailable | Deliberation on whether a private partner can limit the circumstances where it is penalized for breaching environmental standards where such a breach is not within its control. For example, a wastewater treatment plant operator will wish to avoid prosecution or even liability for pollution caused by a pollutant in the influent which the treatment plant cannot treat, or will at least want to have the power to pursue the polluter to stop the pollution and/or obtain compensation. |
| | Is there a local regulation establishing a process for social impact assessment? | Yes/No/Not Applicable/ Unavailable | Details on whether the legal and regulatory framework governing PPPs stipulates a mechanism for managing the social impact of a PPP project, including the potential social issues which could be caused by a PPP project |

*continued on next page*

*continued from previous page*

| Subcategory | Supporting Indicators | Units | Definition |
|---|---|---|---|
| | Is there involuntary land clearance for PPP projects? | Yes/No/Not Applicable/ Unavailable | Deliberation on whether land expropriation is possible for PPP projects |
| Land rights | Which of the following is permitted to the private partner: | | Definition of various mechanisms through which land ownership and/or land use rights could be provided to the private partner in respect of the project site for a PPP project<br><br>Details on land records and registration which could be provided to the private partner |
| | • Transfer land lease/use/ ownership rights to third party | Yes/No/Not Applicable/ Unavailable | |
| | • Use leased/owned land as collateral | Yes/No/Not Applicable/ Unavailable | |
| | • Mortgage leased/owned land | Yes/No/Not Applicable/ Unavailable | |
| | Is there a legal mechanism for granting wayleave rights, for example, laying water pipes or fibre cables over land occupied by persons other than the government or the private partner? | Yes/No/Not Applicable/ Unavailable | |
| | Is there a land registry/cadastre with public information on land plots? | Yes/No/Not Applicable/ Unavailable | |
| | Which of the following information on land plots is available to the private partner: | Yes/No/Not Applicable/ Unavailable | |
| | • Appraisal of land value | Yes/No/Not Applicable/ Unavailable | |
| | • Landowners | Yes/No/Not Applicable/ Unavailable | |
| | • Land boundaries | Yes/No/Not Applicable/ Unavailable | |
| | • Utility connections | Yes/No/Not Applicable/ Unavailable | |
| | • Immovable property on land | Yes/No/Not Applicable/ Unavailable | |
| | • Plots classification | Yes/No/Not Applicable/ Unavailable | |
| Government financial support for PPP projects | Is there a dedicated government financial support mechanism for PPP projects? | Yes/No/Not Applicable/ Unavailable | Details on various mechanisms of government financial support available to make PPP projects financially viable<br><br>Salient features of government financial support mechanisms available |
| | What are the instruments of government financial support available under this government financial support mechanism? | | |
| | • Capital grant | Yes/No/Not Applicable/ Unavailable | |
| | • Operations grant | Yes/No/Not Applicable/ Unavailable | |
| | • Annuity/availability payments | Yes/No/Not Applicable/ Unavailable | |

*continued on next page*

*continued from previous page*

| Subcategory | Supporting Indicators | Units | Definition |
|---|---|---|---|
| | • Guarantees to cover | Yes/No/Not Applicable/ Unavailable | |
| | – Currency inconvertibility and transfer risk | Yes/No/Not Applicable/ Unavailable | |
| | – Foreign exchange risk | Yes/No/Not Applicable/ Unavailable | |
| | – War and civil disturbance risk | Yes/No/Not Applicable/ Unavailable | |
| | – Breach of contract risk | Yes/No/Not Applicable/ Unavailable | |
| | – Regulatory risk | Yes/No/Not Applicable/ Unavailable | |
| | – Expropriation risk | Yes/No/Not Applicable/ Unavailable | |
| | – Government payment obligation risk | Yes/No/Not Applicable/ Unavailable | |
| | – Credit risk | Yes/No/Not Applicable/ Unavailable | |
| | – Minimum demand/revenue risk | Yes/No/Not Applicable/ Unavailable | |
| | – Risk of making annuity/ availability payments in a timely manner | Yes/No/Not Applicable/ Unavailable | |
| | What are the caps/ceilings for the government financial support under each of the abovementioned government financial support instruments? | | |
| | Is there a minimum PPP project size (investment) for a PPP project to be eligible for receiving government financial support? | Yes/No/Not Applicable/ Unavailable | |
| | Are there minimum financial commitment requirements for the private developer equity before the government support could be drawn? | Yes/No/Not Applicable/ Unavailable | |
| | Is the government financial support required, and an allowed bid parameter for PPP projects? | Yes/No/Not Applicable/ Unavailable | |
| | Are unsolicited PPP proposals eligible to receive government financial support? | Yes/No/Not Applicable/ Unavailable | |
| | Are there standard operating procedures for providing government financial support to PPP projects? | Yes/No/Not Applicable/ Unavailable | |

*continued on next page*

*continued from previous page*

| Subcategory | Supporting Indicators | Units | Definition |
|---|---|---|---|
| | • Appraisal and approval process | Yes/No/Not Applicable/ Unavailable | |
| | • Budgeting process | Yes/No/Not Applicable/ Unavailable | |
| | • Disbursement process | Yes/No/Not Applicable/ Unavailable | |
| | • Monitoring process | Yes/No/Not Applicable/ Unavailable | |
| | • Accounting, auditing, and reporting process | Yes/No/Not Applicable/ Unavailable | |
| | Who are the signatories to the Government Financial Support Agreement? | | |
| | Who is responsible for monitoring the performance of PPP projects availing government financial support? | Yes/No/Not Applicable/ Unavailable | |
| | • Independent engineer? | Yes/No/Not Applicable/ Unavailable | |
| | • Government agency? | Yes/No/Not Applicable/ Unavailable | |
| | • Ministry of Finance? | Yes/No/Not Applicable/ Unavailable | |
| | What are the other forms of government support available for PPP projects? | Yes/No/Not Applicable/ Unavailable | |
| | • Land acquisition funding support? | Yes/No/Not Applicable/ Unavailable | |
| | • Funding support for resettlement and rehabilitation of affected parties? | Yes/No/Not Applicable/ Unavailable | |
| | • Tax holidays/exemptions? | Yes/No/Not Applicable/ Unavailable | |
| | • Real estate development rights? | Yes/No/Not Applicable/ Unavailable | |
| | • Advertising and marketing rights? | Yes/No/Not Applicable/ Unavailable | |
| | • Interest rate/cost of debt subventions? | Yes/No/Not Applicable/ Unavailable | |
| | • Other subsidies and subventions? | Yes/No/Not Applicable/ Unavailable | |
| | Can the other forms of government support be availed over and above the government financial support through various instruments listed above? | Yes/No/Not Applicable/ Unavailable | |

*continued on next page*

*continued from previous page*

| Subcategory | Supporting Indicators | Units | Definition |
|---|---|---|---|
| Project develop-ment funding support | What are the various sources of funds for PPP project preparation? | | Details on various sources through which funding could be availed for the development activities (preparation, structuring, and procurement) for a PPP project<br><br>Details on stages of the PPP project development stage during which such funding could be availed and utilized, including payments to transaction advisors |
| | • Budgetary allocations | Yes/No/Not Applicable/ Unavailable | |
| | • Dedicated project preparation/ project development fund | Yes/No/Not Applicable/ Unavailable | |
| | • Technical assistance from multilateral, bilateral, and donor agencies? | Yes/No/Not Applicable/ Unavailable | |
| | • Recovery of project preparation funding from the preferred bidder? | Yes/No/Not Applicable/ Unavailable | |
| | At what stage of the PPP project can the project preparation/ development funding be availed by the government agency? | | |
| | • Pre-feasibility stage | Yes/No/Not Applicable/ Unavailable | |
| | • Detailed feasibility stage | Yes/No/Not Applicable/ Unavailable | |
| | • Transaction stage | Yes/No/Not Applicable/ Unavailable | |
| | Is there a list of project preparation/ project development activities toward which the project development funding can be utilized? | Yes/No/Not Applicable/ Unavailable | |
| | Can the project development funding be utilized to appoint transaction advisors for PPP projects? | Yes/No/Not Applicable/ Unavailable | |
| | Is there a specific process to be followed by government agencies to appoint transaction advisors? | Yes/No/Not Applicable/ Unavailable | |
| | What are the payment mechanisms for making payments to transaction advisors? | Yes/No/Not Applicable/ Unavailable | |
| | • Timesheet based | Yes/No/Not Applicable/ Unavailable | |
| | • Milestone based | Yes/No/Not Applicable/ Unavailable | |
| | Are there standard agreements and documents to avail project development funding? | Yes/No/Not Applicable/ Unavailable | |
| | Who are the signatories to the project development funding agreements? | | |

*continued on next page*

*continued from previous page*

| Subcategory | Supporting Indicators | Units | Definition |
|---|---|---|---|
| PPP project statistics | Is there a National PPP database for the country? | Yes/No/Not Applicable/ Unavailable | Details on the key PPP statistics in the country, such as (i) availability of a PPP database showing distribution of PPP projects across sectors and across various stages of the PPP lifecycle, and (ii) availability of a national PPP project pipeline and its alignment with the National Infrastructure Plan for the country |
| | Is the distribution of PPP projects across infrastructure sectors available? | Yes/No/Not Applicable/ Unavailable | |
| | Is the distribution of PPP projects across various stages of the PPP lifecycle available? | Yes/No/Not Applicable/ Unavailable | |
| | Does the country publish a national PPP project pipeline? | Yes/No/Not Applicable/ Unavailable | |
| | At what frequency is the national PPP project pipeline published? | | |
| | Is the national PPP project pipeline based on the National Infrastructure Plan for the country? | Yes/No/Not Applicable/ Unavailable | |
| Sources of PPP financing | Who are the typical entities financing PPP projects in the country? | Yes/No/Not Applicable/ Unavailable | Details on the sources of financing for PPP projects in the country<br><br>Details on typical key financing terms for various sources of financing, banks active in project finance for the last 24 months, active PPP project sponsors in the country for the last 24 months, availability of derivatives market, and availability of credit rating agencies in the country |
| | • Private developers | Yes/No/Not Applicable/ Unavailable | |
| | • Construction contractors | Yes/No/Not Applicable/ Unavailable | |
| | • Institutional/financial/private equity investors | Yes/No/Not Applicable/ Unavailable | |
| | • Pension funds | Yes/No/Not Applicable/ Unavailable | |
| | • Insurance companies | Yes/No/Not Applicable/ Unavailable | |
| | • Banks | Yes/No/Not Applicable/ Unavailable | |
| | • Non-banking financial corporation/financial institutions | Yes/No/Not Applicable/ Unavailable | |
| | • Donor agencies | Yes/No/Not Applicable/ Unavailable | |
| | • Government agencies and state-owned enterprises | Yes/No/Not Applicable/ Unavailable | |

*continued on next page*

*continued from previous page*

| Subcategory | Supporting Indicators | Units | Definition |
|---|---|---|---|
| | What is the distribution of financing among these entities financing PPP projects? | | |
| | Does the country have the history/ track record of issuing bonds by infrastructure projects? | Yes/No/Not Applicable/ Unavailable | |
| | How many infrastructure projects/ private developers for infrastructure projects have raised funding through bond issuances? | Number | |
| | What is the value of funding raised through capital markets by PPPs? | Number | |
| | Does the country have a matured derivatives market to hedge certain risks associated with PPPs? | Yes/No/Not Applicable/ Unavailable | |
| | Does the country have a national development bank? | Yes/No/Not Applicable/ Unavailable | |
| | Does the country have credit rating agencies to rate infrastructure projects? | Yes/No/Not Applicable/ Unavailable | |
| | Typically, what are the credit ratings achieved/received by infrastructure projects? | Yes/No/Not Applicable/ Unavailable | |
| | Is there a threshold credit rating for infrastructure PPPs below which institutional investors, pension funds, and insurance companies would not invest in infrastructure PPPs? | Yes/No/Not Applicable/ Unavailable | |
| | What is the typical funding model for infrastructure PPPs—corporate finance or project finance? | | |
| | Are there regulatory limits/ restrictions for the maximum exposure that can be taken by banks to infrastructure projects? | Yes/No/Not Applicable/ Unavailable | |

### Table A1.3: Sector-Specific Public–Private Partnership Landscape

| Subcategory | Supporting Indicators | Units | Definition |
|---|---|---|---|
| Contracting agencies in the sector | None | Description | Details on which government agencies could act as the contracting agencies for a PPP project |
| Sector laws and regulations | None | Description | Details on the applicable sector laws and regulations for PPP projects including the sector regulators and their respective functions |
| Foreign investment restrictions in the sector | Maximum allowed foreign ownership of equity in greenfield projects | % | Details on the maximum allowed foreign equity investment in greenfield PPP projects in a particular sector |
| Standard contracts in the sector | PPP/concession agreement | Yes/No/Not Applicable/ Unavailable | Specifics of whether standard contracts are available for PPP projects in a particular sector |
| | Performance-based operation and maintenance contract | Yes/No/Not Applicable/ Unavailable | |
| | Engineering procurement and construction contract | Yes/No/Not Applicable/ Unavailable | |
| Sector master plan | None | Description | Details on the master plan and/or roadmap adopted for infrastructure development in the sector by the national government and the corresponding line ministry<br><br>Details on the pipeline of PPP projects for the sector aligned with the sector master plan and/or roadmap<br><br>Details on the PPP projects under preparation and procurement in the sector |
| Features of past PPP projects | Number of PPP projects procured through various modes of PPP procurement—Direct Appointment, Unsolicited Bids, and Competitive Bids | Number | Features of past PPP projects based on supporting indicators in terms of the number and value (where applicable) of PPP projects for each supporting indicator |
| | Number and value of PPP projects reaching financial closure | Number | |
| | Number of PPP projects with foreign sponsor participation in absolute terms, and as a percentage of total number of PPP projects | Number | |
| | Number of PPP projects supported with various forms of government financial support—Viability Gap Funding, Government Guarantees, and Availability/ Performance Payments | Number | |
| | Number of PPP projects based on various types of payment mechanisms—User Charges, and Government Pay (Off-take) | Number | |

*continued on next page*

*continued from previous page*

| Subcategory | Supporting Indicators | Units | Definition |
|---|---|---|---|
| Tariffs applicable to the sector | None | Description | Details on the indicative tariffs applicable in the sector based on the examples of select PPP or other projects operational in the sector |
| Typical risk allocation for PPP projects in the sector | Traffic risk | Yes/No/Not Applicable/ Unavailable | Details on the typical risk allocation between the government contracting agency and the private partner based on examples of select PPP projects which have achieved commercial close |
| | Collection risk | Yes/No/Not Applicable/ Unavailable | |
| | Competition risk | Yes/No/Not Applicable/ Unavailable | |
| | Government payment risk | Yes/No/Not Applicable/ Unavailable | |
| | Environmental and social risk | Yes/No/Not Applicable/ Unavailable | |
| | Land acquisition risk | Yes/No/Not Applicable/ Unavailable | |
| | Permits | Yes/No/Not Applicable/ Unavailable | |
| | Geotechnical risk | Yes/No/Not Applicable/ Unavailable | |
| | Brownfield risk: inventories studies, property boundaries, project scope | Yes/No/Not Applicable/ Unavailable | |
| | Political risk | Yes/No/Not Applicable/ Unavailable | |
| | Force majeure | Yes/No/Not Applicable/ Unavailable | |
| | Foreign exchange risk | Yes/No/Not Applicable/ Unavailable | |
| | Construction risk | Yes/No/Not Applicable/ Unavailable | |
| Financing details for PPP projects in the sector | PPP projects with foreign lending participation | Number | Typical financing details based on past PPP projects on the lines of the supporting indicators |
| | PPP projects that received export credit agency/international financing institution support | Number | |
| | Typical debt: Equity ratio | Ratio | |
| | Time for financial closure | Months | |
| | Typical concession period | Years | |
| | Typical Financial Internal Rate of Return | % | |
| Challenges associated with PPPs in the sector | None | Description | Details on the PPP-related and sector-specific challenges faced by PPP projects in the sector |

### Table A1.4: Typical Sector-Specific Infrastructure Indicators for the Country

| Subcategory | Supporting Indicators | Units | Definition |
|---|---|---|---|
| Roads | Length of the total road network | kilometers | |
| | Quality of road infrastructure | 1(low) – 7(high) | |
| Railways | Length of total railway network | total route-km | |
| | Total number of passengers carried | Million passenger-km | |
| | Total volume of freight carried | Million ton-km | |
| | Quality of railways infrastructure | 1(low) – 7(high) | |
| Ports | Total number of ports | Number | |
| | Total freight capacity of all ports | MTPA | |
| | Total container traffic at ports | TEUs | |
| | Quality of port infrastructure | 1(low) – 7(high) | |
| | Quality of trade and transport-related infrastructure index | 1=low to 5=high | |
| Airports | No. of airports | Number | |
| | Total passenger capacity | million passengers | |
| | Quality of air transport infrastructure | 1 (low) – 7 (high) | |
| | Total number of projects with cumulative lending, grant, and technical assistance commitments in the transport sector | Number | |
| | Total amount of cumulative lending, grant, and technical assistance commitments in the transport sector | $ million | |
| Energy | Electric power consumption | kilowatt-hour per capita | |
| | Share of clean energy | % of total energy use | |
| | Access to electricity | % of population | |
| | Getting electricity (score out of 100) | Number | |
| | Energy imports | % of total energy use | |
| | Investment in energy with private participation | current $ million | |
| | Total number of projects with cumulative lending, grant, and technical assistance commitments in the energy sector | Number | |
| | Total amount of cumulative lending, grant, and technical assistance commitments in the energy sector | $ million | |
| Water and Wastewater | Improved water source access | % of population with access | |
| | Improved sanitation facilities access | % of population with access | |
| | Investment in water and sanitation with private participation | current $ million | |

*continued on next page*

*continued from previous page*

| Subcategory | Supporting Indicators | Units | Definition |
|---|---|---|---|
| | Total number of projects with cumulative lending, grant, and technical assistance commitments in water and other urban infrastructure and services | Number | |
| | Total amount of cumulative lending, grant, and technical assistance commitments in water and other urban infrastructure and services | $ million | |
| ICT | Telephone subscribers | per 100 inhabitants | |
| | Cellular Phone Subscribers | per 100 inhabitants | |
| | Cellular Network Coverage | % of population covered | |
| | Internet Subscribers | per 100 inhabitants | |
| | Internet Bandwidth per Internet User | kbps | |
| | Total number of projects with Cumulative Lending, Grant, and Technical Assistance Commitments in ICT sector | Number | |
| | Total amount of Cumulative Lending, Grant, and Technical Assistance Commitments in ICT sector | $ million | |
| Social infrastruc-ture | Government Expenditure on Education | % of GDP | |
| | Education spending as % of government spending | % | |
| | Primary School Gross Enrollment | % | |
| | Adult Literacy Rate | % | |
| | Total number of projects with Cumulative Lending, Grant, and Technical Assistance Commitments in education sector | Number | |
| | Total amount of Cumulative Lending, Grant, and Technical Assistance Commitments in education sector | $ million | |
| | Total Health Expenditure | % of GDP | |
| | Health spending per capita | USD | |
| | Maternal Mortality Ratio (modelled estimates per 100,000 live births) | (per 100,000 live births) | |
| | Infant Mortality Rate | (below 1 year/per 1,000 live births) | |
| | Life Expectancy at Birth | (years) | |
| | Child Malnutrition | (% below 5 years old) | |
| | Total number of projects with Cumulative Lending, Grant, and Technical Assistance Commitments in health sector | Number | |
| | Total amount of Cumulative Lending, Grant, and Technical Assistance Commitments in health sector | $ million | |
| | Existing No. of Affordable Housing Units | No. | |
| | Affordable Housing Gap | | |

*continued on next page*

### Table A1.5: Local Government Public–Private Partnership Landscape

| Subcategory | Supporting Indicators | Units | Definition |
|---|---|---|---|
| Key indicators related to local governments in the country | Number of Subnational Governments (SNGs) | | Details on the local governments using select key indicators on (i) the number and levels of local governments, (ii) the typical expenditure profile and heads, (iii) the typical revenue profile and heads, (iv) the typical debt profile and heads, and (v) grants and transfers from the higher levels of government |
| | • Municipal Level | Number | |
| | • Intermediate Level | Number | |
| | • Regional or State Level | Number | |
| | Total number of SNGs | Number | |
| | SNG Expenditure Profile | SNG Expenditure Profile | |
| | Total SNG Expenditure as % of GDP | % | |
| | • SNG Current Expenditure as % of GDP | % | |
| | • SNG Staff Expenditure as % of GDP | % | |
| | • SNG Investment as % of GDP | % | |
| | Total SNG Expenditure as % of the Total General Government (% of Total Public Expenditure) | % | |
| | • SNG Current Expenditure as a % of Total Current Expenditure of the General Government | % | |
| | • SNG Staff Expenditure as a % of Total Staff Expenditure of the General Government | % | |
| | • SNG Investment as a % of Total Investment of the General Government | % | |
| | Current Expenditure of SNG as a % of Total SNG Expenditure | % | |
| | Staff Expenditure of SNG as a % of Total SNG Expenditure | % | |
| | Investments of SNG as a % of Total SNG Expenditure | % | |
| | SNG Expenditure by Function | SNG Expenditure by Function | |
| | • General Public Services | % | |
| | • Defence | % | |
| | • Security and Public Order | % | |

*continued on next page*

*continued from previous page*

| Subcategory | Supporting Indicators | Units | Definition |
|---|---|---|---|
| | • Economic Affairs | % | |
| | • Environmental Protection | % | |
| | • Housing and Community Amenities | % | |
| | • Health | % | |
| | • Recreation, Culture, and Religion | % | |
| | • Education | % | |
| | • Social Protection | % | |
| | SNG Revenue Profile | SNG Revenue Profile | |
| | Total SNG Revenue as a % of GDP | % | |
| | • SNG Tax Revenue as a % of GDP | % | |
| | • SNG Grants and Subsidies as a % of GDP | % | |
| | • SNG Other Revenues as a % of GDP | % | |
| | Total SNG Revenue as % of Total General Government Revenue | % | |
| | • SNG Tax Revenue as a % of Total General Government Tax Revenue | % | |
| | • SNG Grants and Subsidies as a % of Total General Government Grants and Subsidies | % | |
| | • SNG Other Revenues as a % of Total Other Revenues | % | |
| | SNG Tax Revenue as a % of Total SNG Revenue | % | |
| | SNG Grants and Subsidies as a % of Total SNG Revenue | % | |
| | SNG Other Revenues as a % of Total SNG Revenue | % | |
| | SNG Debt Profile | SNG Debt Profile | |
| | Outstanding SNG Debt as % of GDP | % | |
| | Outstanding SNG Debt as % of Total Outstanding Debt of General Government | % | |

*continued on next page*

*continued from previous page*

| Subcategory | Supporting Indicators | Units | Definition |
|---|---|---|---|
| | Parameters for transfers to the Subnational Governments from the National Government | Parameters for transfers to the Subnational Governments from the National Government | |
| | Score on transfers to Subnational Governments | | |
| | • Score on system for allocating transfers | | |
| | • Score on timeliness of information on transfers | | |
| | • Score on extent of collection and reporting of consolidated fiscal data for general government | | |
| | Value of Central Government transfers to Subnational Governments | % of the GDP | |
| | Value of Actual budgetary allocation to Subnational Governments from National Government | % of total expenditure | |
| | Value of Deviation of actual against the budgeted transfers to Subnational Governments | % of budgeted transfers | |
| Local governance system | None | Description | Details on the local governance system in the country, including the various levels of local governments; their roles, responsibilities and functions; and the devolution of powers from the higher levels of government to these various levels of local governments. |
| Infrastruc-ture development plan for local governments | None | Description | Details on the infrastructure development plans prepared by the local governments based on their capital investment projects in the pipeline, and the coverage of such infrastructure development plans. |
| PPP enabling framework for local governments | None | Description | Details on the PPP enabling framework applicable to local government PPP projects, including PPP legal and regulatory framework, PPP policy framework, and PPP institutional framework |

*continued on next page*

*continued from previous page*

| Subcategory | Supporting Indicators | Units | Definition |
|---|---|---|---|
| Eligible sectors for PPPs for local governments | None | Description | Details on the eligible sectors in which PPPs could be undertaken by local government as government contracting agency |
| Revenues for local governments | None | Description | Details on the typical sources of revenue for local governments |
| Borrowings by local governments | None | Description | Details on the typical sources of debt financing available for local governments, the purpose for which borrowed funds could be used, the terms of such borrowings, and the borrowing exposure of select local governments |
| Budgetary allocation to local governments | None | Description | Details on the budgetary allocations and transfers to the local governments from the higher levels of government |
| Credit rating of local governments | None | Description | Details on the precedence of local governments being rated by credit rating agencies in the country<br>Details of credit ratings obtained by select local governments in the past |
| Case study on a local government PPP | None | Description | A case of a PPP project undertaken by a local government in the past, which covers details on project background, project assets, PPP structure for the project, risk allocation among the parties for the project, project finance and project revenue details, and key learnings from the PPP project |

## Table A1.6: Critical Macroeconomic and Infrastructure Sector Indicators for the Country

| Subcategory | Supporting Indicators | Units | Definition |
|---|---|---|---|
| Critical macro-economic and infrastruc-ture sector indicators | Total population | million | Details of major macroeconomic indicators for the country |
| | Average annual population growth rate | % | |
| | Population density | persons per square kilometer (km²) of surface area | |
| | Urban population | % of total population | |
| | Surface area | '000 km² | |
| | Unemployment rate | % | |
| | Proportion of population below $1.90 purchasing power parity (PPP) a day | % | |
| | Nominal gross domestic product (GDP) | $ billion | |
| | | % | |
| | Annual growth rate of GDP (2019) | % | |
| | Annual growth rate of GDP (2020 forecast) | % | |
| | Annual growth rate of GDP (2021 forecast) | % | |
| | GDP at purchasing power parity (PPP) per capita | $ at PPP | |
| | GDP at current market prices | $ billion | |
| | Gross fixed investment at current market prices | % of GDP | |
| | Per capita gross national income (GNI), Atlas Method | $ | |
| | Inflation rate (2019) | % | |
| | Inflation rate (2020 forecast) | % | |
| | Inflation rate (2021 forecast) | % | |
| | Current account (2019) | % of GDP | |
| | External trade, goods, value of imports, CIF (2018) | $ billion | |
| | External trade, goods, value of exports, FOB (2018) | $ billion | |
| | CPI % change over 2018 | % of CPI in 2018 | |
| | Real effective exchange rate | | |
| | Investment in energy with private sector participation | Current $ million | |

*continued on next page*

*continued from previous page*

| Subcategory | Supporting Indicators | Units | Definition |
|---|---|---|---|
| | Investment in transport with private sector participation | Current $ million | |
| | Investment in water and sanitation with private sector participation | Current $ million | |
| | Logistics Performance Index (LPI) rank | Number | |
| | Logistics Performance Index (LPI) score | Number | |
| | Customs rank | Number | |
| | Customs score | Number | |
| | Infrastructure rank | Number | |
| | Infrastructure score | Number | |
| | International shipments rank | Number | |
| | International shipments score | Number | |
| | Logistics competence rank | Number | |
| | Logistics competence score | Number | |
| | Tracking and tracing rank | Number | |
| | Tracking and tracing score | Number | |
| | Timeliness rank | Number | |
| | Timeliness score | Number | |
| | **Structure of Output (% of GDP at current producer \| basic prices)** | | |
| | Agriculture | % | |
| | Industry | % | |
| | Services | % | |
| | Consumer price index (national) | % annual change | |
| | Producer price index | % annual change | |
| | Wholesale price index (national) | % annual change | |
| | Retail price index | % annual change | |
| | Exchange rates (End of period) | Local currency - $ | |
| | **ADF Portfolio** | | |
| | Total number of loans | Number | |
| | 1. Sovereign | Number | |
| | 2. Non-sovereign | Number | |
| | Net loan amount | $ million, cumulative | |
| | 1. Sovereign | $ million, cumulative | |
| | 2. Non-sovereign | $ million, cumulative | |

*continued on next page*

*continued from previous page*

| Subcategory | Supporting Indicators | Units | Definition |
|---|---|---|---|
| | Disbursed amount | $ million, cumulative | |
| | 1. Sovereign | $ million, cumulative | |
| | 2. Non-sovereign | $ million, cumulative | |
| | Net foreign direct investment (FDI) inflows | % of GDP | |
| | Sovereign debt risk rating | Letter rating | |
| | Central government debt | % of GDP | |
| | CPIA quality of budgetary and financial management rating | 1=low to 6=high | |
| | **Ease of Doing Business** | | |
| | Ease of doing business rank | Number | |
| | Starting a business (rank) | Number | |
| | Dealing with construction permits (rank) | Number | |
| | Getting electricity (rank) | Number | |
| | Registering property (rank) | Number | |
| | Getting credit (rank) | Number | |
| | Protecting minority investors (rank) | Number | |
| | Paying taxes (rank) | Number | |
| | Trading across borders (rank) | Number | |
| | Enforcing contracts (rank) | Number | |
| | Resolving insolvency (rank) | Number | |
| | **Corruption and Sustainable Development Index** | | |
| | Corruption Perceptions Index rank (out of 180) | Number | |
| | Corruption Perceptions Index score (out of 100) | Number | |
| | Sustainable Development Index rank | Number | |
| | Sustainable Development Index score | Number | |
| | **Cumulative Lending, Grant, and Technical Assistance Commitments** | | |
| | Number of projects | Number | |
| | Total lending | $ million | |
| | GCI infrastructure score | out of 7 | |
| | **EIU Infra-scope Index Score** | | |
| | PPP regulations score (out of 100) | Number | |
| | PPP regulations rank | Number | |
| | PPP institutions score (out of 100) | Number | |
| | PPP institutions rank | Number | |

*continued on next page*

*continued from previous page*

| Subcategory | Supporting Indicators | Units | Definition |
|---|---|---|---|
| | PPP market maturity score (out of 100) | Number | |
| | PPP market maturity rank | Number | |
| | PPP financing score (out of 100) | Number | |
| | PPP financing rank | Number | |
| | Investment and business climate score (out of 100) | Number | |
| | Investment and business climate rank | Number | |
| Ease of Doing Business | Score of starting a business | (0-100) | Details on the various Ease of Doing Business parameters for the country based on the World Bank's Ease of Doing Business publication |
| | • Procedures | (number) | |
| | • Time | (days) | |
| | • Cost | (number) | |
| | • Paid-in min. capital | (% of income per capita) | |
| | Score of dealing with construction permits | (0-100) | |
| | • Procedures | (number) | |
| | • Time | (days) | |
| | • Cost | (% of warehouse value) | |
| | • Building quality control index | (0-15) | |
| | Score of getting electricity | (0-100) | |
| | • Procedures | (number) | |
| | • Time | (days) | |
| | • Cost | (% of income per capita) | |
| | • Reliability of supply and transparency of tariff index | (0-8) | |
| | Score of registering property | (0-100) | |
| | • Procedures | (number) | |
| | • Time | (days) | |
| | • Cost | (% of property value) | |
| | • Quality of the land administration index | (0-30) | |
| | Score of getting credit | (0-100) | |
| | • Strength of legal rights index | (0-12) | |
| | • Depth of credit information index | (0-8) | |
| | • Credit registry coverage | (% of adults) | |
| | • Credit bureau coverage | (% of adults) | |
| | Score of protecting minority investors | (0-100) | |
| | • Extent of disclosure index | (0-10) | |
| | • Extent of director liability index | (0-10) | |
| | • Ease of shareholder suits index | (0-10) | |

*continued on next page*

*continued from previous page*

| Subcategory | Supporting Indicators | Units | Definition |
|---|---|---|---|
| | • Extent of shareholder rights index | (0-6) | |
| | • Extent of ownership and control index | (0-7) | |
| | • Extent of corporate transparency index | (0-7) | |
| | Score of paying taxes | (0-100) | |
| | • Payments | (number per year) | |
| | • Time | (hours per year) | |
| | • Total tax and contribution rate | (% of profit) | |
| | • Post-filing index | (0-100) | |
| | Score of trading across borders | (0-100) | |
| | ***Time to export*** | | |
| | • Documentary compliance | (hours) | |
| | • Border compliance | (hours) | |
| | ***Cost to export*** | | |
| | Documentary compliance | (USD) | |
| | Border compliance | (USD) | |
| | ***Time to export*** | | |
| | • Documentary compliance | (hours) | |
| | • Border compliance | (hours) | |
| | ***Cost to export*** | | |
| | Documentary compliance | (USD) | |
| | • Border compliance | (USD) | |
| | Score of enforcing contracts | (0-100) | |
| | • Time | (days) | |
| | • Cost | (% of claim value) | |
| | • Quality of judicial processes index | (0-18) | |
| | Score of resolving insolvency | (0-100) | |
| | • Recovery rate | (cents on the dollar) | |
| | • Time | (years) | |
| | • Cost | (% of estate) | |
| | • Outcome | (0 as piecemeal sale and 1 as going concern) | |
| | • Strength of insolvency framework index | (0-16) | |

## 1.3 Comment of Financial Indicators

In regard to indicative loan terms presented in this publication, it should be noted that it is very difficult to generalize the loan terms as the data are dynamic. The data vary from one sector to another, and in a particular sector, the loan terms differ from one project to another depending on the project cash flows and the creditworthiness of the project sponsors. The loan terms are also driven by market forces, monetary policy, fiscal policy, and other macroeconomic variables. Generally, international banks provide project finance in internationally convertible currency and the terms are broadly consistent across countries, given other risk factors are held constant, as country risk is the only risk factor. In general, some of the factors that determine pricing are:

- exposure to market/revenue risk,
- exposure to foreign exchange risk,
- credibility of off-taker,
- credibility of sovereign,
- availability of export credit/multilateral support,
- "proven-ness" of sector and underlying technology, and
- financing market (such as global macroeconomic events) and regulations (i.e., Basel III).

It is understood in project finance that lenders take all securities including security over the "rights" of the concessionaire to operate the asset and collect revenue. The stability of the revenue stream is most important, and most international lenders will require a sovereign guarantee from the Ministry of Finance for the paying authority's obligations. In addition, from a commercial bank's perspective, such sovereign guarantee has to be further guaranteed/insured by export credit agencies and/or multilateral lending agencies.

In general, local banks lending in local currency will have less stringent requirements on a project; however, they will also offer a higher financing cost. From previous market sounding, local banks can generally cope with higher debt–equity ratios, lower debt-service coverage ratio, and no explicit sovereign guarantee where international lenders would require it. They can also cope with some level of revenue and fare risk where international banks demand a guaranteed offtake for greenfield projects. Also, very often banks have the appetite and capacity to finance public–Private Partnerships (PPP) projects; however, the lack of well-prepared and structured projects limits the progress.

Capital markets are expected to play a major role in financing infrastructure PPPs, but are relatively underdeveloped in majority of the developing member countries (DMCs) covered. Capital markets have played a muted role in project financing in such DMCs. DMCs with a relatively matured PPP market and a relatively developed capital market have witnessed some PPPs issuing bonds and raising financing from capital markets. Institutional investors such as insurance companies and pension funds are restricted from taking exposure to PPP projects during construction period due to their internal investment norms and regulatory requirements to invest in investment grade projects and investment avenues, which majority of infrastructure PPPs do not attain during the construction period. Hence majority of such institutional investors take exposure to infrastructure PPPs during the operations period by buying out a part of the equity investment (as allowed by the PPP Agreement) of the project sponsors, or by retiring out bank financing for the project.

## 1.4 Comments on Data Sources

The research was carried out using publicly available sources, including:

- government websites, reports, and publications, including national government line ministries and government contracting agencies;
- annual reports of national government line ministries and government contracting agencies;
- applicable laws and regulations (where regulations were available only in the local language, unofficial translations were used);
- websites and annual reports of sector regulators;
- Asian Development Bank (ADB) reports and publications;
- online publications, including online databases of other multilateral development agencies;
- industry publications and databases such as *Inframation News* and *IJGlobal Project Finance & Infrastructure Journal*;
- publications and websites of reputable consultancy companies and law firms; and
- other publicly available reports, publications, and documents from authentic and globally acceptable sources.

Some of the widely used databases included:

- World Bank Private Participation in Infrastructure (PPI) Database, https://ppi.worldbank.org/en/ppi;
- Inframation database https://www.inframationnews.com/;
- IJGlobal database, https://ijglobal.com/;
- PPP Knowledge Lab, https://pppknowledgelab.org/;
- the Economist Intelligence Unit (EIU) Infrascope Index, https://infrascope.eiu.com/;
- Global Infrastructure Hub, https://www.gihub.org/;
- Organisation for Economic Co-operation and Development (OECD), https://www.oecd.org/;
- TheGlobalEconomy.com, https://www.theglobaleconomy.com/;
- International Monetary Fund (IMF), https://data.imf.org/?sk=388dfa60-1d26-4ade-b505-a05a558d9a42;
- Doing Business, https://www.doingbusiness.org/;
- World Bank Public–Private-Partnership Legal Resource Center, https://ppp.worldbank.org/public-private-partnership/;
- World Economic Forum, *The Global Competitiveness Report*, http://www3.weforum.org/docs/WEF_TheGlobalCompetitivenessReport2019.pdf;
- Global Infrastructure Outlook, https://outlook.gihub.org/; and
- Trading Economics, https://tradingeconomics.com/.

Major sources used

- Asian Development Bank's Country Partnership Strategy, 2018–2023: Philippines.
- https://www.adb.org/documents/philippines-country-partnership-strategy-2018-2023
- Public–Private Partnership Center. https://ppp.gov.ph/
- Investment Opportunities, December 2019, The Public–Private Partnership Center of the Philippines. https://ppp.gov.ph/publications/investment-opportunities-brochure-december-2019/
- Public–Private Partnership Center. https://ppp.gov.ph/
- Investment Opportunities, December 2019, The Public–Private Partnership Center of the Philippines. https://ppp.gov.ph/publications/investment-opportunities-brochure-december-2019/
- Laws and regulations
  - Legal and Regulatory Frameworks. https://ppp.gov.ph/ppp-program/legal-and-regulatory-frameworks/
  - Other Pertinent Laws. https://ppp.gov.ph/other-pertinent-laws/
  - Historical Background. https://ppp.gov.ph/ppp-program/historical-background/
- List of PPP modality and safeguards
  - List of PPP Modality. https://ppp.gov.ph/wp-content/uploads/2015/01/List-of-PPP-Modality.pdf
  - Safeguards in PPP. https://ppp.gov.ph/wp-content/uploads/2019/01/PPPC_PPPGB_Reso-Safeguards-in-PPP.pdf
  - The Project Development and Monitoring Facility Guidelines, January 2020.
  - https://ppp.gov.ph/wp-content/uploads/2020/01/PDMFS_200190128_REP_Revised-Guidelines-January-2020.pdf

A detailed list of sources is provided in the References section of this publication.

In addition to the above-mentioned sources, the research for this report was informed by the internal knowledge of CRISIL Infrastructure Advisory, based on various ongoing and completed PPP consultancy assignments in Indonesia; public sector officials; the ADB team from the Office of Public–Private Partnership (OPPP); the ADB Resident Mission for Indonesia; consultants to the ADB Resident Mission in Indonesia; various government agencies; and contributing legal firms and commercial banks.

It should be noted that, as the research relied primarily on information reported in public sources that have not been verified by the authors and may not be accurate or contain all the required information, there is the risk of inaccuracy and incompleteness, depending on the reliability of sources and the validity of the information used.

For quantitative indicators relating to the number of projects, where there were gaps the total number of cases has been reported based on the limited information available. Therefore, reported numbers of projects in this publication may be an underestimate or overestimate the actual numbers.

Further, for various indicators, this publication captures information based on the provisions of the laws, regulations, policies, and government publications associated with the PPP legal, regulatory, policy, and institutional frameworks in the country. This publication does not provide details on the existing status regarding the adoption or application of such PPP laws, regulations, and policies, and the existing challenges being faced in such applications.

# Appendix 2: Critical Macroeconomic and Infrastructure Sector Indicators

The various macroeconomic and infrastructure sector indicators for Philippines are as provided in the table below:

| Parameter | Value | Unit |
|---|---|---|
| Total population | 108.27 | million |
| Average annual population growth rate | https://www.adb.org/publications/basic-statistics-2020 | % |
| Population density | 361 | persons per square kilometer ($km^2$) of surface area |
| Urban population | 46.91 | % of total population |
| Surface area | 300 | '000 $km^2$ |
| Unemployment rate | 5.3 | % |
| Proportion of population below $1.90 purchasing power parity (PPP) a day | 7.81 | % |
| Nominal gross domestic product (GDP) | 359.35 | $ billion |
| | 5.91 | % |
| Annual growth rate of GDP (2019) | 6.00 | % |
| Annual growth rate of GDP (2020 forecast) | -3.80 | % |
| Annual growth rate of GDP (2021 forecast) | 6.50 | % |
| GDP at purchasing power parity (PPP) per capita | 8352.3 | $ at PPP |
| GDP at current market prices | 313.1 | $ billion |
| Gross fixed investment at current market prices | 25.2 | % of GDP |
| Per capita gross national income (GNI), Atlas Method | 3,830.00 | $ |
| Inflation rate (2019) | 2.50 | % |
| Inflation rate (2020 forecast) | 2.20 | % |
| Inflation rate (2021 forecast) | 2.40 | % |
| Current account (2019) | -0.13 | % of GDP |
| External trade, goods, value of imports, CIF (2018) | 91.42 | $ billion |
| External trade, goods, value of exports, FOB (2018) | 56.12 | $ billion |
| CPI % change over 2018 | 2.48 | % of CPI in 2018 |
| Real effective exchange rate | 112.47 | |
| Investment in energy with private sector participation | 2,478.40 | Current $ million |
| Investment in transport with private sector participation | 2,471.90 | Current $ million |
| Investment in water and sanitation with private sector participation | 488.80 | Current $ million |
| Logistics Performance Index (LPI) rank | 60 | Number |
| Logistics Performance Index (LPI) score | 2.90 | Number |
| Customs rank | 85 | Number |

*continued on next page*

*continued from previous page*

| Parameter | Value | Unit |
|---|---|---|
| Customs score | 2.53 | Number |
| Infrastructure rank | 67 | Number |
| Infrastructure score | 2.73 | Number |
| International shipments rank | 37 | Number |
| International shipments score | 3.29 | Number |
| Logistics competence rank | 69 | Number |
| Logistics competence score | 2.78 | Number |
| Tracking and tracing rank | 57 | Number |
| Tracking and tracing score | 3.06 | Number |
| Timeliness rank | 100 | Number |
| Timeliness score | 2.98 | Number |
| **Structure of Output (% of GDP at current producer \| basic prices)** | | |
| Agriculture | 9.30 | % |
| Industry | 30.80 | % |
| Services | 59.90 | % |
| Consumer price index (national) | 5.20 | % annual change |
| Producer price index | 0.68 | % annual change |
| Wholesale price index (national) | 7.03 | % annual change |
| Retail price index | 3.91 | % annual change |
| Exchange rates (End of period) | 52.72 | Local currency - $ |
| **ADF Portfolio** | | |
| Total number of loans | 18.00 | Number |
| 1. Sovereign | 13.00 | Number |
| 2. Non-sovereign | 5.00 | Number |
| Net loan amount | 2,964.30 | $ million, cumulative |
| 1. Sovereign | 2,710.60 | $ million, cumulative |
| 2. Non-sovereign | 253.70 | $ million, cumulative |
| Disbursed amount | 1,412.10 | $ million, cumulative |
| 1. Sovereign | UA | $ million, cumulative |
| 2. Non-sovereign | UA | $ million, cumulative |
| Net foreign direct investment (FDI) inflows | 2.50 | % of GDP |
| Sovereign debt risk rating | 41.00 | Letter rating |
| Central government debt | 42.10 | % of GDP |
| CPIA quality of budgetary and financial management rating | UA | 1=low to 6=high |
| **Ease of Doing Business** | | |
| Ease of doing business rank | 95.00 | Number |
| Starting a business (rank) | 171.00 | Number |
| Dealing with construction permits (rank) | 85.00 | Number |

*continued on next page*

*continued from previous page*

| Parameter | Value | Unit |
|---|---|---|
| Getting electricity (rank) | 32.00 | Number |
| Registering property (rank) | 120.00 | Number |
| Getting credit (rank) | 132.00 | Number |
| Protecting minority investors (rank) | 72.00 | Number |
| Paying taxes (rank) | 95.00 | Number |
| Trading across borders (rank) | 113.00 | Number |
| Enforcing contracts (rank) | 152.00 | Number |
| Resolving insolvency (rank) | 65.00 | Number |
| **Corruption and Sustainable Development Index** | | |
| Corruption Perceptions Index rank (out of 180) | 113.00 | Number |
| Corruption Perceptions Index score (out of 100) | 34.00 | Number |
| Sustainable Development Index rank | 99.00 | Number |
| Sustainable Development Index score | 65.50 | Number |
| **Cumulative Lending, Grant, and Technical Assistance Commitments** | | |
| Number of projects | 682.00 | Number |
| Total lending | 19,319.02 | $ million |
| GCI infrastructure score | 3.4 | out of 7 |
| **EIU Infra-scope Index Score** | | |
| PPP regulations score (out of 100) | 85 | Number |
| PPP regulations rank | 2 | Number |
| PPP institutions score (out of 100) | 94 | Number |
| PPP institutions rank | 3 | Number |
| PPP market maturity score (out of 100) | 58 | Number |
| PPP market maturity rank | 11 | Number |
| PPP financing score (out of 100) | 68 | Number |
| PPP financing rank | 3 | Number |
| Investment and business climate score (out of 100) | 81 | Number |
| Investment and business climate rank | 1 | Number |

CIF = cost, insurance, and freight; CPI = consumer price index; FOB = freight on board; GCI = global competitive index; GDP = gross domestic product; GNI = gross national income; PPP = purchasing power parity; UA = unavailable.

Sources: ADB. 2020. *Basic Statistics 2020*. Manila. https://www.adb.org/publications/basic-statistics-2020; ADB. 2019. *Key Indicators for Asia and Pacific 2019*. Manila. https://www.adb.org/publications/key-indicators-asia-and-pacific-2019; ADB. GDP Growth in Asia and the Pacific, Asian Development Outlook (ADO). https://data.adb.org/dataset/gdp-growth-asia-and-pacific-asian-development-outlook; IMF. https://data.imf.org/?sk=85b51b5a-b74f-473a-be16-49f1786949b3; IMF. Exchange Rate Selected Indicators. https://data.imf.org/regular.aspx?key=61545850; World Bank. LPI Rankings 2018. https://lpi.worldbank.org/international/global?sort=asc&order=LPI%20Score#datatable; ADB. 2019. *Key Indicators for Asia and Pacific 2019*. Manila. https://www.adb.org/publications/key-indicators-asia-and-pacific-2019; ADB. 2018. *Philippines, 2018–2023—High and Inclusive Growth*. Manila. https://www.adb.org/sites/default/files/institutional-document/456476/cps-phi-2018-2023.pdf; Doing Business. Ease of Doing Business Rankings. https://www.doingbusiness.org/en/rankings; Transparency International. Countries. https://www.transparency.org/en/countries/philippines#; ADB. Cumulative Lending, Grant, and Technical Assistance Commitments. https://data.adb.org/dataset/cumulative-lending-grant-and-technical-assistance-commitments; PPP Knowledge Lab. Philippines. https://pppknowledgelab.org/countries/philippines; https://infrascope.eiu.com/.

# Appendix 3: World Bank's Ease of Doing Business Parameters for the Philippines

| Ease of Doing Business in Philippines | | | Doing Business Rank - 95 | Doing Business Score - 62.8 |
|---|---|---|---|---|
| | Region | East Asia and the Pacific | | |
| | Income category | Lower middle income | | |
| | Population | 109,704,207[a] | | |
| | City covered | Quezon City | | |

[a] Worldometer. Philippines Population. https://www.worldometers.info/world-population/philippines-population/.

Source: World Bank Group. *Doing Business 2020: Economy Profile, Philippines*. https://www.doingbusiness.org/content/dam/doingBusiness/country/p/philippines/PHL.pdf.

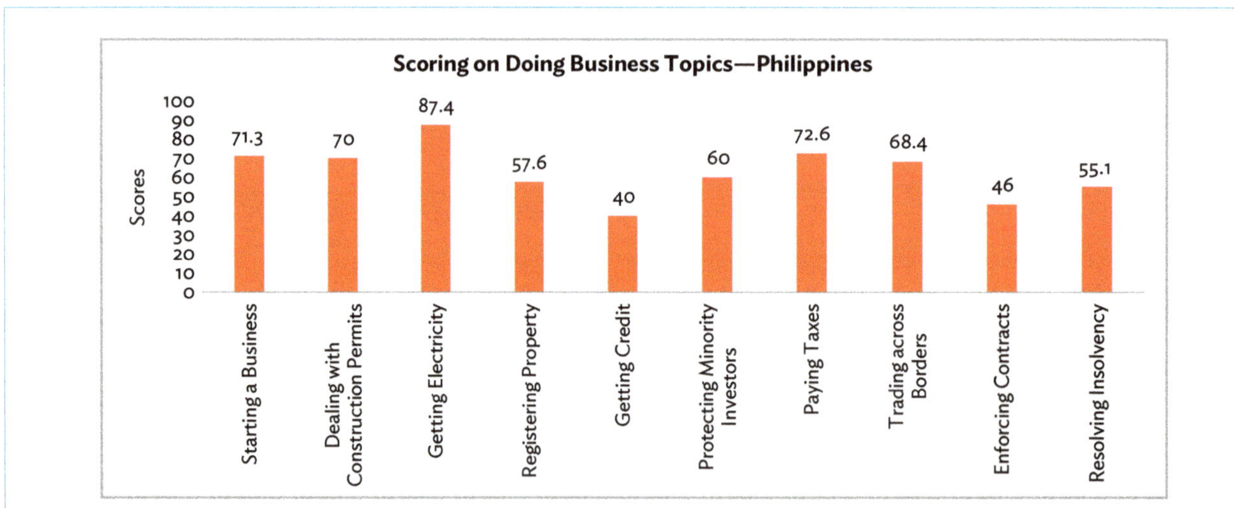


Source: World Bank Group. *Doing Business 2020: Economy Profile, Philippines*. https://www.doingbusiness.org/content/dam/doingBusiness/country/p/philippines/PHL.pdf.

| Starting a Business (rank) | 171 | Dealing with Construction Permits (rank) | 85 | Getting Electricity (rank) | 32 | Registering Property (rank) | 120 |
|---|---|---|---|---|---|---|---|
| Score of starting a business (0–100) | 71.3 | Score of dealing with construction permits (0–100) | 70.0 | Score of getting electricity (0–100) | 87.4 | Score of registering property (0–100) | 57.6 |
| Procedures (number) | 13 | Procedures (number) | 22 | Procedures (number) | 4 | Procedures (number) | 9 |
| Time (days) | 33 | Time (days) | 120 | Time (days) | 37 | Time (days) | 35 |
| Cost (number) | 23.3 | Cost (% of warehouse value) | 2.3 | Cost (% of income per capita) | 24.3 | Cost (% of property value) | 4.3 |
| Paid-in min. capital (% of income per capita) | 0 | Building quality control index (0–15) | 13 | Reliability of supply and transparency of tariff index (0–8) | 6 | Quality of the land administration index (0–30) | 12.5 |

| Getting Credit (rank) | 132 | Protecting Minority Investors (rank) | 72 | Paying Taxes (rank) | 95 |
|---|---|---|---|---|---|
| Score of getting credit (0–100) | 40 | Score of protecting minority investors (0–100) | 60 | Score of paying taxes (0–100) | 72.6 |
| Strength of legal rights index (0–12) | 1 | Extent of disclosure index (0–10) | 9 | Payments (number per year) | 13 |
| Depth of credit information index (0–8) | 7 | Extent of director liability index (0–10) | 4 | Time (hours per year) | 171 |
| Credit registry coverage (% of adults) | 0 | Ease of shareholder suits index (0–10) | 7 | Total tax and contribution rate (% of profit) | 43.1 |
| Credit bureau coverage (% of adults) | 13.5 | Extent of shareholder rights index (0–6) | 1 | Post-filing index (0–100) | 50 |
| | | Extent of ownership and control index (0–7) | 5 | | |
| | | Extent of corporate transparency index (0–7) | 4 | | |

| Trading across Borders (rank) | 113 | Enforcing Contracts (rank) | 152 | Resolving Insolvency (rank) | 65 |
|---|---|---|---|---|---|
| Score of trading across borders (0–100) | 68.4 | Score of enforcing contracts (0–100) | 46 | Score of resolving insolvency (0–100) | 55.1 |
| *Time to export* | | Time (days) | 962 | Recovery rate (cents on the dollar) | 21.1 |
| Documentary compliance (hours) | 36 | Cost (% of claim value) | 31 | Time (years) | 2.7 |
| Border compliance (hours) | 42 | Quality of judicial processes index (0–18) | 7.5 | Cost (% of estate) | 32 |

*continued on next page*

*continued from previous page*

| Trading across Borders (rank) | 113 | Enforcing Contracts (rank) | 152 | Resolving Insolvency (rank) | 65 |
|---|---|---|---|---|---|
| *Cost to export* | | | | Outcome (0 as piecemeal sale and 1 as going concern) | 0 |
| Documentary compliance (USD) | 53 | | | Strength of insolvency framework index (0–16) | 14 |
| Border compliance (USD) | 456 | | | | |
| *Time to export* | | | | | |
| Documentary compliance (hours) | 96 | | | | |
| Border compliance (hours) | 120 | | | | |
| *Cost to export* | | | | | |
| Documentary compliance (USD) | 68 | | | | |
| Border compliance (USD) | 690 | | | | [a] |

[a] Doing Business. Home. https://www.doingbusiness.org/.

# Appendix 4: Assessment of the Public Financial Management System in the Philippines, 2016

The latest assessment of the Public Financial Management System (PFMS), based on the Public Expenditure and Financial Accountability (PEFA) framework (2013), states that the Philippines has an overall rating of A (on a four-point scale with A as the best and D as the worst) for the transparency of intergovernmental fiscal relations.

| Parameter/Sub-parameter | Score | Justification for Score |
|---|---|---|
| Transfers to subnational governments | A | Overall rating based on M2 methodology |
| System for allocating transfers | A | All transfers to the LGUs are based on clearly defined set of rules and procedures. |
| Timeliness of information on transfers | A | Information on transfers is provided by the Department of Budget and Management early in the budget cycle. |
| Extent of collection and reporting of consolidated fiscal data for general government | UA | – |

UA = Unavailable

## Public Expenditure and Financial Accountability Assessment of Public Financial Management System in the Philippines

| Parameter | Value | Unit |
|---|---|---|
| Central government transfers to subnational governments | UA | % of the GDP |
| Actual budgetary allocation to subnational governments from the national government | UA | % of total expenditure |
| Deviation of actual against the budgeted transfers to subnational governments | UA | % of budgeted transfers |

UA = Unavailable

Source: PEFA. 2016. *Republic of the Philippines: PFM Strategy Implementation Support—Public Financial Management and Accountability Assessment.* Manila. https://www.pefa.org/sites/pefa/files/assessments/reports/PH-Jun16-PFMPR-Public-with-PEFA-Check-Meth16.pdf.

# References

Asian Development Bank (ADB). 2014. *Philippines: Public–Private Partnerships by Local Government Units*. Manila. https://www.adb.org/sites/default/files/publication/213606/philippines-ppp-lgus.pdf.

ADB. 2018. *Philippines—Energy Sector Assessment, Strategy, and Road Map*. Manila. https://www.adb.org/sites/default/files/publication/463306/philippines-energy-assessment-strategy-road-map.pdf.

ADB. 2018. *Philippines, 2018–2023 — High and Inclusive Growth*. Manila. https://www.adb.org/sites/default/files/institutional-document/456476/cps-phi-2018-2023.pdf.

ADB. 2019. *Credit Financing for Local Development: The Subnational Debt in the Philippines*. Manila. https://www.adb.org/sites/default/files/publication/506931/adbi-wp966.pdf.

ADB. 2019. *Key Indicators for Asia and the Pacific, 2019*. Manila. https://www.adb.org/publications/key-indicators-asia-and-pacific-2019.

ADB. 2019. *Public–Private Partnership Monitor.* Second Edition. Manila. https://www.adb.org/sites/default/files/publication/509426/ppp-monitor-second-edition.pdf.

ADB. 2020. *Basic Statistics 2020.* Manila. https://www.adb.org/publications/basic-statistics-2020.

ADB. Cumulative Lending, Grant, and Technical Assistance Commitments. https://data.adb.org/dataset/cumulative-lending-grant-and-technical-assistance-commitments.

ADB. GDP Growth in Asia and the Pacific, Asian Development Outlook (ADO). https://data.adb.org/dataset/gdp-growth-asia-and-pacific-asian-development-outlook.

Boholanoko 100. Republic Acts of Philippines. https://boholanoko100.wordpress.com/.

City Population. Airports. https://www.citypopulation.de/en/world/bymap/Airports.html.

Commission on Audit. Service Concession Arrangements: Grantor. https://www.coa.gov.ph/phocadownload/userupload/ABC-Help/GAM_B/sc1.2.htm.

Department of Transportation and Communications and the Philippine Ports Authority. 2015. *Davao Sasa Port Modernization Project. Information Memorandum*. Manila. http://dotr.gov.ph/images/PPP/2015/P17BDavaoSasaPortMP/filepart1.pdf.

Doing Business. Ease of Doing Business Rankings. https://www.doingbusiness.org/en/rankings.

Doing Business. Getting Electricity. https://www.doingbusiness.org/en/data/doing-business-score?topic=getting-electricity.

Doing Business. https://www.doingbusiness.org/.

Department of Transportation and Communications. http://www.dotc.gov.ph/.

Department of Public Works and Highways. About DPWH. https://www.dpwh.gov.ph/dpwh/content/about-dpwh.

Department of Public Works and Highways. News. https://www.dpwh.gov.ph/DPWH/news/15539.

Department of Public Works and Highways. PPP Menu. http://www.dpwh.gov.ph/dpwh/ppp/priority.

Economic and Social Commission for Asia and the Pacific. 2008. *Case Study 6: The Mandaluyong Market, Philippines*. Manila. https://www.unescap.org/ttdw/ppp/ppp_primer/96_the_mandaluyong_market_philippines.html.

École Supérieure de Commerce. 2012. *Case Study (Public Buildings), Philippines*. https://www.esc-pau.fr/ppp/documents/featured_projects/philippines_mandaluyong_city.pdf.

GI Hub InfraCompass. Philippines. https://infracompass.gihub.org/ind_country_profile/phl.

Global Infrastructure Hub. https://www.gihub.org/.

Government of the Philippines, Department of Energy. 2017. *Power Development Plan and Status of Renewable and Fossil-Based Power Sources*. Manila. http://erdt.coe.upd.edu.ph/images/congress/6thERDTCongress/01_Nuclear%20Energy%20Forum_Aug%2018%20no%20script.pdf.

Government of the Philippines, Investment Coordination Committee. 2014. *Generic Preferred Risk Allocation Matrix (GPRAM)*. Manila. https://ppp.gov.ph/wp-content/uploads/2015/04/Generic-Preferred-Risk-Allocation-Matrix.pdf.

Government of the Philippines, National Economic and Development Authority. 2009. *Structuring Public–Private Partnerships (PPPs)*. Manila. http://www.neda.gov.ph/wp-content/uploads/2014/01/Structuring-Public–Private-Partnerships-PPPs-Handbook.pdf.

Government of the Philippines, Public–Private Partnership Center. 2015. *Republic Act 8974*. Manila. https://ppp.gov.ph/wp-content/uploads/2015/01/Republic-Act-8974.pdf.

Government of the Philippines, Public–Private Partnership Center. 2016. *Right of Way Act*. Manila. https://ppp.gov.ph/wp-content/uploads/2016/03/Right-of-Way-Act-RA10752.pdf.

Government of the Philippines, Public–Private Partnership Center. 2012. *A PPP Manual for LGUs*. Manila. https://ppp.gov.ph/wp-content/uploads/2012/07/PPP-Manual-for-LGUs-Volume-1.pdf.

Government of the Philippines, Public–Private Partnership Center. 2012. *The Philippine Amended BOT Law*. Manila. https://ppp.gov.ph/wp-content/uploads/2013/02/BOT-IRR-2012_FINAL.pdf.

Government of the Philippines, Public–Private Partnership Center. https://ppp.gov.ph/.

Government of the Philippines, Public–Private Partnership Center. 2019. *Investment Opportunities*. Manila. https://ppp.gov.ph/investors-corner/investment-opportunities-2/.

Government of the Philippines, Public–Private Partnership Center. 2001. *The Project Development and Monitoring Facility*. Manila. https://ppp.gov.ph/wp-content/uploads/2020/01/PDMFS_200190128_REP_Revised-Guidelines-January-2020.pdf.

Government of the Philippines, Public–Private Partnership Center. 2012. *A PPP Manual for LGUs*. Manila. https://ppp.gov.ph/wp-content/uploads/2012/03/Volume-2-LGU-PPP-Manual.pdf.

Government of the Philippines, Public–Private Partnership Center. 2015. *PPP Contractual Arrangements*. Manila. https://ppp.gov.ph/wp-content/uploads/2015/01/List-of-PPP-Modality.pdf.

Government of the Philippines, Public–Private Partnership Center. 2018. *Public–Private Partnership Projects Monitoring Framework and Protocols*. Manila. https://ppp.gov.ph/wp-content/uploads/2018/07/PPPC_GUIDE_Monitoring-Framework-Protocols-20150825.pdf.

Government of the Philippines, Public–Private Partnership Center. 2019. *Reporting of PPP Project Spending and Contingent Liabilities*. Manila. https://ppp.gov.ph/wp-content/uploads/2019/10/PPPC_POL_JMC-Reporting-of-PPP-Project-Spending.pdf.

Government of the Philippines, Public–Private Partnership Center. Historical Background. https://ppp.gov.ph/ppp-program/historical-background/.

Government of the Philippines, Public–Private Partnership Center. List of Projects. https://ppp.gov.ph/list-of-projects/ (accessed 28 August 2020).

Government of the Philippines, Public–Private Partnership Center. Other Pertinent Laws and Issuances. https://ppp.gov.ph/other-pertinent-laws/.

Government of the Philippines, Public–Private Partnership Center. PDMF. PDMF Process. https://ppp.gov.ph/pdmf/pdmf-process/.

Government of the Philippines, Public–Private Partnership Center. PPP Processes. https://ppp.gov.ph/ppp-program/ppp-processes/.

Government of the Philippines, Public–Private Partnership Center. PPPGB Guidelines and Issuances. https://ppp.gov.ph/guidelines-and-issuances/.

Government of the Philippines, Public–Private Partnership Center. Projects Database. https://ppp.gov.ph/project-database/.

Government of the Philippines, Public–Private Partnership Center. What is PPP? https://ppp.gov.ph/ppp-program/what-is-ppp/.

Government of the Philippines. 2012. *PPP Manual for LGUs – Volume 3: Utilizing LGU PPP Project Templates and Bid Documents*. Manila. https://ppp.gov.ph/wp-content/uploads/2012/03/Volume-3-LGU-PPP-Manual.pdf.

Government of the Philippines. 2012. *The Philippine Amended BOT Law Republic Act 7718 and its Revised Implementing Rules and Regulations*. Manila. https://ppp.gov.ph/wp-content/uploads/2017/04/BOT-IRR-2012_2017-printing.pdf.

Government of the Philippines. 2016. *Generic Preferred Risk Allocation Matrix*. Manila. https://ppp.gov.ph/wp-content/uploads/2017/02/GPRAM_2Aug2016.pdf.

Government of the Philippines. 2018. *The Omnibus Investments Code*. Manila. http://boi.gov.ph/wp-content/uploads/2018/02/EO-226-omnibus-investments-code.pdf.

Government of the Philippines. Commission on Audit. Downloads. https://www.coa.gov.ph/phocadownload/userupload/ABC-Help/BOT_LAW/BOT/Section13.3.htm.

Government of the Philippines. Local Government Code of 1991. Section 17. https://www.officialgazette.gov.ph/1991/10/10/republic-act-no-7160/#:~:text=SECTION%2017.,functions%20currently%20vested%20upon%20them.

Government of the Philippines. Presidential Decree No. 198. https://lwua.gov.ph/about-us/mandate-and-functions/#:~:text=The%20Local%20Water%20Utilities%20Administration,law%20on%20May%2025%2C%201973.

Government of the Philippines. Republic Act No. 2000. Limited Access Highway Act. https://peatc.gov.ph/sites/default/files/REPUBLIC%20ACT%20NO%202000.pdf.

Government of the Philippines. Republic Act No. 6234. http://mwss.gov.ph/wp-content/uploads/RA-6234-1.pdf.

Government of the Philippines. Republic Act No. 9136. https://www.napocor.gov.ph/images/about_us/EPIRA_RA9136.pdf.

Government Procurement Policy Board. Republic Act 7718. *An Act Authorizing the Financing, Construction, Operation and Maintenance of Infrastructure Projects by the Private Sector, and for Other Purposes*. Manila. https://www.gppb.gov.ph/laws/laws/RA_6957.pdf.

International Benchmarking Network. 2020. IBNET Database. https://database.ib-net.org/DefaultNew.aspx.

International Comparative Legal Guides. Practice Areas. Litigation and Disputes. https://iclg.com/practice-areas/litigation-and-dispute-resolution-laws-and-regulations/philippines.

International Energy Agency. Feed-in Tariff Rules. http://www.iea.org/policies/4805-feed-in-tariff-rules.

International Monetary Fund. Exchange Rate selected indicators. https://data.imf.org/regular.aspx?key=61545850.

International Monetary Fund. https://data.imf.org/?sk=85b51b5a-b74f-473a-be16-49f1786949b3.

Infrascope. https://infrascope.eiu.com/.

Law Business Research. 2015. *The Public–Private Partnership Law Review*. London. https://www.syciplaw.com/Documents/LegalResources/2015/PPP%20Law%20Review%20-%20Philippines%202015.pdf.

Manila Water Company, Maynilad Water Services. https://www.mayniladwater.com.ph/maynilad-to-adjust-water-tariff-by-april/.

Maritime Industry Authority. 2007. *Annual Report 2007*. Manila. https://marina.gov.ph/wp-content/uploads/2018/07/AR2017-1.pdf.

Municipal Development Fund Office. www.mdfo.gov.ph.

National Economic Development Authority. 2020. *Revised List of Infrastructure Flagship Projects*. 17 February. Manila. https://www.neda.gov.ph/infrastructure-flagship-projects/.

National Economic Development Authority. *Joint Memorandum Circular No. 1 Series of 2016*. http://blgf.gov.ph/wp-content/uploads/2017/10/JMC-No.-1-DILG-DBM-DOF-BLGF-NEDA.pdf.

Organisation for Economic Co-operation and Development. *Regional Policy—Philippines*. Paris. https://www.oecd.org/regional/regional-policy/profile-Philippines.pdf.

Official Gazette. Presidential Decree No. 1067. https://www.officialgazette.gov.ph/1976/12/31/presidential-decree-no-1067-s-1976/#:~:text=the%20utilization%2c%20exploitation%2c%20development%2c,e.

Official Gazette. Presidential Decree No. 17. https://www.officialgazette.gov.ph/1972/10/05/presidential-decree-no-17-s-1972/.

Official Gazette. Republic Act No. 8545. https://www.officialgazette.gov.ph/1998/02/24/republic-act-no-8545/.

Official Gazette. *Republic Act No. 9497*. https://www.officialgazette.gov.ph/2008/03/04/republic-act-no-9497/.

Philippine Dispute Resolution Center, Inc. News. www.pdrci.org.

Public Expenditure and Financial Accountability. 2016. *Republic of the Philippines PFM Strategy Implementation Support*. Manila. https://www.pefa.org/sites/pefa/files/assessments/reports/PH-Jun16-PFMPR-Public-with-PEFA-Check-Meth16.pdf.

Public Expenditure and Financial Accountability. 2016. *Republic of the Philippines PFM Strategy Implementation Support Public Financial Management and Accountability Assessment*. Manila. https://www.pefa.org/sites/pefa/files/assessments/reports/PH-Jun16-PFMPR-Public-with-PEFA-Check-Meth16.pdf.

Philippines Ports Authority. https://www.ppa.com.ph/.

PPP Knowledge Hub. http://pppknowledgehub.org/.

PPP Knowledge Lab. Philippines. https://pppknowledgelab.org/countries/philippines.

Public–Private Partnerships Governing Board. 2015. *Policy on Viability Gap Funding (VGF) for Public–Private Partnership (PPP) Projects*. Manila. https://ppp.gov.ph/wp-content/uploads/2015/04/PPP-Governing-Board-Policy-Circular-No-04-2015.pdf.

Public–Private Partnerships Governing Board. 2018. *Guidelines on Identification, Selection, and Prioritization of Public–Private Partnership Project*. Manila. https://ppp.gov.ph/wp-content/uploads/2018/07/PPPC_GUIDE-Identification-Selection-Prioritization-20150325.pdf.

Public–Private Partnerships Governing Board. 2018. *Safeguards in PPPs: Mainstreaming Environmental, Displacement, Social, and Gender Concerns*. Manila. https://ppp.gov.ph/wp-content/uploads/2019/01/PPPC_PPPGB_Reso-Safeguards-in-PPP.pdf.

PSALM. https://www.psalm.gov.ph/.

Rappler. Nation. https://www.rappler.com/nation/223856-new-law-creates-department-housing-urban-development.

Republic Act 6957. An Act Authorizing the Financing, Construction, Operation and Maintenance of Infrastructure Projects by the Private Sector, and for other Purposes. https://ppp.gov.ph/ppp-program/historical-background/#:~:text=In%201986%2C%20right%20after%20the,also%20enacted%20Presidential%20Proclamation%20No.

Securities and Exchange Commission. *Uploads*. https://www.sec.gov.ph/wp-content/uploads/2020/01/2016_PressReleases_SECApprovedPublicPrivatePartnershipListingRules.pdf.

National Transmission Corporation. 2018–2019. *Feed-In-Tariff Allowance Rate Application. ERC Case No. 2018-085. RC Expository Presentation*. Manila. https://www.transco.ph/downloads/fitall/2019FIT-AllRateExpositoryPresentation-Davao.pdf.

The Global Economy. Compare Countries. https://www.theglobaleconomy.com/compare-countries/.

The Global Economy. Education Spending, Percent of Government Spending—Country Rankings. https://www.theglobaleconomy.com/rankings/Education_spending_percent_of_government_spending/.

The Global Economy. Energy Imports. https://www.theglobaleconomy.com/rankings/Energy_imports/.

The Global Economy. Health Spending per Capita—Country Rankings. https://www.theglobaleconomy.com/rankings/Health_spending_per_capita/.

The Global Economy. Port Traffic—Country Rankings. https://www.theglobaleconomy.com/rankings/Port_traffic/ https://infrascope.eiu.com/.

The Global Economy. Railroad Infrastructure Quality—Country Rankings. https://www.theglobaleconomy.com/rankings/railroad_quality/.

The Global Economy. Railway Passengers—Country Rankings. https://www.theglobaleconomy.com/rankings/railway_passengers/.

The Global Economy. Railway Transport of Goods—Country Rankings. https://www.theglobaleconomy.com/rankings/Railway_transport_of_goods/.

The Global Economy. Share of Clean Energy—Country Rankings. https://www.theglobaleconomy.com/rankings/share_of_clean_energy/.

The LawPhil Project. Republic Act No. 1383. https://lawphil.net/statutes/repacts/ra1955/ra_1383_1955.html#:~:text=1383&text=AN%20ACT%20CREATING%20A%20PUBLIC,of%20business%20of%20the%20corporation.

Toll Regulatory Board. http://trb.gov.ph./ (accessed 4 July 2020).

Trading Economics. Philippines-Road Total Network. https://tradingeconomics.com/philippines/roads-total-network-km-wb-data.html.

Transparency International. Countries. https://www.transparency.org/en/countries/philippines#.

United Cities and Local Governments. 2016. *Subnational Governments Around the World—Structure and Finance*. https://www.uclg.org/sites/default/files/global_observatory_of_local_finance-part_iii.pdf.

United Cities and Local Governments. https://www.uclg.org/.

World Education News + Reviews. https://wenr.wes.org/.

World Bank Group. *Doing Business 2020: Economy Profile, Philippines*. Washington DC. https://www.doingbusiness.org/content/dam/doingBusiness/country/p/philippines/PHL.pdf.

World Bank Group. 2016. *Closing the Gap in Affordable Housing in the Philippines*. Washington DC. http://documents1.worldbank.org/curated/en/547171468059364837/pdf/AUS13470-REVISED-PUBLIC-WBNationalHousingSummitFinalReport.pdf.

World Bank Group. 2016. *Private Sector Provision of Water and Sanitation Services in Rural Areas and Small Towns: The Role of the Public Sector—Philippines.* Washington DC. https://www.wsp.org/sites/wsp/files/publications/WSP%20SPI%20Country%20Report%20-%20Philippines%20final.pdf.

World Bank Group. Access to Electricity. https://data.worldbank.org/indicator/EG.ELC.ACCS.ZS?end=2018&locations=MM-KH-UZ-CN-BD-GE-IN-ID-KZ-PK-PH-LK-TH-VN&start=2018&view=bar.

World Bank Group. Air Transport, Passengers Carried. https://data.worldbank.org/indicator/IS.AIR.PSGR?locations=BD-KH-GE-KZ-MM-PK-PG-LK-UZ-VN-CN-IN-ID-PH-TH.

World Bank Group. Benchmarking Infrastructure Development. https://bpp.worldbank.org/.

World Bank Group. Infrastructure Finance, PPPs and Guarantees. Country Snapshots. Philippines. https://ppi.worldbank.org/en/snapshots/country/philippines (accessed 28 August 2020).

World Bank Group. LPI Rankings 2018. https://lpi.worldbank.org/international/global?sort=asc&order=LPI%20Score#datatable.

World Bank Group. PPI Database. https://ppi.worldbank.org/en/ppi.

World Bank Group. PPP. Library. https://ppp.worldbank.org/public-private-partnership/library/ppp-legal-framework-snapshot-philippines.

World Bank Group. PPP. Library. https://ppp.worldbank.org/public-private-partnership/library/national-government-public-private-partnership-manual-draft.

World Bank Group. PPP. Library. https://ppp.worldbank.org/public-private-partnership/library/public-private-partnership-law-review-philippines.

World Bank Group. PPP. Library. https://ppp.worldbank.org/public-private-partnership/library/standard-provisions-announcement-and-amendment-contracts.

World Health Organization, South-East Asia Regional Office. 2017. Executive Summary. Philippines. http://www.searo.who.int/entity/asia_pacific_observatory/publications/hits/executive_summary_philippines_hit_ii.pdf?ua=1.

World Port Source. Ports. http://www.worldportsource.com/countries.php.

www.ingramcontent.com/pod-product-compliance
Lightning Source LLC
LaVergne TN
LVHW060617110826
845147LV00019B/1042

* 9 7 8 9 2 9 2 6 2 6 4 8 8 *